THE VIETNAM WAR IN HISTORY,
LITERATURE AND FILM

BAAS Paperbacks

Series Editors: Philip John Davies, Professor of American Studies at De Montfort University; George McKay, Professor of English and American Studies at the University of Central Lancashire; Simon Newman, Sir Denis Brogan Chair in American Studies at the University of Glasgow; and Carol R. Smith, Senior Lecturer in English and American Studies at King Alfred's College, Winchester.

Published in association with the British Association for American Studies, this exciting series has become an indispensable collection in American Studies. Each volume tackles an important area and is written by an accepted academic expert within the discipline. Books selected for the series are clearly written introductions designed to offer students definitive short surveys of key topics in the field.

Titles in the series include:

The Cultures of the American New West
Neil Campbell

Gender, Ethnicity and Sexuality in Contemporary American Film
Jude Davies and Carol R. Smith

The United States and World War II
Martin Folly

The Sixties in America: History, Politics and Protest
M. J. Heale

The United States and European Reconstruction
John Killick

Religion in America to 1865
Bryan F. LeBeau

American Exceptionalism
Deborah L. Madsen

The American Landscape
Stephen F. Mills

Slavery and Servitude in North America, 1607–1800
Kenneth Morgan

Jazz in American Culture
Peter Townsend

The New Deal
Fiona Venn

Animation and America
Paul Wells

Political Scandals in the USA
Robert Williams

The Vietnam War in History, Literature and Film

MARK TAYLOR

EDINBURGH UNIVERSITY PRESS
OCM 59368702

© Mark Taylor, 2003

Edinburgh University Press Ltd
22 George Square, Edinburgh

Typeset in Fournier by
Koinonia, Manchester, and
printed and bound in Great Britain by
MPG Books Ltd, Bodmin

A CIP Record for this book is available from the British Library

ISBN 0 7486 1533 4 (paperback)

Contents

List of Illustrations   vi

Map of South-east Asia   vii

Timeline   viii

Introduction: Understanding America's War in Vietnam   1

1   Telling True War Stories   10

2   Heroes   33

3   Cinematic History: The Case of *JFK*   58

4   Battles   84

5   Villains   104

6   Veterans   131

Conclusion: Telling Differences   148

A Guide to Further Reading   151

Glossary   154

Index   155

Illustrations

1 Map of South-east Asia (1954–75)   vii

2 American soldiers in Vietnam   34

3 President Johnson listening to a tape sent to him by his
   son-in-law, Captain Charles Robb   62

4 American soldiers carry a wounded comrade out of combat   85

5 Map of Son My   108

6 Some of the dead at My Lai 4   111

7 Vietnam veterans at the memorial wall in Washington DC   136

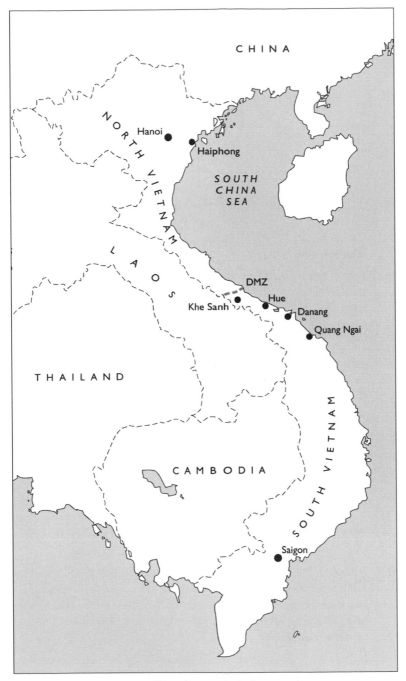

Map of South-east Asia (1954–75)

Timeline

1887   The French established the Indochinese Union, made up of Annam, Cambodia, Cochin China and Tonkin. Laos was added to the Union in 1893. Tonkin, Annam and Cochin China constituted the territory known previously as Vietnam.

1940   France fell to the Germans in June and, after fighting along the border between Tonkin and China in September, the French colonial government in Indochina allowed the Japanese to station troops in Tonkin and to use airfields there.

1941   In July the French ceded military control of Cochin China to the Japanese but administration of the Union's civilian affairs remained in French hands. Meanwhile, the Viet Minh was formed to oppose the French and the Japanese.

1945   After removing the French from power in Indochina on 9 March, the Japanese surrendered to the Allies on 15 August. The withdrawal of Japanese troops from Indochina gave the Viet Minh the opportunity to seize power in Vietnam and, on 2 September 1945, Ho Chi Minh declared Vietnamese independence. In the following weeks, British, Chinese Nationalist, French and Indian troops entered Vietnam and, despite Viet Minh resistance, the French were re-installed as colonial rulers. Harry S Truman had become President of the United States after Roosevelt's death on 12 April.

1946   Almost a year of negotiations between the French and the Viet Minh about the future of Vietnam ended with French warships shelling Vietnamese civilians in Haiphong on 23 November and the Viet Minh attacking French forces in Tonkin on 19 December. The war would last until 1954.

1949   In August the Soviet Union successfully detonated a nuclear device and in October Communists in China completed the defeat of Chiang

Kai-shek's Nationalist forces. Fears about the activities of Communists in America, which Senator McCarthy would take advantage of in subsequent years, were sharpened by accusations that Alger Hiss, a former employee of the State Department, had passed secrets to the Soviet Union.

1950 On 14 January the Democratic Republic of Vietnam was proclaimed by Ho Chi Minh and recognised by China and the Soviet Union. In March Truman agreed to provide military assistance to the French in Indochina. After war broke out in Korea on 25 June, America accelerated its provision of military and economic assistance to the French. In the autumn Viet Minh attacks intensified.

1953 Under President Eisenhower, who took office in January, an armistice was signed in July to end the war in Korea. He continued Truman's policy of assisting the French in Indochina, agreeing an additional 385 million dollars of aid in September. In November the French began to establish a large base at Dien Bien Phu.

1954 Despite receiving two billion dollars in military aid from the Americans during the previous four years, the French suffered a decisive defeat at Dien Bien Phu in May. In July agreement was reached at the Geneva Conference that Vietnam would be temporarily partitioned near the seventeenth parallel until elections to reunify the country were held in 1956. In the North the Communist Lao Dong party, led by Ho Chi Minh, took control, and in the South Ngo Dinh Diem became premier. The agreement allowed refugees to cross the border in either direction. The American Navy assisted as more than 900,000 Vietnamese moved to South Vietnam. Less than 90,000 moved in the opposite direction, leaving about 10,000 Viet Minh in the South. More than 200,000 Viet Minh had been killed in a war which also cost 75,000 lives on the French side.

1955 America began to aid the South Vietnamese government in January. Having defeated his domestic opponents, the Binh Xuyen, the Cao Dai and the Hoa Hao, Diem announced himself President of the Republic of Vietnam on 26 October. In July, with American backing, he had asserted that South Vietnam would not participate in the planned elections in 1956.

1956 As American advisors trained the South Vietnamese Army, Diem made plans to eradicate the Viet Minh in the South.

1957   More than 400 South Vietnamese government officials were killed as the Viet Minh took up arms once again.

1959   The North Vietnamese sent personnel and supplies into the South by land, along the Ho Chi Minh trail, and by sea. Two American military advisors were killed at Bien Hoa. Twenty-three years later their names would be the first of more than 58,000 inscribed on the Vietnam Veterans Memorial in Washington DC.

1960   In America John F. Kennedy was elected to the presidency. On 20 December the formation of the National Liberation Front (referred to as the Viet Cong by the South Vietnamese government) was announced in Hanoi.

1961   Having declared a state of emergency in October, Diem asked Kennedy for additional military aid. The American military force grew from 900 to 3,200 and some took part in combat against NLF forces.

1962   General Paul D. Harkins, commander of Military Assistance Command, Vietnam (MACV), controlled over 11,000 American advisors. The American Special Forces had begun to train the Montagnards as a paramilitary force and the Strategic Hamlet Program, an American-funded effort to remove villagers from NLF areas, had been launched. Nevertheless, NLF forces continued to grow in strength and confidence.

1963   On 2 January South Vietnamese forces suffered a humiliating defeat in a battle at Ap Bac. By the summer, demonstrations against the government, the violence with which Diem and his brother Nhu attempted to crush Buddhist activists and Diem's failure to deliver reforms persuaded Kennedy that a change was needed. Aware of the support of the American government, South Vietnamese generals staged a successful coup on 1 November. Diem and Nhu were killed. Lyndon B. Johnson succeeded to the presidency when Kennedy was assassinated on 22 November. At that time the American force in South Vietnam was in excess of 16,000. In December the North Vietnamese agreed to provide NLF forces with Chinese and Soviet weaponry and additional personnel.

1964: General Nguyen Khanh seized power in South Vietnam on 30 January. General William Westmoreland took command of MACV on 20 June. On 2 August North Vietnamese boats attacked an

American destroyer in the Gulf of Tonkin. Reports of a second attack on 4 August led to the bombing of North Vietnam by American planes and a congressional resolution which enabled Johnson to 'take all necessary measures ... to prevent further aggression'. The dispute over the reliability of the reports of a second attack would remain unsettled. The first North Vietnamese infantry regiments moved into South Vietnam where more than 23,000 Americans were serving.

1965 Another coup removed Khanh from power in February. A further change of government followed in June. In response to NLF attacks on American bases a campaign of bombing codenamed 'Rolling Thunder' was launched against North Vietnam on 2 March. Six days later the first American combat troops landed at Danang, their mission to protect American bases from attack. On 6 April their role was widened to include offensive operations. In November heavy fighting occurred when American troops clashed with North Vietnamese regulars in the Ia Drang Valley. By the end of the year there were over 184,000 American troops in South Vietnam. More than 1,300 of them lost their lives during the year.

1966 After a thirty-seven-day bombing halt designed to encourage peace negotiations, Johnson recommenced attacks on 31 January. During the year, in which the American force in South Vietnam increased to 385,000, over 5,000 Americans were killed as Westmoreland endeavoured to wage a war of attrition against NLF forces and their North Vietnamese allies.

1967 Nguyen Van Thieu was elected President of South Vietnam on 3 September. As domestic opposition to the war increased, Johnson tried to convince the American people that progress was being made in Vietnam. Westmoreland returned to America in November to add his weight to the argument that the enemy was being defeated. The resignation of Secretary of Defense Robert McNamara, who privately disagreed, was announced in November. More than 485,000 Americans were serving in Vietnam. Over 9,000 were killed.

1968 The Tet Offensive began on 30 January. The American public was shocked by the scale of the offensive and by the prospect that the Marine force besieged at Khe Sanh might be overrun. As American units counter-attacked the NLF suffered heavy losses, but the offensive provoked a change of heart in the American government. Clark Clifford, the new Secretary of Defense, concluded that military escalation was not working. On March 31 Johnson announced that he would devote the remainder of his presidency to the pursuit of peace in Vietnam and that he would not stand for re-election. General Creighton Adams took over from Westmoreland on 3 July. On 31 October Johnson ended the bombing of North Vietnam. Five days later Richard Nixon was elected to the presidency. During the year more than 14,500 Americans were killed. Both sides were responsible for the massacre of civilians. In February NLF forces murdered over 2,000 of the inhabitants of Hue. On 16 March, in Son My, American troops killed hundreds of Vietnamese villagers, many of them women and children.

1969   Having authorised the secret bombing of enemy bases in Cambodia, Nixon announced in June that the American force in Vietnam was to be reduced. Secretary of Defense Melvin Laird had announced the policy of 'Vietnamization' in March and Nixon hoped to neutralise domestic opposition to the war by limiting American casualties, relying upon air power and shifting the responsibility for fighting the war on the ground to the South Vietnamese. Even so, 9,400 Americans died in combat, poor morale hindered military effectiveness and large anti-war demonstrations took place across America.

1970   In February secret peace talks took place between American and North Vietnamese representatives. The announcement on 30 April that American units were to support a South Vietnamese operation across the Cambodian border triggered further anti-war protests in America. General Adams still had more than 334,000 Americans under his command.

1971:   Intended to demonstrate the effectiveness of 'Vietnamization', an assault into Laos by South Vietnamese forces ended in disarray. In June the *New York Times* began the publication of excerpts from the *Pentagon Papers*. Nixon announced in November that American troops would no longer take part in offensive operations, although over 150,000 of them remained in South Vietnam.

1972:   On 30 March the North Vietnamese began the Easter Offensive and Nixon responded by increasing the bombing of the North.

With American support, the South Vietnamese managed to contain the attacks. General Frederick Weyand became commander of MACV and, in November, Nixon was re-elected to the presidency. He ordered further bombing when renewed peace talks stalled in December.

1973 On 27 January a cease-fire was formally agreed. The last American troops left South Vietnam on 29 March and the last American POWs were released on 1 April although claims that other American POWs remained in captivity would continue to be a source of contention.

1974 As the Watergate scandal unfolded in America, Congress cut aid to South Vietnam. Nixon resigned in August to be succeeded by Gerald Ford. In December the North Vietnamese commenced another offensive.

1975 Without American support, South Vietnamese forces were rapidly driven southwards by the advancing North Vietnamese. On 30 April Saigon fell. The last Americans, including Ambassador Graham Martin, had departed by helicopter hours before. America would refuse to trade with Vietnam until 1994 and full diplomatic relations would not be established until the following year.

Understanding America's War in Vietnam

It is the purpose of this book to explore the different ways in which America's war in Vietnam has been portrayed in history, literature and film and the nature of the truths which historians, other writers and film makers have tried to tell about it. There has been no shortage of attempts to make sense out of America's defeat in Vietnam but decades of soul searching and study have not resolved the disagreements which provoked so much bitterness during the war. Why could America not win? What would victory have consisted of? And was America engaged in a noble effort to defend a small, young country against an invading Communist force or guilty of an aggressive war against a people seeking the right of self-determination? Plenty of Americans remain certain that the war was noble in intention, or at least a necessary evil, and some have concluded that the war's major injustice was the treatment of American prisoners by the North Vietnamese. The number of public buildings in America continuing to fly the black and white POW/MIA flag over a quarter of a century after the fall of Saigon testifies to the power of the notion that Americans who had been declared missing in action were secretly kept in prison by the Vietnamese after the war: that, finally, Americans were the victims. Meanwhile, those considering the war an act of American immorality have pointed out the damage wrought upon the Vietnamese people and their land. For some Americans who served in Vietnam, however, events were distinguished by their senselessness. The phrase 'It don't mean nothin'' was commonly used by American soldiers to express their alienation from their surroundings and from the acts they performed and witnessed.[1] So, confronted by such a variety of entrenched attitudes and beliefs, how should those who want to understand America's war in Vietnam proceed?

The challenge for Americans writing and making films about what the Vietnamese call the American War has been to communicate truths about a war which, in its divisive effect upon the American people, in much of its combat and in its result, was confusingly different from other twentieth-century wars in which Americans were involved. This book will consider the extent to which history, literature and film offer compatible approaches to understanding America's war in Vietnam and, indeed, the world in which we live. It will suggest that, having been tested in unprecedented ways by the complexities of America's involvement in Vietnam, historians, writers of literature and film makers have revealed distinctive strengths and weaknesses when trying to explain the political and cultural origins of the war and when trying to illuminate the experiences of the men and women who served there, especially those engaged in what Roger J. Spiller accurately characterised as history's 'darkest corner': combat.[2]

In the context of the Vietnam War, questions about the helpfulness of particular disciplines are particularly relevant because of the scepticism with which many attempts to portray the war have been received. History, it has been alleged by some, cannot fully explain this first 'postmodern' war. The scale, confusion and 'unknowability' of events in Vietnam require, according to this view, alternative forms of representation which writers of fiction are best equipped to provide. Of course, the notion that writers of literature can present truths as well as, or more effectively than, historians is not a recent one. Henry James suggested that it was an error to believe 'that the novelist is less occupied in looking for the truth ... than the historian'.[3] And, more provocatively, literary critic R. W. B. Lewis asserted in 1955 that one of Nathaniel Hawthorne's short stories was 'like every good story ... truer than history'.[4] However, the argument that America's war in Vietnam particularly demands interpretation by creative artists raises some difficult questions. Does this mean that Michael Herr's novel *Dispatches* might be a more useful path to an understanding of the war than Stanley Karnow's *Vietnam: A History*? Or that a feature film like Oliver Stone's *Platoon* (1986) is able to represent the Vietnam War 'the way it really was', whilst historians cannot?[5] And if writers of literature or film makers are to be used as the sources of truths about historical events, what sort of dangers might be associated with this?

Chapter 1 provides a detailed investigation of the difficulties attached to the telling of true war stories. The five chapters which follow explore the extent to which an inter-disciplinary approach to America's war in Vietnam can solve these difficulties. Analysis of the ways in which particular aspects of the war have been depicted by historians, journalists, novelists, memoirists (who can better be described as autobiographical novelists) and film makers suggests how true war stories can be told and reveals the sorts of truths which each can tell. The usefulness of studying texts which present false images of the war is also examined. Like more accurate texts, they can suggest the influence of ideas current in the period of their composition as well as ideas about the period in which they were set, thereby contributing to an understanding of the attitudes present at either time. In the process of these different analyses, the nature of the boundaries between the individual disciplines of history, literature and film can be clarified.

Chapter 2 considers the American Special Forces and their portrayal by journalists, historians, novelist Robin Moore and, doubling as film maker and actor, John Wayne. The Special Forces, who were more popularly known as the Green Berets, were the Army's specialists in guerrilla warfare. They are important because they were, for many, the heroes of America's efforts in Vietnam. It is no coincidence that, in 2001, the media was quick to stress the involvement of American Special Forces personnel in Afghanistan. Moore's book *The Green Berets*, published in 1965, and Wayne's similarly titled film, released in 1968, were savaged by critics and yet were highly popular – Moore's book has sold more copies than any other novel about the war. Their study, and study of the ways in which journalists presented the Special Forces to the American public in the early 1960s, when the Kennedys were hopeful that the Special Forces might be an answer to Communist insurgencies in the Third World, disclose some of the ideas which fostered support for America's involvement in Vietnam. Moore's 'book of truth' and Wayne's film are also surprisingly useful in other ways, Moore's book exhibiting some of the attitudes held by soldiers in the Special Forces and Wayne's film detailing the ways in which President Johnson's administration tried to justify the war to the American people.[6]

Whilst study of the Special Forces demonstrates the advantages of an inter-disciplinary approach which uses film and literature to shed light on the war and its cultural origins, study of Oliver Stone's film *JFK* (1991) in Chapter 3 highlights the necessity of treating with caution films which offer a recreation of specific events in history. Stone argued in *JFK* that had President Kennedy survived he would have found a way to extricate America from Vietnam and that President Johnson manipulated policy to ensure the escalation of America's military effort. 'Cinematic History: the Case of *JFK*' shows how Stone manipulated primary sources in order to persuade viewers towards a version of events which suited his own political agenda. Nevertheless, despite its failure as history, *JFK* provoked an important debate about the relationship between film and history and analysis of its faults suggests some of the criteria which ought to be applied to film that recreates history, as well as pointing to more effective means of establishing the causes of American escalation in Vietnam.

If combat is history's 'darkest corner', it is also, to cite Spiller once more, 'war's essential, defining feature'.[7] One does not understand a war without appreciating the nature of the combat which occurred. Frequently, the desire to make events comprehensible to a reader or a cinema audience has robbed attempts to render combat, in which disorder is frequently the most striking characteristic, of their authenticity. In Vietnam, Americans were confronted by enemies whose variety of strategy and tactics added to the confusion of the combat experience. The North Vietnamese Army (NVA) and the range of forces operating under the banner of the National Liberation Front (NLF) fought different types of war in a bid to limit the impact of American firepower and, rather than inflicting a decisive military blow upon their enemy, simply to frustrate and outlast them. Study of the writing and film which has endeavoured to overcome the difficulties involved in the portrayal of the various sorts of combat in Vietnam provides the focus for Chapters 4 and 5, 'Battles' and 'Villains'.

'Battles' explores the question of where to look for the most truthful representations of two battles which took place at the height of the war: the siege at Khe Sanh in early 1968, when American Marines were surrounded and outnumbered by the NVA, and the fighting in the Ashau Valley in 1969, when American forces suffered heavy casualties in securing an objective, only to abandon it shortly afterwards. Are Army reports, journalism, oral testimony by participants or works of history sufficient for the recording of such engagements, conventional in some ways, but highly distinctive in others? Or can fictional works based on fact, like Michael Herr's highly regarded *Dispatches* or John Irvin's *Hamburger Hill* (1987), provide more honest and enlightening accounts?

'Villains' considers the massacres at Son My in March 1968 when American troops, apparently frustrated to the point of murder by their inability to find a conventional war to fight, slaughtered approximately 500 Vietnamese noncombatants. This chapter asks whether fictional works, like Tim O'Brien's novel *In the Lake of the Woods* or Oliver

Stone's *Platoon*, can add anything to the official investigation carried out by the Peers Inquiry, the Inquiry's conclusions being reliant to some extent on the flawed evidence of confused, partial or mendacious participants. Can a novel or film recreate the horror of such episodes more adequately than more dispassionate descriptions or offer explanations of why such atrocities occur?

Having offered perspectives on American soldiers in the guise of heroes, as villains and in combat, the sixth chapter deals with the experience of veterans returning to America and their treatment by film makers. For several years during and after the war the Vietnam veteran was depicted on the screen as out of control and often violent. Michael Cimino's *The Deer Hunter*, which won the Academy Award for Best Picture in 1978, signalled Hollywood's acceptance of a need to produce films which emphasised the suffering of the veteran and offered a closure to the trauma of American defeat. Although the depiction of veterans in *The Deer Hunter* and other films which achieved critical or commercial success provides a useful index of cultural attitudes towards the war, it is notable that the temptation to sensationalise the experience of the veteran has persisted. The most powerful example of this is provided by films like George Pan Cosmatos' *Rambo: First Blood Part II* (1985), starring Sylvester Stallone, which feature veterans returning to Vietnam after the war to rescue American POWs. In such films the figure of the veteran has been manipulated in a manner intended to re-write the history of the war.

Before embarking upon the inter-disciplinary studies which are the substance of this book some background is called for. What follows is a tentative outline of the events and decisions which led America to invest so heavily in a land war in South-east Asia. This may usefully be read in tandem with the Timeline which appears on pages viii–xiii above.

Why Did America Fight a War in Vietnam?

America's war in Vietnam was, it may be suggested, a consequence of fear, misunderstanding and an optimism borne initially of arrogance and later of desperation. Successive administrations, beginning with Harry S Truman's post-war government, were frightened by the prospect of a Communist Vietnam. China's 'fall' to Communism in 1949 and America's indecisive conflict with Communists in Korea might have been the focus of Truman's concerns in Asia but global politics dictated that America's reputation would be dealt a blow if any country in the region became Communist. By 1954 President Eisenhower was warning the American people that South-east Asia was vulnerable to the 'domino effect': the idea that if one country became Communist, others would follow.[8] However, few Americans understood Vietnamese history, the character of the people or the extent to which some of them were prepared to go to achieve a unified, independent and Communist Vietnam. And even if Americans in the 1950s and 1960s had grasped the circumstances in Vietnam more clearly, they would have found it hard to accept that, having won two World Wars, with wealth and technology at their command and a brimming confidence in their ability to get a job done, they might be unable to secure a satisfactory settlement in Vietnam.

When Presidents Kennedy and Johnson took decisions which tied America more firmly to the fates of the Vietnamese people, they did so in the hope that the resolve of the South Vietnamese might be stiffened and that the North Vietnamese and the southern insurgents led by the NLF might back down. As the American commitment in economic, military and human terms grew, so too did the sense amongst America's leaders that too much had been contributed to allow an admission of failure. By June 1965 President Johnson was privately confessing his doubts about the war to his Secretary of Defense, Robert McNamara:

> I'm very depressed about it. Because I see no program from either Defense or State that gives me much hope of doing anything, except just praying and gasping to hold on during the monsoon and hope they'll quit.
>
> I don't believe they're *ever* going to quit.[9]

In public, however, Johnson continued to express an optimism that he did not feel, apparently convinced that he was restricted to a single, unappealing option on Vietnam: to hang on and hope that matters would soon improve. Meanwhile, the North Vietnamese leadership had settled in for the long haul.

Vietnamese history includes a struggle for independence from the Chinese, their northern neighbour, which, at its conclusion in 1428, had lasted for over a thousand years. The ineptitude of the French colonial administration which, from 1887, ruled the three provinces of Vietnam, Annam, Cochinchina and Tonkin, as part of the Indochinese Union, had merely added to the bitterness of a Vietnamese people whose national heroes were those who had resisted foreign invaders. The Viet Minh, an independence movement led by Ho Chi Minh, took the opportunity to seize power from the occupying Japanese at the end of World War II before the French could reinstate the colonial arrangements which had existed before the war.

Having declared Vietnamese independence in September 1945 the Viet Minh were to be frustrated for another nine years. The French, with American support, regained nominal control of Vietnam with talk of independence in the future. If America's leaders were prompted by historical sentiment to sympathise with a small country seeking to escape the yoke of colonialism, their political priorities were the retention of sound relations with a European ally and the drawing of cold war battle-lines. The French, however, continued to conduct themselves as the imperial masters of Vietnam and by 1946 the Viet Minh had been stung into military action against them. President Truman, like his successor Eisenhower, supplied the French with military aid while remaining doubt-ful that the French could be relied upon to settle matters effectively. Each president found himself confronted by the same limited set of discour-aging options: the Communist sympathies of Ho Chi Minh, French colonialism, or an acceptance of increased American responsibility in the region.

After the Viet Minh had decisively defeated the French at the battle of Dien Bien Phu in 1954, an international conference in Geneva 'tempor-arily' partitioned Vietnam into North and South. With the Viet Minh in control of the North, Eisenhower committed limited American resources towards the protection and nurturing of a non-Communist South. Declaring after the Geneva conference that: 'We must work with these people, and then they themselves will soon find out that we are their friends and that they can't live without us', Eisenhower set the tone of a relationship which would be characterised by American condescension and Vietnamese stubbornness.[10]

Perhaps blinded by a sense of their own capability, the Americans failed to appreciate both the depth of the nationalist sentiment which motivated their enemy and the unwillingness of their South Vietnamese allies to adapt to American imperatives. The words of an American colonel to a subordinate in Stanley Kubrick's *Full Metal Jacket* (1987) suggest the arrogance of this particular misunderstanding: 'We are here to help the Vietnamese because inside of every gook there's an American trying to get out.'[11] As the war became more Americanised the resent-ment of the South Vietnamese at such attitudes often expressed itself in a reluctance to take the initiative and an unwillingness to co-operate with American ideas. Instead, successive South Vietnamese administrations concentrated on ensuring their own continuance in power and the South Vietnamese people, frequently the victims of the American war effort, accepted the economic advantages of the American presence without committing their 'hearts and minds' to the American priority of nation building. The North Vietnamese and the forces of the NLF, in contrast, were committed to the notion that, eventually, the Americans would give up and go home.

It may be argued that fear, misunderstanding and an optimism which, until 1968 and the Tet Offensive, was self-perpetuating do not account for all of America's difficulties in Vietnam. Indeed, the explanation may be disputed at each of its stages: some, for example, may consider America's determination to prevent Vietnam falling into the hands of the Communists as an act of courage rather than a demonstration of fear, or Johnson's military escalation as war-mongering rather than an act of desperation. The explanation has been offered here as a possible context for the studies which follow and an illustration of some of the dilemmas faced by America's leaders. What probably can be agreed is that while Vietnam was, in 1945, a relatively unimportant factor in discussions of what the post-war world might look like, the beginning of the cold war transformed the future of Vietnam into a frustrating priority for America. By April 1975, the war in Vietnam had cost the lives of over 58,000 Americans and, at a conservative estimate, of more than one million Vietnamese.[12] How an inter-disciplinary approach can help to explain this descent into tragedy is the focus of the analyses which follow. Chapter 1, however, looks in more detail at this question: how do you tell true war stories?

Notes

1. 'It Don't Mean Nothin': The Vietnam Experience', an essay by William P. Mahedy, begins with a veteran's comment: 'When I went to Vietnam, I believed in Jesus Christ and John Wayne. After Vietnam, both went down the tubes. It don't mean nothin'.' Mahedy, who worked in a Vet Center, observed: 'I have heard other veterans say the same thing a thousand times in different ways.' In Walter Capps (ed.), *The Vietnam Reader* (New York: Routledge, 1991), p. 33.
2. Roger J. Spiller cited in Paul Fussell (ed.), *The Bloody Game* (London: Scribner's, 1991), p. 313.
3. Henry James, 'The Art of Fiction', in Leon Edel (ed.), *The Future of the Novel* (New York: Vintage Books, 1956), p. 6.
4. R. W. B. Lewis, *The American Adam: Innocence, Tragedy, and Tradition in the Nineteenth Century* (Chicago: University of Chicago Press, [1955] 1971), p. 14.

5. *Time* headlined its review of Oliver Stone's *Platoon*: 'Viet Nam, the way it really was, on film'. Richard Corliss, 26 January 1987.
6. Moore's first line is '*The Green Berets* is a book of truth.' Robin Moore, *The Green Berets* (New York: Crown Publishers, 1965), p. 1. Although John Wayne shared directorial credit for *The Green Berets* with Ray Kellogg it is referred to throughout this book as Wayne's film because of the dominant influence he had upon it.
7. Spiller cited in Fussell (ed.), *The Bloody Game*, p. 313.
8. At a television news conference on 7 April 1954, Eisenhower said: 'You have a row of dominoes set up and you knock over the first one, and what will happen to the last one is the certainty that it will go over very quickly ... The loss of Indochina will cause the fall of Southeast Asia like a set of dominoes.' Cited in Robert D. Schulzinger, *A Time For War: The United States and Vietnam, 1941–1975* (New York: Oxford University Press, [1997] 1998), pp. 66–7.
9. Telephone conversation between Johnson and McNamara, 21 June 1965. Printed in Michael Beschloss (ed.), *Reaching for Glory: Lyndon Johnson's Secret White House Tapes, 1964–1965* (New York: Simon and Schuster, 2001), p. 365. The emphasis in this and all other quotations is in the original.
10. Eisenhower cited in George C. Herring, *America's Longest War: The United States and Vietnam, 1950–1975*, 3rd edn (New York: McGraw-Hill, Inc., 1996), p. 44.
11. From *Full Metal Jacket*, directed by Stanley Kubrick (Warner Bros, 1987).
12. There is considerable disagreement about Vietnamese casualty figures. Guenter Lewy suggested an 'overall casualty toll of 1,313,000' for the period 1965 to 1974, of whom 'about 365,000' were Vietnamese civilians, in Lewy, *America in Vietnam* (New York: Oxford University Press, 1978), p. 451. Loren Baritz, however, estimated that '2,000,000 Vietnamese were killed', of whom 400,000 were civilians, in Baritz, *Backfire: A History of How American Culture Led Us Into Vietnam and Made Us Fight The Way We Did* (Baltimore: The Johns Hopkins University Press, [1985] 1998), p. 344.

CHAPTER I

Telling True War Stories

Thirty years from now, people will think of the Viet Nam War as Platoon.[1]
David Halberstam (journalist and novelist) January 1987

While Oliver Stone might have enjoyed the idea that future generations would base their understanding of America's war in Vietnam on *Platoon*, his partly autobiographical film about American soldiers in combat there, many historians would have shuddered with horror at David Halberstam's suggestion that the war would be remembered by Stone's representation of it. In 1968, the same year that Stone was slogging through the bush on the Vietnamese–Cambodian border, historian A. J. P. Taylor had warned that 'film as well as being very useful is a very dangerous instrument for historical study'.[2] Thirty years later, Arthur Marwick observed in his social and political history, *The Sixties*, that 'Films and novels have to be handled with particular care: invoking the occasional fictional character or quoting the odd striking phrase may ornament the historian's discourse, but seldom adds weight to it.'[3] And in the wake of Oliver Stone's versions of the Kennedy assassination in *JFK* and Nixon's presidency in *Nixon* (1995) historians might have felt that any film by Oliver Stone required extra labels indicating 'Danger! Handle With Care'. However, Halberstam's prophecy was based on persuasive precedent. American veterans of the war in Vietnam had frequently claimed that their expectations of combat had their origins in Hollywood's versions of World War II, of John Wayne charging up the slopes of Mount Suribachi in *Sands of Iwo Jima* (1949) or Audie Murphy playing himself in *To Hell and Back* (1955).[4] The Academy Award-winning *Platoon* is a dramatic, memorable movie which *Time* headlined 'Viet Nam, the way it really was, on film', and Stone's empassioned manipulation of a variety of cinematic techniques to depict the physical experiences of a group of infantrymen is horribly convincing in many of the scenes. Historians have to accept, however grudgingly, that Stone's film 'is' the Vietnam War for many people, especially those too young to remember the war itself. Historians must also recognise that their versions of events reach a much smaller audience than films or even moderately successful fiction dealing with the same period and that history books rarely have the immediate, emotional impact of film or fiction.

Nevertheless, to 'think of the Viet Nam War as *Platoon*', or as Michael Herr's *Dispatches*, Tim O'Brien's *Going After Cacciato* or, indeed, historian George C. Herring's *The Longest War* is to simplify and to limit one's understanding of America's most controversial war. As Tim O'Brien's short story 'How to Tell a True War Story' suggested, communicating or detecting the truth about war is not an easy matter. For O'Brien, or at least for his narrator, 'Absolute occurence is irrelevant. A thing may happen and be a total lie; another thing may happen and be truer than the truth' or as O'Brien wrote in 'Good Form', another of his stories, 'story truth is truer sometimes than happening truth'.[5] On the other hand, it is usually assumed that the historian believes the opposite, that the truths of history are built upon what *has* happened. It is important, although not necessarily easy, to try to establish what happened in the Gulf of Tonkin on 4 August 1964 which might have justified President Johnson's decision to use American planes to bomb North Vietnam for the first time, for example, or what happened during the massacres at Son My.

The particular problems of the historian require some clarification. Over a century ago Thoreau asked: 'How do you make a fact flower into a truth?'[6] At the time, many of his readers would have been content to leave the task in the safe keeping of a historian. The following sections of this chapter will explore whether history still inspires similar confidence and the ways in which war in the twentieth century, and specifically the Vietnam War, has posed new challenges for history.

If history is not a science, then are historians any different in essence from novelists ... ?[7] Richard J. Evans

The problems confronted by historians of America's war in Vietnam are not limited to Oliver Stone's predilection for making films about American history. Not only must historians compete with Hollywood and the bookshelves groaning under the weight of novels, memoirs, journals, plays and collections of poetry, most of which claim to be telling their own particular truths, but they must, at the beginning of the twenty-first century, be ready to argue for the distinctiveness of the historical enterprise. At the end of the nineteenth century, historians could believe, in the words of Lord Acton, that 'all information is within reach, and every problem has become capable of solution.'[8] In 1903 the Regius Professor of Modern History at Cambridge, J. B. Bury, could claim a secure role for the discipline when he delivered his inaugural lecture: 'History is a science, no less and no more ... History is not a branch of literature.'[9] Then, historians could take refuge in the notion that novelists might sell more books but it was historians who, in scientific fashion, discovered truths about the past. Crucially, there was a firm boundary between truth and fiction. The definition of historical objectivity which Peter Novick offered in the opening pages of *That Noble Dream: The 'Objectivity Question' and the American Historical Profession* illustrates the principles upon which most historians in Bury's era based their work:

> The assumptions on which [historical objectivity] rests include a commitment to the reality of the past, and to truth as correspondence to that reality; a sharp separation between knower and known, between fact and value, and above all between history and fiction. Historical facts are seen as prior to and independent of interpretation: the value of an interpretation is judged by how well it accounts for the facts; if contradicted by the facts, it must be abandoned. Truth is one, not perspectival. Whatever patterns exist in history are 'found', not 'made'.[10]

Novick goes on to trace in detail the ways in which the idea of 'historical objectivity' was staggered by the publication of Einstein's 'General Theory of Relativity' in 1913 and by the experience of World War I. By revealing the uncertainty of the foundations upon which scientists had worked, Einstein's theory led some historians to revise their claims about telling *the* truth and to accept that history's purpose was to construct interpretations of the past which must be affected by their own perspective of the world. The scale and apparent senselessness of the slaughter on the Western Front induced many to believe that some of mankind's behaviour was beyond rational explanation while the prostitution of history to the demands of propaganda on both sides of the conflict further damaged historians' claims to be entirely neutral observers.

The notion of historical objectivity was periodically revived during the twentieth century, notably in cold war America in order to demonstrate the 'rightness' of western democracy and the 'wrongness' of Communism, and some historians simply chose to ignore any doubts they might harbour about the philosophical foundations of their discipline.

Nevertheless, by the 1960s there was an acceptance of the progressive rather than the absolute nature of historical enquiry. In 1967 G. R. Elton wrote of the historian's task: 'His can never be the last word, an ambition in any case bred out of vanity, but he can establish new footholds in the territory of truth.'[11] The image of territory demonstrates the size of the task and the notion of footholds its tentative nature, a far cry from Bury's confident claims of scientific certitude or Lord Acton's optimism. Two years after Elton's remarks in *The Practice of History*, Sir Charles Oman accepted the limits of the historian's role in *On the Writing of History* with words which questioned the distinction between history and literature: 'for History is not a purely objective thing, it is the historian's way of envisaging and correlating a certain series of events. As the Frenchman said, "Il n'y a pas d'histoire, mais seulement des histoires."'[12] No history, but only stories – the words might have become a slogan for the New Journalists whose writing in the 1960s and '70s explored and manipulated whatever boundaries there were between fact and fiction.

By 1988, Ellen Somekawa and Elizabeth A. Smith could publish an essay in the *Journal of Social History* entitled 'Theorizing the writing of history, or "I can't think why it should be so dull, for a great deal of it must be invention"' and assume that most of their readers would be unsurprised by the suggestion in their title.[13] Few historians in the 1980s considered themselves engaged in scientific projects which resulted in objective accounts of the past based entirely upon the facts they had researched. As Hayden White had written: 'Neither the reality nor the meaning of history is "out there" in the form of a story awaiting only a historian to discern its outline and identify the plot that comprises its meaning.'[14] In other words, historians cannot *discover* the past. Instead they can invent a story or stories about it, based on the 'facts' as they understand them, but imposing their own order and meaning upon those 'facts' by the structure of their argument and their choice of language.

The soldier's history of war does not readily submit to the orderly require-ments of history.[15] Roger J. Spiller

Historians writing about war, especially about combat, have frequently encountered additional obstacles. The most basic information – casualty figures, the disposition of the different forces and the actions of the combatants – often remains in question because of the confusion that war brings. And as Michael Walzer pointed out in *Just and Unjust Wars*:

'Hypocrisy is rife in wartime discourse, because it is especially important at such a time to appear to be in the right.'[16]

The closer the historian gets to the heart of combat, the greater the problems. Soldiers expecting a violent end, in the clamour and horror and chaos of battle, do not make reliable eyewitnesses and it is upon eyewitnesses that those who seek the truth about combat must usually depend. Investigating and interpreting what happens at the heart of the combat experience involves wrestling with the confused, the contradictory, the irrational and often the incredible. It involves trying to strip away and analyse layers of deception, self-deception and reorganisation applied with a variety of intentions – perhaps to make the experience comprehensible or credible or tolerable. It is significant that philosophers of history have often couched their strategies of historical interpretation in terms that effectively exclude combat, history's 'darkest corner'. Agnes Heller's attempt to define a theory of history, for example, relied on concepts of plausibility and coherence:

> Plausibility is the verisimilitude of everyday life, thinking and *judgment*. We normally accept the most plausible interpretation. The interpretation of any event is most plausible if it provides an explanation of the event by creating a connection between the characters and the situations of all persons involved in the event, and does so in a coherent way.[17]

Yet combat has little to do with 'everyday life' and events in combat may be highly implausible, demonstrating irrational behaviour by the participants and resulting in incoherence rather than order.

Amongst the most persuasive descriptions of battle in nineteenth-century literature are those which accept its chaos: Stendahl's description of Waterloo in *The Charterhouse of Parma*, for example, or Stephen Crane's account of the battle at Chancellorsville in *The Red Badge of Courage*. Twentieth-century combat, with its greater, more rapid and more varied destructive capacity, is even more difficult to explain. Those portrayals of combat which offer 'the most plausible explanation' are likely to be the most superficial, for 'plausible' means 'seeming reasonable' and reason is often absent in combat.[18]

Indeed the accurate portrayal of combat is so difficult that there is a widely held theory that non-combatants can never understand it and that, as Walt Whitman wrote of the American Civil War: 'The Real War Will Never Get In The Books'.[19] Writing about twentieth-century wars offers plenty of examples of the feeling amongst combatants that it is not possible to explain the truth about combat. The partly autobiographical novel *All Quiet On The Western Front* was written by Erich Maria Remarque, a veteran of World War I. Remarque's hero confessed that he could not properly describe his experience of combat: 'I cannot even say myself exactly what I mean.' After World War II Eugene B. Sledge described his experiences in combat in the Pacific as 'totally incomprehensible' in his memoir *With the Old Breed at Peleliu and Okinawa*. And, in the partly autobiographical *Dispatches*, Michael Herr claimed to recall a story told to him by an American soldier in Vietnam which took him a year to understand: 'Patrol went up the mountain. One man came back. He died before he could tell us what happened.'[20] Herr's tale marked off the experience of combat as an area which must remain a mystery to the non-combatant. Of course, each of these examples comes from a text which sought to do that which it accepted, momentarily at least, as impossible and it is no answer simply to dismiss every attempt to depict combat as doomed to failure. The world of war may not be entirely comprehensible but it seems not to be escapable either and in history, literature and film efforts continue to offer insights into the experience of combat and the nature of war. The question is: which forms provide the most effective insights?

Paul Fussell attempted to clarify the specific problems of writing about combat in his book *The Great War and Modern Memory*, published in 1975. Using World War I as his model, Fussell argued that the horror of combat defied the attempts of language to represent it. Having indicated the past failure of the enterprise, Fussell then wondered about the effects of attempting to write about combat and about which styles of writing about battle, if any, may be 'suitable for history'. Fussell's concern reflected a general awareness that the ways in which language is used inevitably imposes patterns of thought and emphases which are originated by the historian, or indeed by any writer or artist, rather than the events themselves: 'How are actual events deformed by the application to them of metaphor, rhetorical comparison, prose rhythm, assonance, alliteration, allusion and sentence structures and connectives implying clear causality?'[21] (Although Fussell does not extend his argument to other media it is relevant. For example, artists working in the medium of film, even documentary film makers, 'deform' events by, amongst other techniques, the selection of camera shot, juxtaposing shots, editing, adding music, using lighting and choosing perspective.)

Fussell's conclusion was that 'it would seem impossible to write an account of anything without some literature creeping in.'[22] The consequence of this conclusion is that there can be no distinction between historical descriptions of battles which attempt anything beyond simple chronology, war memoirs, war reportage and novels because the act of organising material into intelligibility immediately transforms it into fiction. Fussell quoted Robert Kee, an RAF flyer in World War II, with approval:

> There's nothing you could really get hold of if you were trying to write a proper, historical account of it all. No wonder the stuff slips away mercury-wise from proper historians. No wonder they have to erect artificial structures of one sort or another in its place. No wonder it is those artists who re-create life rather than try to re-capture it who, in one way, provide the good historians in the end.[23]

Fussell also offered the idea of novelist Wright Morris who believed that 'Anything processed by memory is fiction' and delved back into the seventeenth century to cite Thomas Hobbes' comment in *Leviathan* that 'Imagination and memory are but one thing.'[24] Thus, the implication of Fussell's argument is that writers of informed imagination are as likely to produce credible versions of combat as those who claim to write non-fiction. This is, firstly, because of the way in which the application of language must add the writer's conscious or unconscious nuances of meaning and pattern to the events that are under description and thereby alter them. Secondly, it is because partial, frightened, confused participants in combat, men or women who are perhaps exhausted, feverish or injured, perceive events incompletely or inaccurately and almost certainly readjust them in the act of telling. Clearly there is a difference between writing history and writing memories, but in combat it is memory that is the main resource of the historian as there is little opportunity to make records or take notes about what is happening while a battle is raging.

Historians have been troubled by the implications of Fussell's argument about the status of non-fiction. They have also been justly irritated by the dismissive tone he adopted. In *The Great War and Modern Memory* he complained of the falsity of traditional descriptions of warfare:

> *battles* is perhaps not the best word, having been visited upon these events by subsequent historiography in the interest of neatness and

the assumption of something like a rational causality ... to imply an understandable continuity with earlier British history and to imply that the war makes sense in a traditional way.[25]

The accusation that historians have peddled inaccuracy in order to retain a neat view of the world predictably attracted hostility. His highly selective use of evidence and the demonstrable inaccuracy of some of his own historical statements left his work vulnerable to attack. 'Paul Fussell at War', an article by Robin Prior and Trevor Wilson published in *War in History* in 1994, demonstrated the weakness of his history although, significantly, it failed to dent the strength of his argument about the difficulties the portrayal of combat presents to historians. Having commented that Fussell was a Professor of English writing about history, Prior and Wilson gave their own, rather bitter, version of Fussell's argument in their introduction: 'Conventional historians in his opinion, only dress up the distorted, fanciful version of official apologists.'[26] There followed an extremely effective attack on some of Fussell's pronouncements about World War I. His claim that the British Army suffered 7,000 casualties a day on the Western Front during World War I was correctly ridiculed with the observation that, if this were the case: 'Britain's forces, without launching or sustaining a single attack, would thereby have suffered 10 million casualties – the equivalent of some 600 divisions.' As the British only raised five million fighting men during the four years of the war, Fussell's proposition was 'plainly fanciful'.[27]

Nevertheless, historians are left with Fussell's central argument. In the introduction to their article Prior and Wilson asked the question:

> If diplomatic documents and battle narratives will not explicate all facets of modern war, will literary sources reveal the entire story? Or is modern war too complex and perhaps too self-contradictory to be wholly revealed even by imaginative writings and personal accounts? [28]

Prior and Wilson devoted their article to disproving Fussell's historical pronouncements and the issue of how historians should pursue the truth about combat and to what extent it is possible was not addressed. Fussell's original question about the most effective way to portray combat remained unanswered.

History is the fiction and fiction is the history.[29] Donald Ringnalda

Between the arrival of American troops in Vietnam in 1965 and their departure in 1973 radical changes took place in the writing of journalism and fiction. Encouraged by the atmosphere of experimentation abroad in the 1960s and conscious of growing scepticism about the authority of official sources, the attempts of American writers to 'tell the truth' became more self-conscious and the uncertainty of the dividing line between fiction and non-fiction was foregrounded rather than obscured. In particular, the development of the various styles of writing that became known as New Journalism altered the perceptions of many writers about their craft. Although novelists Truman Capote and Norman Mailer were the most famous of the writers who were identified with New Journalism, most of the early New Journalists were reporters, working for magazines like *Esquire* or Sunday supplements like *New York*. The questions raised by New Journalism and the techniques they adopted to tell the truth made a powerful impression on the writing of history, investigative journalism and fiction in America and elsewhere.

In 1965 Truman Capote presented his account of a multiple murder in what he described as a 'non-fiction novel' called *In Cold Blood*.[30] Basing his work on official records, interviews and 'my own observation', Capote was able to describe the events and re-create the thoughts and motives of the people involved, whilst retaining the dual authority of a writer of history and the omniscience of a novelist.[31] Three years later Norman Mailer produced *The Armies of the Night*, which documented the demonstration against the Vietnam War held in Washington DC in October 1967. Mailer entitled the first part of his book 'History as a Novel' and the second part 'The Novel as History'. Half way through his second section, however, Mailer admitted that the titles were interchangeable and argued that the writing of history is not always the best route to the truth:

> this first book [is] a personal history which while written as a novel was to the best of the author's memory scrupulous to facts and there-fore a document; whereas the second, while dutiful to all newspaper accounts, eyewitness reports, and historic inductions available, while even obedient to a general style of historical writing ... is finally now to be disclosed as some sort of condensation of a collective novel – which is to admit that an explanation of the events at the Pentagon

cannot be developed by the methods of history – only by the instincts of a novelist.[32]

Mailer's argument illustrates the climate in which the New Journalists worked and the radical re-structuring of literary, journalistic and historical categories which was being attempted. The use of documentation did not automatically imply historical accuracy and writing in the form of a novel did not prevent the expression of truth. The New Journalists' vigorous combination of fictional techniques with the detailed observations of reports also conveyed the confusion of the times. Like Mailer, some of them would use the novel to:

> replace history at precisely that point where experience is sufficiently emotional, spiritual, psychical, moral, existential or supernatural to expose the fact that the historian in pursuing the experience would be obliged to quit the clearly demarcated limits of historic enquiry.[33]

This was the atmosphere in which many of the writers about the Vietnam War worked, or at least read, and served some sort of writer's apprenticeship. The notion that the nature of the war in Vietnam made it especially difficult to distinguish between fact and fiction, and the widening 'credibility gap' between official pronouncements and the perceptions of participants and observers of the war in Vietnam, seemed to render the styles of New Journalism particularly appropriate.

Featured in Tom Wolfe and E. W. Johnson's anthology *The New Journalism*, John Sack's *M*, published in 1966, demonstrates the originality of technique which New Journalism offered to writing about the Vietnam War and the uncertainties that it evoked. Sack used the interviews he conducted with the soldiers of a company of the First Infantry Division to construct a narrative which was widely accepted as reportage. Tom Wolfe's introduction to the extract anthologised in *The New Journalism* referred to the difficulties Sack had with the initial publication of parts of his book in *Esquire* magazine:

> Sack interviewed the soldiers of M company about what had been going through their minds during certain adventures, then made these thoughts and feelings part of the action itself as he described it. Sometimes this took the form of brief interior monologues ... *Esquire*'s lawyers threw up their hands over this use of other people's thoughts on the grounds that it opened the way to invasion of privacy suits unless Sack could get written consent from each soldier involved. It is

an indication of Sack's perseverance, not to mention his accuracy, that he thereupon backtracked and got in touch with every living soldier that was mentioned ... showed them the manuscript and got their OKs.[34]

However, Wolfe's praise for Sack's accuracy was mistaken in a very important way. Sack confessed to Eric James Schroeder in *Vietnam, We've All Been There: Interviews with American Writers*:

> I'm playing a diabolical trick on the reader of *M* ...You can never tell which scenes I witnessed and which were reported to me second-hand ... I want the reader to feel that he or she is being handed raw information, raw facts ... This is a shuck. Obviously everything has been passed through my consciousness, and I'm just taking advantage of this whole American belief in objectivity. I myself don't believe in objectivity – no New Journalist does.[35]

So where does this leave the historian, or indeed the literary critic? Both might regard Sack's book as a confidence trick. Unable to distinguish between verifiable facts, subjective impression and what might be pure fiction, the book was reportage in almost the same sense as F. Scott Fitzgerald's *This Side of Paradise* and other autobiographical novels. The only important difference seems to be that Sack sought to invest *M* with an aura of authenticity which was entirely spurious. He did this by retaining the names of the people upon whom his characters were based in his final chapter, 'Roll-Call'; by writing without using a first person narrator to strengthen the impression that the reader was receiving 'raw information'; and by ensuring that his photograph did not appear on the book cover in case it reminded the reader that someone had 'arranged and interpreted the facts'.[36]

A look at three of the reviews of *M* which prefaced the Corgi edition of Sack's book demonstrates the confusion these techniques aroused. The *Los Angeles Times* enthused about it: 'This is the whole story, one of the most compelling ever told about men in war.' *Saturday Review*'s critic found it: 'Unforgettable ... *M* comes closer to the reality of Vietnam than anything else I have yet read' and *Bookweek* eulogised: 'Splendid ... One of the finest, most perceptive books of reportage on any subject in recent years'.[37]

These three comments reveal the bewilderment caused by Sack's version of New Journalism. *Bookweek* thought that it was reportage, which presumably implied factually accurate. Like Wolfe, this reviewer felt that Sack was an entirely reliable and credible witness. It is ironic that Wolfe, the editor of an anthology of New Journalism, should have mis-read *M* in the same way, failing to recognise that it was essentially a novel masquerading as history. *The Saturday Review* was more cautious. *M* came closer to reality than anything else the critic had read. This suggests an awareness of two things: firstly, that Sack's book might not be entirely factual and, secondly, that it is possible to approach the truth in a book whether it is fiction or non-fiction. By accident or design the *Los Angeles Times* evaded the issue, referring to *M* as a story which made 'compelling' reading, thus leaving open the question of whether it was a book of truth or not.

Sack's book is important because it demonstrated the way in which the line between fiction and non-fiction could be manipulated. The nature of the war in Vietnam was such that the most experienced journalists found it perplexing. Sack had experience as a war correspondent in Korea and obviously decided that conventional reportage about Vietnam was inappropriate or impossible. As Sack said to Schroeder: 'Anybody in his forties or fifties would have been interpreting things so much from the point of view of his recollections of World War II that he would not have been able to grasp what was going on over there.'[38]

Certainly anybody who relied exclusively upon official accounts of what was happening in Vietnam would have received an inaccurate version of events. In *Vietnam: A History*, Stanley Karnow referred to the 'stupendous amount of paper' generated during the Vietnam War and offered the warning: 'Documents, whatever their origin, ought to be approached with caution.' Turning to interviews with participants in an attempt to overcome the difficulties created by the quantity and uncertain status of documentation produced during the war, Karnow recognised that 'the participants in the war were rarely models of dispassionate objectivity.'[39] He was left offering a synthesis of the information which he found the most credible, based on sources that he admitted were dubious.

Sack's response was to ignore established categories of fiction and non-fiction, to rely upon the tendency to accept anything written in documentary style and to deliver a version of the truth which, he would have argued, was sincere in intention if imaginary in detail. Towards the end of his book Sack described an attack on an American camp:

The communists still keep coming – damn. The camp is frightfully shy of rifle soldiers, some are in Army hospitals, irregular holes in their arms or legs, malaria, gonorrhea, some are on pacification work and Demirgian is fast asleep, the artillery officer is a playboy in Tokyo on a rest and recreation leave, a terror-stricken lieutenant is still in his little cotton tent, his shoes shined, his belt buckle bright with metal polish. Outside of the company camp the barbed wire is absent – orders, we've got to show the Vietnamese we aren't a bunch of scaredies, damn! On one whole side of the triangle not a rifle is functioning, double damn – the bullets are stuck inside of them and of the machine guns, too ... The communists are coming over the earthen walls now! Are we down-hearted? YES![40]

Here, in microcosm, was criticism of America's performance in Vietnam. Sack attacked the Army's disorganisation and its leadership – one officer was a playboy on leave, the other, an obsessively neat and terrified lieutenant, remained in his tent. The equipment was inadequate and the camp's defences incomplete, because, in an ironic reversal of the commonly made accusation that the great weakness of the Vietnamese was fear of losing face, the Americans could not use barbed wire in case they appeared frightened of attack.[41] The ordinary soldiers, although Sack implied sympathy for those in hospital with 'irregular holes in their arms or legs', were presented as frightened, confused and 'down-hearted'. The description was not historically true and Sack's position, as he stated it to Schroeder, was that it could not be, because 'Objectivity is just impossible.'[42] Sack's writing had the merit of challenging the official version of the truth in a convincing fashion and it prepared the ground for writers like Michael Herr and Tim O'Brien, who would experiment further with strategies intended to portray the truth about combat in Vietnam. Also, of course, it implied that whatever truths there were to tell about the Vietnam War were in the hands of writers of fiction, that 'history is the fiction and fiction is the history'.

He did not know where truth lay.[43] Tim O'Brien

All of this is not to say that historical investigations into other periods and other events have not required scepticism in the scrutiny of documentation and testimony – historians, as the case of the 'Hitler Diaries' illustrated, have always needed to be on guard.[44] Nevertheless, the

Vietnam War presented a new set of challenges to historians: even Oliver Stone has confessed that it was an 'extremely complicated war'.[45]

Consider the task undertaken by President Lyndon Johnson in the words of an American officer serving in Vietnam in 1967:

> The magnitude of what he is trying to accomplish here can only be realised when you firmly establish in your own mind that Johnson is trying to take 5,000 villages living on a rice economy with a 2,000-year-old Asian tradition of chieftain rule warped by 100 years of ugly colonialism and *build a nation* with an industrial base and a democratic tradition in the midst of a twenty-year-old war.[46]

In subsequent years Johnson's efforts to '*build a nation*' would be presented as a noble undertaking, an American (rather than a Vietnamese) tragedy, or an immoral act of imperialism. Each of these positions would be held by significant numbers of Americans in civilian life and in the services. Which was the more correct? As Timothy J. Lomperis has observed, 'the real Gordian knot to the understanding of the Vietnam War [is] not complications over unfathomable facts but a deep-seated clash over values.'[47] Two recent books exemplify this. Michael Lind's *Vietnam: The Necessary War*, published in 1999, concluded with the sentence: 'the greatest danger is that the Vietnam War will be treated by mainstream historians as an inexplicable mistake ... The Vietnam War was neither a mistake nor a betrayal nor a crime. It was a military defeat.'[48] Published a year earlier, Jim Neilson's *Warring Fictions* complained that: 'Vietnam War literature ... does not challenge the fundamental morality of U.S. aims, nor does it document the large-scale killing of Vietnamese.'[49] Lind and Neilson's dispute, over twenty years after the war ended, is one of political motive rather than a disagreement about 'unfathomable facts'.

The words of another American who served in Vietnam highlight the importance of the war's motive for individual veterans: 'The notion that [the war] was for nothing is intolerable ... The minute I think we were doing the wrong thing ... I go from being a fighting man to being a butcher'.[50] In national terms the stakes were just as high, as President Bush's enthusiastic words in the aftermath of the Gulf War illustrated: 'By God, we've kicked the Vietnam syndrome once and for all!'[51] America's defeat in Vietnam left so much confusion, shame and rage and so much eagerness for personal and national anguish to be resolved that emotional and spiritual closure came to be in greater demand than historical accounts of events. Novelist, veteran and government official James Webb has written:

> Only the arts will provide resolution to our national angst over Vietnam. Only a good book or painting or play or movie can conjure the emotions and ambiguities of an experience, and through such exorcism affect attitudes that shape consciousness.[52]

Which leaves historians on the sidelines again, apparently.

Webb's words, part of a review he wrote of Francis Ford Coppola's 1979 film *Apocalypse Now*, demonstrate one of the ways in which the historian's role has been revised by some who feel new approaches are required in order to understand America's war in Vietnam. Conjuring emotions and exorcising psychic demons might have traditionally fallen into the province of the artist, but even exploration of the 'ambiguities of an experience', surely an activity for which historians have the necessary skills, has been annexed by the writers of fiction, the painters, the playwrights and the film makers according to Webb.

It would be harsh to accuse Webb and other artists of leaving historians to pick through the paperstorm generated by the American presence in Vietnam while the artists shared novelist Tim O'Brien's approach to writing about the war and told 'lies to get at the truth.'[53] Nevertheless, it has become a widely held assumption that, as a postmodern war, portrayals of the war in Vietnam demand a postmodern style to be meaningful, or indeed to be meaningless in order to reflect the meaninglessness of the war. Writers and critics of literature often give the impression that there is diminishing room in which the historian can usefully work.

Donald Ringnalda, for example, has argued in the preface to his 1994 book, *Fighting and Writing the Vietnam War*, that clarifying the war's history would be counter-productive: 'One of the essential points of my study is that the last thing America needs to do with the Vietnam experience is to make sense of it ... we need to articulate the contours of *nonsense* that culminated in the war.'[54]

Pursuing a similar point, Kate Beaird Meyers had suggested six years previously that traditional history reached an impasse with the Vietnam War: 'Because Vietnam is so different from other wars in modern memory, no good model exists for translating it into a traditional chronological historical narrative.'[55] At least novelist and journalist Jack Fuller, speaking in 1986 at a conference about the literature of the Vietnam War, had allowed historians the task of drawing up the war's calendar, 'What we find out as we write is a different kind of truth than the things historians record in the books of days and hours', even if the implication seemed to be that historians should leave the revelation of more sophisticated truths to the writers of literature.[56]

Literature by American veterans of the war in Vietnam has frequently contrasted the certainties associated with World War II with the lack of purpose perceived by soldiers in Vietnam in order to highlight the futility and meaninglessness of the Vietnam War. The protagonist of David Halberstam's novel, *One Very Hot Day*, published in 1967, was a veteran of the Normandy invasion, reluctantly serving in Vietnam. His description of the two wars shows their essential difference:

> We didn't know how simple it was, and how good we had it. Sure we walked, but in a straight line. Boom, Normandy beaches, and then you set off for Paris and Berlin. Just like that ... All you needed was a compass and good sense. But here you walk in a goddamn circle, and then you go home, and then you go out the next day and wade through a circle, and then you go home and the next day you go out and reverse the circle you did before, erasing it. Every day the circles get bigger and emptier.[57]

Halberstam's erasure of empty circles (or zeros) provides an image which suggests that seeking a meaning in America's actions in Vietnam is bound to fail: there is no meaning. Tim O'Brien's *Going After Cacciato*, published in 1978, makes an associated point:

> They did not know even the simple things: a sense of victory, or satisfaction, or necessary sacrifice. They did not know the feeling of taking a place and keeping it, securing a village and then raising the flag and calling it a victory. No sense of order or momentum. No front, no rear, no trenches laid out in neat parallels. No Patton rushing for the Rhine ... They did not have targets ... They did not know strategies ... They did not know how to feel ... they did not know which stories to believe ... They did not know good from evil.[58]

O'Brien's Vietnam, like Halberstam's, lacked the comfort of straight lines and his protagonist, ironically named Berlin, a target in World War II, found it impossible to distinguish truth from falsehood or right from wrong.

Spatial uncertainty and reference to the 'simple' ideas associated with World War II, or rather Hollywood's films about World War II, are elements in another text which has received much critical attention for its suggestions of how a 'different kind of truth' can be presented: Michael Herr's *Dispatches*, published in 1977. A journalist who spent a year in Vietnam, Herr spent seven years writing *Dispatches*, which he has described as a novel.[59] Nevertheless, Herr based his book on his experiences and used the form of the novel to challenge the traditional historical notion that facts are the source of understanding about the past:

> Maps, charts, figures, projections, fly fantasies, names of places, of operations, of commanders, of weapons; memories, guesses, second guesses, experiences (new, old, real, imagined, stolen); histories, attitudes – you could let it all go, let it all go. If you wanted some war news in Saigon you had to hear it in stories brought from the fields by friends, see it in the lost watchful eyes of the Saigonese, or do it like Trashman, reading the cracks in the sidewalk.[60]

Herr opted to write 'a secret history' which reflected the chaos of America's war in Vietnam in its structure and language rather than a conventional set of dispatches from the front. According to Donald Ringnalda, Herr's book exposed: 'One of the most profound problems in studies of the Vietnam War ... the stubborn Euclidean assurance that fact and fiction are easily recognized opposites from two different worlds.'[61]

The chronology of Herr's experiences during his year in Vietnam was deliberately disrupted in order to mirror the confusion he had experienced during his year in Vietnam and to underline the difficulty of establishing a coherent narrative about the war – here the historian is denied even 'the books of days and hours'. Herr's point about the difficulty of deciding on the war's starting point illustrates his lack of confidence in traditional history. Herr observed:

> You couldn't find two people who agreed about when it began ... intellectuals like 1954 as the reference date; if you saw as far back as War 2 and the Japanese occupation you were practically a historical visionary. 'Realists' said that it began for us in 1961, and the common run of Mission flack insisted on 1965, post-Tonkin Resolution ... Anyway, you couldn't use standard methods to date the doom ... Straight history, auto-revised history, history without handles, for all the books and articles and white papers, all the talk and the miles of film, something wasn't answered, it wasn't even asked ... hiding low under the fact-figure crossfire there was a secret history, and not a lot of people felt like running in there to bring it out.[62]

Had Herr asked a historian for an opinion on this part of his book he might have been told that the absence of a declaration of war did not preclude an explanation of the events that led to American intervention and that entry into some of the other wars in America's history had proceeded incrementally. (Roosevelt's Lend-Lease Act could have been perceived as a step towards war with Germany, for example.) Similarly, as he admits, drafted American soldiers were very clear about one aspect of the 'fact-figure crossfire': the number of days each had left 'in country'.[63] But by suggesting that historians were not capable of solving the mystery of the war's beginnings, Herr freed himself to speculate about its cultural origins and what John Hellmann called the 'unconscious desire which [American] culture projected onto Southeast Asia'.[64]

As well as stressing the impossibility of 'using standard methods to date the doom', Herr was also at pains to remind the reader of the contradictions and lack of meaning in America's presence in Vietnam. By citing an American pilot's comment, 'Vietnam, man. Bomb 'em and feed 'em, bomb 'em and feed 'em' and re-telling the probably apocryphal tale of an American major who explained, 'We had to destroy Ben Tre in order to save it', Herr pointed out, in Ringnalda's words, that 'our linguistic certainties no longer obtain.'[65] However, Jim Neilson has shown, in *Warring Fictions*, the danger of arguing that the American military's contradictory and distorted use of language in the Vietnam War is evidence that 'an accurate accounting of the war is impossible'.[66] The precise number of Vietnamese civilians who died during the war as a result of America's military policies may be subject to dispute, but the deaths that did occur are facts which cannot be altered or ignored and language remains the most effective form in which such facts can be communicated. The structure and content of *Dispatches* can aid an understanding of how confused an individual might have found the experience of being in Vietnam during 1967 and 1968 – it should not be taken, however, as evidence that explanation of the war is beyond us.

The rest of this book is devoted to showing that demeaning the efforts of other disciplines to clarify the past is misguided, that America's war in Vietnam was such a complicated war that inter-disciplinary study, in this case the consideration of film, history and literature, is an essential aid to understanding what the war was like, especially when it is applied to particular episodes in the war. An inter-disciplinary approach can ensure that historians and students of literature and film are suitably sceptical about claims of authenticity, whilst clarifying the importance of those works which provide credible, if fictional, accounts of combat.

Ringnalda commented that the section in *Dispatches* entitled 'Illumination Rounds', an apparently random collection of memories of incidents and characters: 'would likely make writers of straight history squirm, because it offers them no kernel, no hook, no linear progression, no angle – actually far too many angles.'[67] It is characteristic of the arguments adduced against the ability of 'straight history' to deal with America's war in Vietnam that historians are presumed to be powerless in the face of complexity and disorder. On the other hand, to return to the comments by A. J. P. Taylor and Arthur Marwick cited at the beginning of this chapter, historians often find the efforts of film makers and writers of literature to explain the past to be potentially dangerous or lacking in substance.

The major problem here (the minor one is the apparently instinctual urge of scholars to engage in inter-disciplinary warfare) is that literature and film, especially feature films, tend to deal with the war as it has been experienced by individuals, whereas history often seeks a more detached and general perspective. This has been helpfully expressed by Milton J. Bates in his book *The Wars We Took to Vietnam*, published in 1996. Bates cited a CIA case officer featured in Al Santoli's oral history, *Everything We Had*, who commented:

> I'm grateful that I went to Vietnam in the position I went in because I knew what was going on. I read the cables. When there was a new offensive or a new strategy, I knew what it was and I could relate it to what was happening in the village. But I knew grunts – the poor bastards jumped out of helicopters in hot LZs [Landing Zones] and didn't even know where the fuck they were except that guys were shooting at them and mortars were coming in and people were dying and screaming.

As Bates noted, there are two types of knowledge about the war referred to here, that of the 'man in the valley' – the grunt who was directly involved in the heat of the action and whose memories might be of value – and the 'man on the hilltop', the case officer whose perspective was less direct, although broader and based upon documentation.[68] The information provided by either the grunt or the case officer might be false and the stories about the past told by each would be just that: stories. Nevertheless, in the pursuit of knowledge about the past, either of these men would be potential sources, offering different sorts of material, but each having experiences or knowledge that might render their stories particularly credible. In the same way, the ideas about the war of an individual offered in a novel or a feature film and the more distanced perspective of a historian who has studied the *Pentagon Papers* both contribute to an understanding of the war, providing each is received with the necessary scepticism.

The pursuit of truth, Henry James believed, must be the guiding principle for the novelist as it is for the historian. Referring to the novel as history, James wrote: 'That is the only general description (which does it justice) that we may give of the novel.'[69] The world which James described in his novels is a long way from the world of combat but his confidence that the truth of the novelist may be as valuable as the truth of the historian encourages the idea that fiction, properly handled, may offer one solution to the problem of representing the truth about combat. Historians interested in the nature of combat, or indeed the past, should recognise the value of imaginative writing and film as an aid to their enquiries. Writing and film can be studied as historical artefacts, demonstrating the types of communication engaged in by particular cultures. Yet writing and film can also be used, with the necessary scepticism, as a means of gaining 'new footholds in the territory of truth.' The credibility of the stories told to get at the truth becomes the key, and historians and critics of literature and film can usefully share the portrayals of America's war in Vietnam to be found in film and literature. It is, however, as Richard King suggested in his 1991 article 'The Discipline of Fact/The Freedom of Fiction?' the role of history to 'restrain the wilder probes and speculations of fiction.'[70]

It is appropriate that a novelist, Julian Barnes, should have delineated the role of the historian so clearly in *A History of the World in 10½ Chapters*, reminding us that writing about the past is always subject to improvement:

> We all know objective truth is not attainable, that when some event occurs we shall have a multiplicity of subjective truths which we assess and then fabulate into history, into some God-eyed version of what 'really' happened. This God-eyed version is a fake ... But while we know this, we must still believe that objective truth is obtainable; or we must believe that it is 99 per cent obtainable; or if we can't believe this we must believe that 43 per cent objective truth is better

than 41 per cent. We must do so, because if we don't we're lost, we fall into beguiling relativity, we value one liar's version as much as another liar's, we throw up our hands at the puzzle of it all, we admit that the victor has the right not just to the spoils but also to the truth.[71]

Notes

1. David Halberstam cited in Fred Turner, *Echoes of Combat: The Vietnam War in American Memory* (New York: Anchor Books, 1996), p. 135.
2. A. J. P. Taylor cited in Nicholas Pronay, 'The Moving Picture and Historical Research', *Journal of Contemporary History*, July 1983.
3. Arthur Marwick, *The Sixties* (Oxford: Oxford University Press, 1998), p. 532.
4. See Ron Kovic, *Born on the Fourth of July* (London: Corgi Books, 1976), for example. *To Hell and Back*, directed by Jesse Hibbs, was based on Murphy's autobiography and gave the star the opportunity to re-enact some of the exploits which had made him America's most decorated soldier of World War II. Jeanine Basinger suggests that Murphy may have got his ideas about war from watching *Sergeant York* (1941), a film about an American hero of World War I. Basinger, *The World War II Combat Film: Anatomy of a Genre* (New York: Columbia University Press, 1986), p. 175.
5. Tim O'Brien, *The Things They Carried* (London: Flamingo, 1991), p. 79 and p. 179.
6. Henry David Thoreau cited in Timothy J. Lomperis, *'Reading the Wind': The Literature of the Vietnam War* (Durham: Duke University Press, 1987), p. 51.
7. Richard J. Evans, *In Defence of History* (London: Granta Books, 1997), p. 62.
8. A comment made by Lord Acton in October 1896, cited in Peter Novick, *That Noble Dream: The 'Objectivity Question' and the American Historical Profession* (Cambridge: Cambridge University Press, 1988), p. 40.
9. J. B. Bury cited in Evans, *In Defence of History*, p. 26.
10. Novick, *That Noble Dream*, pp. 1–2.
11. G. R. Elton, *The Practice of History* (London: Sydney University Press, 1967), p.141.
12. Sir Charles Oman, *On the Writing of History* (London: Methuen, 1969), pp. 7–8.
13. Ellen Somekawa and Elizabeth A. Smith, 'Theorizing the writing of history, or "I can't think why it should be so dull, for a great deal of it must be invention"', *Journal of Social History*, vol. 22, 1988.
14. Hayden White cited in Novick, *That Noble Dream*, p. 600.
15. Roger J. Spiller cited in Paul Fussell (ed.), *The Bloody Game* (London: Scribner's, 1991), p. 313.
16. Michael Walzer, *Just and Unjust Wars: A Moral Argument with Historical Illustrations* (New York: Basic Books, 1977), p. 20.
17. Agnes Heller, *A Theory of History* (London: Routledge and Kegan Paul, 1982), p. 63.
18. Definition of 'plausible' found in Judy Pearsall and Bill Trumble (eds), *The Oxford English Reference Dictionary*, 2nd edn (Oxford: Oxford University Press, 1996), s.v.
19. Cited, and used as a chapter title, in Paul Fussell, *Wartime* (New York: Oxford University Press, 1989), p. 290.
20. Erich Maria Remarque, trans. A. W. Wheen, *All Quiet on the Western Front* (London: Heinemann, [1929] 1976), p. 146; Eugene B. Sledge, *With the Old Breed at Peleliu*

and Okinawa (New York: Oxford University Press, 1981), p. 121; Michael Herr, *Dispatches* (London: Picador, 1977), p. 14. Although the first and last of these texts are novels they are based upon the authors' personal experiences of battle and represent an apparently sincere attempt to describe combat.

21. Paul Fussell, *The Great War and Modern Memory* (London: Oxford University Press, [1975] 1977), p. 172.

22. Ibid. p. 173.

23. Robert Kee cited in ibid. p. 311.

24. Wright Morris and Thomas Hobbes cited in ibid. p. 205.

25. Ibid. pp. 8–9.

26. Robin Prior and Trevor Wilson, 'Paul Fussell at War', *War in History*, vol. 1, no. 1, March 1994.

27. Ibid.

28. Ibid.

29. Donald Ringnalda, *Fighting and Writing the Vietnam War* (Jackson: University Press of Mississippi, 1994), p. 75. Apparently a paraphrase of a remark by novelist William Eastlake although Ringnalda offers no source.

30. Capote's description of his book as a 'non-fiction novel' was cited in Tom Wolfe and E. W. Johnson (eds), *The New Journalism* (London: Picador, [1975] 1990), p. 41.

31. Truman Capote, *In Cold Blood* (London: Penguin, 1965), p. 9.

32. Norman Mailer, *The Armies of the Night* (London: Penguin, 1968), pp. 267–8.

33. Ibid. p. 268.

34. Wolfe and Johnson, *The New Journalism*, p. 321.

35. Eric James Schroeder, *Vietnam, We've All Been There: Interviews with American Writers* (Westport, CT: Praeger, 1992), p. 20.

36. Ibid. p. 20.

37. John Sack, *M* (London: Corgi, 1986), p. i.

38. Schroeder, *Vietnam, We've All Been There*, p. 19. There are examples of journalists working during World War II who experimented with different techniques in order to write more effectively about combat. John Hersey recorded how his interest in 'using novelistic techniques in journalism' resulted in his 1944 magazine article, 'Survival', an account of the sinking of John F. Kennedy's motor torpedo boat (PT 109). Hersey's comment was cited in Nigel Hamilton, *JFK: Reckless Youth* (New York: Random House, 1992) p. 664.

39. Stanley Karnow, *Vietnam: A History* (London: Guild Publishing, [1983] 1985), p. 710.

40. Sack, *M*, p. 196.

41. Robin Moore's collection of stories, *The Green Berets* (New York: Crown, 1965), contains the following example: 'That Viet intelligence crew is scared of only one thing more than physical danger, and that's loss of face.' p. 241.

42. Schroeder, *Vietnam, We've All Been There*, p. 31.

43. Tim O'Brien, *Going After Cacciato* (London: Flamingo, [1978] 1988), p. 249.

44. The 'Hitler Diaries', which were published in April 1983 by the *Sunday Times* and the German magazine *Stern*, were revealed as fakes when the paper on which they were written was shown to have been manufactured in the 1950s.

45. Oliver Stone in an interview on *Moving Pictures*, BBC2, 1995.

46. Letter written to his brother by Captain Rodney R. Chastant dated 10 September 1967. Printed in Bernard Edelman (ed.), *Dear America: Letters Home From Vietnam*

(New York: W. W. Norton, 1985), p. 210. Just over a year after writing this letter Chastant was killed in Vietnam.

47. Lomperis, 'Reading the Wind', p. 99.
48. Michael Lind, Vietnam: The Necessary War – A Re-interpretation of America's Most Disastrous Military Conflict (New York: The Free Press, 1999), p. 284.
49. Jim Neilson, Warring Fictions: Cultural Politics and the Vietnam War (Jackson: University Press of Mississippi, 1998), p. 54.
50. Kurt Ocher cited in Turner, Echoes of Combat, p. 188.
51. President George Bush cited in Washington Post, 4 March 1991.
52. Lomperis, 'Reading the Wind', p. 15.
53. Schroeder, Vietnam, We've All Been There, p. 132.
54. Ringnalda, Fighting and Writing the Vietnam War, p. ix.
55. Kate Beaird Meyers, 'Fragmentary Mosaics: Vietnam War "Histories" and Postmodern Epistemology', Genre, Winter 1988.
56. Lomperis, 'Reading the Wind', p. 46.
57. David Halberstam, One Very Hot Day (Boston: Houghton Mifflin, 1967), p. 114.
58. O'Brien, Going After Cacciato, pp. 255–6.
59. Schroeder, Vietnam, We've All Been There, p. 35. Despite Herr's designation of Dispatches as a novel it was recommended for the National Book Award for non-fiction in 1978.
60. Herr, Dispatches, p. 41.
61. Ringnalda, Fighting and Writing the Vietnam War, p. 75.
62. Herr, Dispatches, p. 46.
63. Americans in the Army served twelve months in Vietnam, Marines served thirteen months. Herr observes of one soldier at Khe Sanh: 'Like every American in Vietnam he had his obsession with time ... [his] brain cells were arranged like jewels in the finest chronometer.' Dispatches, p. 99.
64. John Hellmann, American Myth and the Legacy of Vietnam (New York: Columbia University Press, 1986), p. 153.
65. Herr, Dispatches, p. 17 and p. 63; Ringnalda, Fighting and Writing the Vietnam War, p. 77.
66. Neilson, Warring Fictions, p. 155.
67. Ringnalda, Fighting and Writing the Vietnam War, p. 87.
68. Milton J. Bates, The Wars We Took to Vietnam: Cultural Conflict and Storytelling (Berkeley and Los Angeles: University of California Press, 1996), p. 220.
69. Henry James, 'The Art of Fiction', in Leon Edel (ed.), The Future of the Novel (New York: Vintage Books, 1956), pp. 5–6.
70. Richard King, 'The Discipline of Fact/The Freedom of Fiction?', Journal of American Studies, 25, 1991.
71. Julian Barnes, A History of the World in 10½ Chapters (London: Picador, 1990), pp. 245–6.

CHAPTER 2

Heroes

Today, America's war in Vietnam is usually associated with images of defeat, confusion or shame: newsreels of the last American helicopters departing hours before the fall of Saigon or of frantic attempts to regain areas lost to NLF forces during the Tet Offensive; photographs of American soldiers traumatised by their experiences of combat or of the women and children who were their victims at My Lai 4. Americans were once given a different impression of events in Vietnam. In the early 1960s the coverage offered by the American media was limited but frequently positive. Couched in terms of resistance to a Communist threat, there was approval for what *Time* magazine described in May 1962 as 'a remarkable U.S. military effort' and praise for those Americans who were showing the South Vietnamese how to fight.[1] Soldiers of the Special Forces were given especially appreciative treatment. *Time* referred to them in March 1962 as the 'best combat troops in the Army' and identified them as the sort of 'individual soldiers' responsible for the government's new counter-insurgency effort in South Vietnam.[2] They enjoyed a far bigger share of the public's attention than might have been expected for a force that, in South Vietnam, numbered less than a thousand in the summer of 1962.[3] As William Prochnau observed in *Once Upon a Distant War*: 'The Green Berets made great Sunday supplement reading.'[4] Indeed, celebrations of the Green Berets continued to prove highly compelling to the American people throughout the decade, whether support for the war was rising or falling.

Amongst the works stimulated by the activities of the Special Forces in Vietnam, three were particularly successful. Published in 1965, Robin Moore's *The Green Berets* became the year's fifth best selling book in America. As Eric James Schroeder commented in *Vietnam, We've All Been There*: 'for years [*The Green Berets*] was the final word on Vietnam: it was one of the first books to come out of the American experience in Vietnam, and the American public bought it like candy – it sold several million copies.'⁵ In 1966 a song entitled 'The Ballad of the Green Berets' by Staff Sergeant Barry Sadler became the best selling single of the year. Like Sadler's album *Ballads of the Green Berets*, it sold over a million copies. And as the American public turned against the war in increasing numbers in the aftermath of the Tet Offensive in 1968, John Wayne's film *The Green Berets*, loosely based on Moore's book and using 'The Ballad of the Green Berets' on its soundtrack, did good business at the box office despite the timing of its release and the hostility of its critical reception. The popularity of these works, each of which emphasised the superior qualities and heroism of the Green Berets, is instructive. Their audiences found in them reflections of attitudes about the war and about America's identity as a nation which they shared, attitudes which need to be recognised by those who want to understand the war and its support by so many Americans. Moore's book and Wayne's film are helpful resources in other ways. Despite Moore's eagerness to present the men of the Special Forces in a glamorous light, their thinking about the war is depicted with some accuracy whilst Wayne's propaganda film provides a register of the arguments of the Johnson administration in support of its actions in Vietnam.

American soldiers in Vietnam (Rex/SIPA).

The training of Special Forces soldiers by the US Army had begun in June 1952 at Fort Bragg in North Carolina. As Shelby L. Stanton explained in his combat history of the American Special Forces, *Green Berets at War*, the first cohort of trainees was deployed to Germany in November 1953 in order to 'organize, train, and equip guerrilla forces, conduct sabotage operations, support resistance movements and to evade and, if necessary, escape from enemy forces', in the event of a Soviet invasion in Europe.[6] In 1957 another group was ordered to 'support unconventional warfare missions in the Far East' and by 1961 members of the Special Forces were working in Vietnam and Laos, 'primarily as mobile training teams for indigenous counterparts.'[7] Nevertheless, there were only 2,000 men attached to the Special Forces worldwide by 1961, a tiny proportion of an American Army whose leaders tended to object to the elitism on which the concept of Special Forces was based.[8]

In Vietnam, the organisation and training of paramilitary defence units became the major responsibility of the Special Forces throughout the 1960s. Working with different Montagnard tribes in the Vietnamese Central Highlands to develop the Civilian Irregular Defense Group (CIDG) programme, the Special Forces had to accept a role for which they had not been directly prepared. As Francis J. Kelly noted in *The Green Berets in Vietnam, 1961–1971*: 'Instead of waging guerrilla warfare against conventional forces in enemy territory, the U.S. Special Forces troops were to find themselves attempting to thwart guerrilla insurgency in "friendly" territory.'[9] Despite such unpromising beginnings – limited manpower, the suspicion of military leaders and an unfamiliar task – their reputation grew. In his 1993 study, *Working-Class War: American Combat Soldiers and Vietnam*, Christian G. Appy observed that 'throughout the early 1960s' the Special Forces were 'perhaps the most significant symbol of the American military, and ... an extremely positive symbol'.[10]

The reputation which the Special Forces enjoyed was substantially the consequence of President Kennedy's enthusiasm for the doctrine of counter-insurgency, an enthusiasm which was shared by others in his administration and acted upon within weeks of his inauguration. Kennedy's belief that the war against Communism urgently required new strategies had been evidenced before his election by his admiration for *The Ugly American*, a novel by William Lederer and Eugene Burdick published in 1958. *The Ugly American*, which sold over four million copies and was later made into a film, was 'written as fiction ... based on fact' and warned that Asia would be lost to Communism without a more dynamic and imaginative American response.[11] In 'A Factual Epilogue' to the novel the authors observed that America needed:

a small force of well-trained, well-chosen, hard-working, and dedi-
cated professionals. They must be willing to risk their comforts and –
in some lands – their health. They must go equipped to apply a
positive policy promulgated by a clear-thinking government. They
must speak the language of the land of their assignment, and they
must be more expert in its problems than are the natives.[12]

Like Lederer and Burdick, Kennedy was convinced of the importance of
sending highly motivated Americans, both military and civilian, to work
with Asian villagers. He was so impressed by *The Ugly American* that his
was one of the signatures on an advertisement in the *New York Times* in
January 1959 announcing that a copy of the book had been sent to each
member of the Senate.[13] On becoming president, he demonstrated in word
and deed his conviction that sending small forces of American soldiers
and civilians to work intensively with villagers in underdeveloped coun-
tries offered an effective means of countering Communist insurgencies.

His inaugural address, delivered on 20 January 1961, was almost
entirely devoted to mapping out America's role as a world power.
Intended as a response to Soviet leader Khrushchev's claims that the
world was destined to become Communist, it emphasised Kennedy's
excitement at the challenges he and the American people confronted on
the world's stage and the special nature of the contribution that American
individuals could make in the struggle against Communism:

> In the long history of the world only a few generations have been
> granted the role of defending freedom in its hour of maximum danger. I
> do not shrink from this responsibility – I welcome it. I do not believe
> that any of us would exchange places with any other people or any
> other generation. The energy, the faith, the devotion which we bring
> to this endeavour will light our country and all who serve it – and the
> glow from that fire can truly light the world.
>
> And so, my fellow Americans: ask not what your country can do
> for you – ask what you can do for your country.[14]

Two of the measures intended to provide substance to this rhetoric were
confirmed within weeks. The president provided an additional nineteen
million dollars for the training of elite troops who would specialise in
unconventional warfare and the techniques of counter-insurgency. He
also signed the Peace Corps into existence. As Richard Reeves has pointed
out, these early foreign policy decisions were: 'an institutionalizing of

The Ugly American.'[15] Each step was intended to address failings of the sort that Lederer and Burdick had described in their novel. The Peace Corps would concentrate on civic action projects and the Special Forces would serve a variety of purposes, contributing medical and technical aid as well as fighting and training others to fight.

Kennedy's determination to encourage an elite force, one which looked, trained and performed differently to conventional forces, was highlighted by his reversal of the Army's decision to prohibit the wearing of the distinctive green beret. A message from the president confirmed the new prestige of the Special Forces. The men were told to 'wear the beret proudly', that it would 'be a mark of distinction and a badge of courage in the difficult days ahead.'[16] He sent a Special Forces Group of 400 men to Vietnam in May 1961 in order to accelerate the training of the South Vietnamese Special Forces, the Luc-Luong Dac Biet (LLDB), and by February 1962 the CIDG programme had begun in the Central Highlands, a programme which Stanton described in *Green Berets at War* as 'the most crucial Special Forces task throughout the Vietnam War.'[17] When this programme expanded, further Special Forces detachments were required to supplement the 991 Special Forces soldiers already in South Vietnam by June 1962.[18] On 6 June the president spoke, in his address to the graduating class of 1962 at West Point, of the need for 'a whole new kind of strategy, a wholly different kind of force' to apply in Vietnam where, he believed, 'another type of war' was being fought 'by guerrillas, subversives, insurgents'.[19]

Unfortunately for Kennedy, the argument about the beret was a reflection of more profound disagreements with his military leaders. Most of his generals were highly sceptical of the president's conviction that the war in Vietnam was a special sort of war which required a special sort of soldier. They shied away from the identification of an elite, especially one whose training encouraged less conventional solutions than the massing of firepower which had become their mantra. The suggestion that the work of the Special Forces could involve a political dimension was troubling to them because it implied that some wars were not susceptible to a purely military solution. There might also have been a suspicion that Kennedy's enthusiasm for the Special Forces was reinforced by budgetary considerations: a few hundred Green Berets were a lot cheaper than the units of conventional troops that the generals were recommending for use in Vietnam. After the president's speech at West Point it was reported that General Lemnitzer, Chairman of the

Joint Chiefs of Staff, believed that the President had been 'oversold' on the strategy of counter-insurgency. Later in the year, General Earle G. Wheeler, who would become the Chairman of the Joint Chiefs under President Johnson, complained that: 'It is fashionable in some quarters … to say that the problems in Southeast Asia are primarily political and economic rather than military. I do not agree. The essence of the problem is military.'[20] Such comments suggested the military's resentment of civilian pressure to adopt a 'fashionable' strategy which threatened to move it away from the ground on which it felt most secure: using hardware to destroy the enemy.

Whilst, as Richard Reeves has observed, Kennedy's view of the Green Berets was 'a rather romantic one', the president had grasped that America's effort in Vietnam would be assisted if soldiers could gain the trust of communities by living and working with them.[21] This understanding was not, however, to be put to any decisive use. As Guenter Lewy wrote in *America in Vietnam*: 'The … Green Berets and similar units in the other services remained small-scale efforts outside the main career stream.'[22] By rendering the Special Forces a promotional cul-de-sac, the military bureaucracy ensured that Kennedy's elite force remained peripheral to events in Vietnam. The hopes of the president's foreign policy advisors that the war would be won by 'brilliant, young, great physical specimens in their green berets, swinging through the trees … arm over arm, and speaking six languages, including Chinese and Russian, and who had Ph.D.'s in history and literature, and ate snake meat at night', as journalist David Halberstam rather cynically put it, were not fulfilled.[23] In the public consciousness, though, the Green Berets were not so easily marginalised.

Kennedy's assassination imparted a nostalgic glow to the reputation of the unit he had encouraged but the 'best combat troops in the Army' were already associated with a variety of qualities which set them apart from other servicemen. In March 1961 an article in *Time* magazine had set the tone:

> [Green Berets] can remove an appendix, fire a foreign-made or obsolete gun, blow up a bridge, handle a bow and arrow, sweet-talk some bread out of a native in his own language, fashion explosives out of chemical fertilizer, cut an enemy's throat … live off the land.[24]

Highly trained but comfortable with the most primitive of weapons, highly educated but able to cope in the most basic of environments, the Special

Forces were presented as innovators who got the job done. In the article
Time ran twelve months later the image was reinforced but adjusted in an
important way: 'The training is intensive: demolition experts can fashion
explosives out of fertilizer; medics can amputate limbs and treat any kind
of gunshot wound under field conditions. (One sergeant delivered 32
babies during a tour in Laos.)'[25] Depicted as life givers as well as life
takers, the men of the Special Forces were moving closer to an ideal-
isation of American soldiership. In each article readers were assured that
such men would not tolerate indiscipline or immodesty. The unit was 'no
place for the hot-blooded hero type' or 'for the man who ... swaggers
into a bar and starts telling everyone he's an American superman.'[26]
Thus the individualism which was a key feature of the Special Forces'
characterisation was tempered by the need for self-control and obedience
to the requirements of the team. As John Hellmann has pointed out in
American Myth and the Legacy of Vietnam:

> the Green Berets of the periodical press occupied in a single timeless
> moment the whole of American myth. Hunter ... builder and teacher
> ... This new western hero carried within him both America's return
> to the frontier and its advance to the millennium.[27]

Primitive and advanced, killer and healer, highly trained yet full of initiative, the Green Beret of the popular imagination promised to merge the
commitment to collective progress of Kennedy's New Frontier with the
self-reliance of the old one.

Evidence that the *Time* articles captured aspects of the self-image to
which members of the Special Forces aspired is available in two books
written by veterans of the Special Forces: Stanton's *Green Berets at War*
and Kelly's *The Green Berets in Vietnam*, both published in 1985. Stanton
depicted the Green Berets as 'rugged individuals' who could 'survive the
most hostile environment' and 'independent thinkers ... able to grasp
opportunities and innovate with the materials at hand'.[28] He also contrasted the willingness of Special Forces personnel to adapt to primitive
conditions with the hidebound outlook of disapproving Army leaders,
thus reminding his readers that the Special Forces had a further appeal:
their ability to antagonise the bureaucracy. Explaining that, whilst
working with the various Montagnard tribes in the CIDG programme,
the men 'carefully learned tribal customs and studied the local dialects,
ate the tribal foods, endured the cold, mixed indigenous garb with their
uniforms and participated in the rituals and ceremonies', Stanton noted

with approval that: 'Many senior MACV officers viewed this ... rugged and independent Special Forces effort with extreme displeasure'.[29]

In *The Green Berets in Vietnam* Kelly, who commanded the 5th Special Forces Group (Airborne) in Vietnam between June 1966 and June 1967, praised the selflessness and integrity of his men. They were 'firmly committed to their motto of "Free the Oppressed" and with equal firmness to their unofficial yardstick: "We are known by what we do, not by what we say we are going to do".'[30] He also cited a report by Colonel William A. McKean, the previous commander of the 5th Special Forces, which was specific in its identification of the unit's heritage: 'If today's Special Forces NCO has ever had any peer, it was probably the tough, self-reliant, combat-tested soldier who fought on the Indian frontier of our own country during the 1870s.'[31] Kennedy's elite unit might have been shuffled to the edges of the American effort in Vietnam but in the popular press, in unit histories written by its veterans and in the perceptions of its leaders, the identity of the Special Forces became an increasingly well defined ideal, linked to powerful and widely acknowledged strands in America's cultural history.

Robin Moore contributed to the development of this mythology and profited from it in *The Green Berets*, a collection of stories about the work of Special Forces detachments in Indo-China in 1963 and 1964. As John Hellmann noted, the paperback edition has been referred to as 'the phenomenon of [1965], with 1,200,000 printed in only two months' and, such was the seductiveness of Moore's image of the Special Forces: 'It reportedly induced so many enlistments of young men hoping to become Green Berets that the Selective Service was able to suspend draft calls during the first four months of 1966.'[32] Moore's work has not appealed to the critics. Emile Capouya complained of Moore's 'boyish enthusiasm for the trickery and butchery he reports' in the August 1965 issue of *Commonweal* and, nearly thirty years later, Donald Ringnalda correctly described *The Green Berets* as having 'absolutely no sense of irony: we were the good guys, they were the bad guys, and therefore, we'll win'.[33] Nevertheless, analysis of Moore's work is revealing. He concentrated on the soldierly virtues of his heroes, rather than 'the civic action portion' of their role, and suggested that their superiority to enemy and ally could ensure victory over the Communists in Vietnam as long as they were given a free hand.[34] Such a suggestion mirrored the attitude of a significant proportion of the American people. Gallup polls demonstrated that Americans believed escalation of the war in Vietnam to be preferable to withdrawal. In April 1965, for example, a poll showed that 31 per cent of respondents considered escalation to be the correct course against only 17 per cent who opted for withdrawal. Later in the decade the trend was even more marked. In November 1967, 55 per cent of respondents to a poll approved escalation and only 10 per cent chose withdrawal. Males, who presumably constituted the bulk of Moore's readership, reacted even more emphatically. In 1964, 55 per cent of male respondents recommended escalation and two years later the figure was 56 per cent. In contrast, public support for the war in Vietnam fell. In August 1965 Gallup found that 61 per cent of those polled believed it had not been a mistake to send troops to fight in Vietnam whilst only 44 per cent were of the same opinion in October 1967.[35] The implications of this, that many Americans thought victory was only a matter of a more determined military effort and that increasing numbers believed the attempt to 'save' the South Vietnamese to be an error, are ideas that appear in *The Green Berets*.

Moore's celebration of the Green Berets includes descriptions of clandestine Special Forces activities in Cambodia in 'A Green Beret – All The Way', in Laos in 'Home to Nanette' and of a CIA-organised infiltration into North Vietnam in the final story in the collection, 'Hit 'em Where They Live'. By showing the successful outcome of cross-border operations, Moore suggested that American victory over the Communists could be secured by allowing the Special Forces, who understood what the war was really like, the freedom to fight as they thought best. In 'A Green Beret – All the Way' Colonel Train, whose 'background was Regular Army', complains that the hero of the story, Sven Kornie, 'is too damned independent and unorthodox'.[36] By the end of the story, in which Kornie has organised an illegal raid into Cambodia and mined the positions of his South Vietnamese allies in the correct expectation that they would turn out to be traitors, Train has been converted to the hero's way of thinking. Kornie's background is significant. Originally from Finland, he had fought in the German Army against the Russians during World War II and the narrator's guess that he would collect 'a Germanic-Viking crew' to serve with him in Vietnam seems to be confirmed.[37] He is not the only one of Moore's heroes with such a background. In 'Coup de Grace', there is a reference to Fritz Scharne's membership of the Hitler Youth. These encounters with German militarism, Moore implied, were effective preparation for a career in the Special Forces. Borne of Aryan discipline and American independence of mind the soldiership practised by Kornie and Scharne under the aegis of the Special Forces seemed to guarantee victory. It is no coincidence that the most succesful incarnation of the Green Beret, Sylvester Stallone's John Rambo, has a similar heritage. In an early scene in *Rambo: First Blood Part II* the audience is told that he is 'of German-Indian descent', apparently a mix that enables him to win battles against regiments of enemies single-handedly.[38]

Characteristic of Moore's writing and his vaunting of the Green Berets' military prowess is a section towards the end of 'Coup de Grace' which describes Scharne's killing of the French leader of a Viet Cong battalion named Huyot, whom the Americans refer to as 'the cowboy'. In a previous operation Huyot has executed a wounded American and this offers a justification for the fate he suffers at Scharne's hands. Having outwitted Huyot in battle and mortally wounded him with a grenade, Scharne and the narrator watch as he dies:

> Huyot was still alive ... though almost unrecognizable. His handsome face had been torn badly by shrapnel, his nose lying on his cheek. Blood burbled from ugly rents in his bare chest. Wounds in his arms, groin and legs bled profusely. His eyes were open, fixed on Scharne who stood looking down at him.
>
> Huyot's lips moved but no words would come ...
>
> Other Rangers gathered to look at the formidable cowboy, barely identifiable as a Caucasian now ... Scharne stared down at him impassively until finally with a grating moan Huyot gave in to his wounds and died.
>
> Fritz turned from the dead Frenchman to me. 'He knew who I was. He knew who it was got him.'[39]

The passage is worthy of close examination. The graphic descriptions humiliate the victim, his once handsome face now 'torn badly', his 'nose lying on his cheek' and the epithet 'ugly' applied to reinforce the loss of his good looks. His impotence is emphasised by the wound to his groin and his inability to speak. Huyot's weakness is observed by Scharne, whom Moore twice describes as looking 'down' at his defeated opponent. Aware of the voyeuristic Scharne, the Frenchman, who is now 'barely identifiable as a Caucasian', dies with his eyes 'fixed' on the victor. His final submission, 'with a grating moan Huyot gave in to his wounds', is observed 'impassively' by the German-American, until he expresses his satisfaction that Huyot was aware of his killer. By encouraging his readers to revel in such a racist manner at Huyot's defeat, Moore stressed the superiority of the Green Beret, the primacy of military skill in solving America's problems in South Vietnam and the personal fulfilment to be gained from victory. Huyot, the 'poor, misguided sonofabitch', apparently represents colonial decadence and, on a simpler level, the idea that the French, who had been defeated in Vietnam, were hostile to the prospect of American success there.[40]

Despite the European origins of the two combatants, however, Moore dramatised the duel between the two men in a context that his American readers would quickly recognise. Huyot can be perceived as the villain in a cowboy film because he 'wears a Stetson' and 'always has on a pair of Levis and Western boots'.[41] Similarly, the opening sentence of 'A Green Beret – All The Way' displays Moore's determination to present the war in familiar terms and to connect the Special Forces' mission in Vietnam with an appropriate precedent: 'The headquarters of Special Forces Detachment B–520 in one of Vietnam's most active war zones looks exactly like a fort out of the old West.'[42] To reassure his readers further that the war in Vietnam could be seen as straightforwardly as the battles fought in the American West, Moore used the terms Viet Cong and Communist as synonyms throughout the book. This made America's enemy, as Jim Neilson pointed out in *Warring Fictions*, 'seem part of the global red menace rather than an indigenous force.'[43] Thus, as their troops poured into South Vietnam in the summer of 1965, Americans were presented with a simplified war, a war responsive to solutions which harnessed military determination and gave free rein to the skills of the Green Berets.

Unfortunately, many of the South Vietnamese were not worth saving according to Moore. In *The Green Berets* their weaknesses are legion. In addition to treachery, they are often guilty of cowardice. In 'Two Birds With One Stone' Sergeant Ossidian claims that there 'isn't a battalion commander in the ARVN that would take a chance on getting himself or his officers shot' and in 'A Green Beret – All the Way', as Kornie and Train expose themselves to danger, 'the Vietnamese camp commander is below in the nearly impregnable bunker'.[44] More explicitly, the Americans' Special Forces' counterparts, the LLDB, are referred to as 'lousy little dirty bug-outs' and, in 'The Immodest Mr. Pomfret', a South Vietnamese helicopter pilot is criticised because he failed to live up to the standards of the Americans: ' "That chopper pilot could have made it easily," Raskin cursed. "Sonofabitch, one sniper and he's scared off." '[45]

Their unworthiness has other aspects. In 'Fourteen VC POW's' Captain Locke has to trick the South Vietnamese into transporting fourteen wounded children to a hospital. Locke then tells the South Vietnamese Captain Nim: 'I have three kids of my own, and I and most Americans love all children. It makes me, and it makes the men on my team sick that we have to use tricks to save these children.'[46] Having established the caring nature of the Special Forces soldiers, who are often family men, Moore reassured his readers that the Americans' trick to save the children would not cause 'a flap' and indicates another form of their allies' cowardice: 'That Viet intelligence crew is scared of only one thing more than physical danger, and that's loss of face.'[47] Whilst Locke's trickery is offered as an example of the initiative with which the Special Forces were associated, deceptions practised by the South Vietnamese attract Moore's condemnation and the assurance that the Americans will not be fooled: 'By this time I had learned to understand the deviousness of the Vietnamese mind and I knew exactly what Chi must be thinking.'[48]

The shabby quality of South Vietnamese soldiers is a frequent feature of the stories. In 'A Green Beret – All The Way' Sergeant Ngoc tortures a Viet Cong suspect and in 'Two Birds With One Stone' the Americans acquire 'about 100 assorted thieves, rapists, muggers, dope pushers, homosexuals, and murderers' from the Saigon jail because of the difficulty of finding suitable recruits for a strike force. A 'hard-fighting group', the company of ex-prisoners were 'given to various types of body mutilation after a battle'.[49] Others are less dangerous to the enemy. In 'Coup de Grace' Scharne relies upon the failure of the South Vietnamese officers to get their men on the march before dawn as part of his plan to trap Huyot. On the march the soldiers make so much noise 'shambling' and 'crashing through the jungle' that they can be heard kilometres away.[50] Frustratingly, the South Vietnamese even resist American instruction. As Lieutenant Barton complains in 'Two Birds With One Stone': 'You can't teach them'.[51]

Refusing to benefit from the experience of Special Forces' soldiers is a weakness of another of Moore's targets, the military bureaucracy. In 'Coup de Grace' Moore described 'the arrival of a jetload of high U.S. administration officials from Washington' and the 'blanket requests ... for optimistic progress reports' that MACV had made in preparation for their visit. As Scharne explains, a decision had also been taken to send 'All of us who have been known to talk too loud at the wrong time ... out of Saigon.' However, Moore's objection that 'the unpalatable truths

[Scharne] would have liked to pass on to the Washington decision makers were rejected out of hand' is followed by Scharne's observation: 'So it goes in an election year.'[52] The suggestion that the government and its military leaders were conspiring to hide the reality of the war, not only from the American people but also from themselves, was not an idle one. It was not until later in the sixties that the daily US military briefing to reporters in Saigon became known as the 'Five O'Clock Follies' but earlier evidence abounds that Scharne's view was justified. In May 1962, when in command of MACV, General Paul Harkins had proclaimed: 'I am an optimist, and I am not going to allow my staff to be pessimistic'.[53] In *The Making of a Quagmire*, published in 1965, David Halberstam noted: 'One's impression was always that MACV's figures reflected what MACV wanted to hear' and referred to 'the automatic we-are-winning push-button chant' that emanated from senior Americans.[54] Both Halberstam and Neil Sheehan have written about Lieutenant Colonel John Paul Vann's experience on returning to Washington in 1963.[55] An American advisor with considerable knowledge of the war and its problems, Vann's briefing of the Joint Chiefs of Staff was cancelled by Maxwell Taylor, the Chairman of the Joint Chiefs, because Vann planned to be critical of the South Vietnamese military effort. As William Prochnau has observed, the war in Vietnam prompted America's leaders to adopt 'an extraordinarily self-destructive policy, one that began with lies to the public and press and soon led to the government lying to itself.'[56]

Moore's preface opens with the statement that '*The Green Berets* is a book of truth' although this is qualified by his explanation that 'I decided I could present the truth better and more accurately in the form of fiction'.[57] The preface also claims that Moore had personal experience of the work of the Special Forces in Vietnam where he spent six months during 1964 in which he was 'allowed to go into combat all over the country just as though I were a Special Forces trooper'.[58] In June 1965 a reviewer in *Time* wrote that Moore: 'fought in more than a dozen actions [and] was credited with several kills.'[59] Stanton included *The Green Berets* in the Sources and Bibliography section of his history *Green Berets at War*, with the comment: 'This gripping "novel" by a famous correspondent was actually a true account of SF action in Vietnam, with only the names of individuals and minor facts changed.'[60] Stanton's status as a veteran of the Special Forces probably explains his willingness to accept so completely Moore's lionization of his comrades but there is evidence that the criticism of America's military bureaucracy is not the only instance of 'true accounting' in *The Green Berets*. Whether Moore had personal experience of the war or, as Richard Slotkin suggested, his book was 'based on interviews with Special Forces veterans', Moore's contact with the men in the Special Forces did reveal something of their activities.[61] More usefully, it imbued him with some of their most profound convictions.

The contradictory objections of the Defense Department to Moore's book are instructive. Whilst complaining that *The Green Berets* falsely gave the impression of being a true story, the Department also observed that it contained sixteen security violations. The stories 'Hit 'em Where They Live' and 'Home to Nanette' would certainly have touched a nerve at the Pentagon. Although there is no evidence that Americans took part in cross-border forays into North Vietnam as Moore suggested in 'Hit 'em Where They Live', teams of South Vietnamese trained by the Americans had been sent into the North, 'to attack enemy supply lines, sabotage military and civilian targets, and agitate against the Hanoi regime', as George C. Herring has observed.[62] Set in 1963, 'Home to Nanette' described a Green Beret under CIA control leading Meo tribesmen into battle against Communists in Laos. This was closer to reality because, to cite Herring again, in 1961 the CIA had 'initiated its "secret war" in Laos, arming some 9,000 Hmong tribesmen for actions against the Ho Chi Minh trail in what would become one of the largest paramilitary operations ever undertaken', an operation that continued after the agreement for a neutral Laos made in Geneva in July 1962.[63] Moore's presentation of such missions as highly organised games in which Americans, several steps ahead of their enemy, were sure to emerge victorious justified the Pentagon's charge of falsehood. Harder to deny, however, was the authenticity of Moore's portrayal of the persistent denigration of the South Vietnamese by the Green Berets.

The hostility of Moore's Green Berets towards the South Vietnamese was embarrassingly accurate, a representation of attitudes towards their allies that existed amongst the Green Berets and other American units in Vietnam. Al Santoli's oral history *To Bear Any Burden* includes the views of Chuck Allen, a Special Forces officer who served in South Vietnam from October 1962 to April 1963. Allen referred to the 'tremendous sense of pride and accomplishment' felt by the Americans he worked with but his attitude towards the South Vietnamese Special Forces makes him sound like a character out of *The Green Berets*:

working with the LLDB – Lousy Little Dirty Bastards ... there was a tremendous sense of frustration ... They didn't want to leave the camp. Sometimes we had to bribe them ... at night we'd catch them cooking rice with an eight-foot bonfire ... We knew damn well that they wanted to give their positions away to try to avoid a firefight.[64]

In *Green Berets at War* Stanton's view of the relationships between Special Forces units and their LLDB counterparts is similar, if more restrained. Summarising the relationship as 'generally poor', he noted: 'many Special Forces soldiers firmly believed that they would be deserted in adverse combat'.[65] Elsewhere his criticism was stronger: 'Special Forces found many of their LLDB counterparts to be incompetent, self-serving individuals who were unco-operative and who actively sabotaged mission accomplishment.'[66]

In contrast, the attitudes of Green Berets towards the Montagnard tribes tended to be patronising but positive. Vietnamese dislike of the Montagnard peoples probably contributed to the Americans' sympathy for them. Chuck Allen remembered: 'All the Montagnards I worked with were pure, good-hearted, hard-working people ... And most of the Special Forces people respected them as individuals. We didn't treat them like *moi*, which means "dog" like the Vietnamese traditionally did.'[67] Visiting a Special Forces Camp on the Vietnamese–Laotian border in 1970, reporter Gloria Emerson found the Green Berets there unresponsive to her questions, except on the same point:

> The Americans loved the Yards. On this subject they would speak. It was an old litany, and their favourite. Yards were uncorrupted by the vile cities, did not cheat or lie, were superior to the Vietnamese, they said. Yards were their kind of men.[68]

Again this was represented by Moore. His depiction of 'the hard-fighting, squat, barrel-chested Meo[s]', one of the Montagnard peoples, is approving.[69] The Meo villagers are eager to learn from the American, Bernard Arklin, who has come to lead them in 'Home to Nanette' and Moore emphasised the tribesmen's superiority to the slovenly and reluctant South Vietnamese: 'Their high morale showed in their gleaming dark eyes, sparkling white-toothed grins and quick gait ... Those not encumbered with weapons quickly unloaded the U-10, and in a mere six minutes the plane was aloft again.'[70] The Meos respond to Arklin's advice because he is prepared 'to live ... as one of them', as he tells an enraged MACV colonel who visits him.[71] The colonel's objection that 'You Special Forces people always go native or something' anticipates Stanton's observation that MACV officers disapproved of such 'rugged and independent' Special Forces activity and exemplifies another widely held conception amongst the Green Berets.[72] As Kelly put it in *The Green Berets in Vietnam*: 'the Special Forces troops were continually conscious of mistrust and suspicion on the part of many relatively senior field grade U.S. military men'.[73] The detail of Stanton's description of the criticisms levelled at the Green Berets by MACV officers might have been written with Moore's 'Home to Nanette' in mind: 'MACV staff officers carped constantly about Special Forces excessive drinking, overt living arrangements with local women ... and other practices not tolerated in conventional Army units. Perhaps most discomfiting to these staid Army fundamentalists were the "outlandish uniforms"'.[74] In 'Home to Nanette', the MACV colonel arrives in the Meo camp to find Arklin participating in a 'drinking party', co-habiting with a Meo woman and wearing a loin cloth.[75]

Although Moore encouraged his audience to revel in a fictional world where the breaking of military regulations is justified, racism indulged and killing celebrated, a reading of *The Green Berets* still provides something more than 'the gabble of cheerful idiocy' that Capouya perceived.[76] As well as emphasising aspects of the Green Berets' image and their connection to America's mythic past, the popularity of Moore's portrayal of the war demonstrated the accuracy with which he reflected the attitudes which led to its support by millions of Americans. His uncritical presentation of the prejudices of the Green Berets he encountered also enables his readers to experience something of their views on the war.

Like Moore's book and Barry Sadler's 'The Ballad of the Green Berets', John Wayne's *The Green Berets* was intended to reassure Americans that they were engaged in a national errand which was commendable. Released in July 1968, the film showed the Green Berets as brave, expert and, though outnumbered, victorious. The South Vietnamese, whom Wayne portrayed with some sympathy and much condescension, are appreciative of what American determination and know-how can achieve in a war which, in Wayne's version, is reminiscent of films about World War II and the winning of the American West. As Richard Schickel commented in a review of the film in *Life* magazine in July 1968, Wayne's 'reference point is not life but movie tradition.'[77] By the end of the film, audiences had seen the Communist enemy bewildered by American ingenuity and slaughtered by American firepower, just as they had watched Wayne defeat the Japanese in his World War II movies and the Indians in his westerns. Wayne also identified a second enemy, a sceptical domestic media which did not understand what the war was really like. Represented in the film by the hostile Beckworth, played by David Janssen, the journalist's conversion is ensured by the simple expedient of allowing him to see the war for himself. Wayne made no attempt to disguise the film's intentions. Asked in *Playboy* magazine if he resented those who accused his film of being 'shameless propaganda', he replied: 'I agreed with them. It was an American film about American boys who were heroes over there. In that sense, it was propaganda.'[78]

By the time the film appeared, however, the Tet Offensive had convinced much of the American media that the effort in Vietnam was doomed. The *Wall Street Journal* had concluded that 'everyone had better be prepared for the bitter taste of a defeat beyond America's power to prevent' and President Johnson had announced his decision not to stand for another term so that he could devote himself to the search for a peaceful solution to the war.[79] In such a context, soldiers who had fought in Vietnam found Wayne's facile optimism comic. As one veteran commented: 'That wasn't no Nam. I laughed about it'.[80] Critics were less tolerant. In the *New York Times* Renata Adler snarled:

> *The Green Berets* is a film so unspeakable, so stupid, so rotten and false that it passes through being funny, through being camp, through everything and becomes an invitation to grieve not so much for our soldiers or Vietnam (the film could not be more false or do greater disservice to them) but for what has happened to the fantasy-making apparatus of this country.[81]

Despite such responses Wayne's film performed well at the box office, taking over nine million dollars in America and Canada alone.[82] It was successful for two reasons. As John Hellmann put it: '*The Green Berets* could be enjoyed as the way Vietnam ought to be, if only someone – the government, the protesters, the press, the South Vietnamese – would let it.'[83] Although this included drawing parallels between the conflict in Vietnam and Hollywood's version of World War II, particularly Edward Dmytryk's 1945 film *Back to Bataan* in which Wayne had starred, it was the genre of the western which provided *The Green Berets* with much of its context. Having called his character Kirby, the name of a cavalry officer he had played in John Ford's *Fort Apache*, made in 1948, Wayne's language frequently suggested that Vietnam was an extension of the American West. Looking off into the distance he observes: 'This'd be great country if it weren't for the war.' Later, as he organises the recovery of 'Dodge City', the Special Forces camp temporarily lost to the Viet Cong, another cliché transforms the cultural and geographical setting: 'We can probably move in there tomorrow, God willing and the river don't rise.' Sounding like a Western gunman, Wayne adds his perspective on the abuse of a Viet Cong prisoner by remarking: 'Out here due process is a bullet.'[84] Wayne's son, Michael, the film's producer, made the connection clear in an interview: 'when you are making a picture, the Indians are the bad guys.'[85] Not only did these details evoke the atmosphere of the western and enable contemporary audiences to put recent events in Vietnam to the back of their minds, they also reminded Americans that they were winners and reinforced an important aspect of the Special Forces' heritage: 'the tough, self-reliant, combat-tested soldier who fought on the Indian frontier of our own country during the 1870s'. No wonder one Green Beret thought Wayne had made 'a real fine film' and another could call it a 'good, low-key, accurate picture'.[86] *The Green Berets* conformed to key elements in their self-image.

The second reason for the success of *The Green Berets* was John Wayne. As Garry Wills pointed out in *John Wayne: The Politics of Celebrity*: 'For twenty-five out of twenty-six years – from 1949 to 1974 – Wayne made the top ten in distributors' lists of stars with commercial appeal'.[87] More consistently popular than any other actor, Wayne's reputation had been made in westerns and combat films. In *Gunfighter Nation* Slotkin described Wayne as 'a cultural symbol whose role in public mythology is akin to that of figures like Daniel Boone, Davy Crockett, and Buffalo Bill.'[88] Although Wayne did not serve in the forces, opting to remain in Hollywood during World War II, General Douglas MacArthur 'thought he was the model of an American soldier' and the Marine Corps awarded him their 'Iron Mike' award.[89] The Veterans of Foreign Wars gave him their gold medal and in 1979 Congress would have a special medal struck for him enscribed 'John Wayne, American'. The consistency of his screen presence had become part of Americans' lives, as Joan Didion recognised in her 1965 essay 'John Wayne: A Love Song': 'when John Wayne rode through my childhood ... he determined forever the shape of some of our dreams.'[90] That presence encouraged his audiences to believe that Americans were just, their victory inevitable and their fighting men heroes in a combat arena which was always comprehensible and meaningful. Such comforting notions had, of course, contributed to support for the war in Vietnam. Wayne, as Schickel had written in *Life* in 1967, reminded Americans: 'of a time when right was right, wrong was wrong, and the differences between them could be set right by the simplest means.'[91] As the real war continued to smash the myths that Wayne had embodied, the force of his screen persona was such that his audiences were able to suspend their disbelief, forget about Vietnam and, despite an uncharacteristically clumsy performance, watch Wayne win again. His propaganda, heavy handed and out of date, could be forgotten amidst the killing of all the Indians.

When he wrote to President Johnson in December 1965 seeking support for a film about the Green Berets in Vietnam, Wayne had been explicit about its purpose. He told Johnson of his conviction that: 'not only the people of the United States but those all over the world should know why it is necessary for us to be [in Vietnam]'.[92] Convinced of Wayne's sincerity, presidential aide Jack Valenti assured Johnson: 'If he made the picture he would be saying the things that we want said.'[93] Nevertheless, the Defense Department demanded three sets of alterations to the script, relating to plot and dialogue, before it agreed to provide Wayne with the military equipment and personnel that he needed to make the film. Amongst other changes, a Special Forces' raid into North Vietnam which Wayne had based upon 'Hit 'em Where They Live' became a raid into a Viet Cong stronghold and a reference to 'war as a game' was dropped. Dialogue was amended to remove the impression that South Vietnam was engaged in a civil war and to emphasise North Vietnamese aggression.[94] By the time Wayne began shooting the film in August 1967 it had become an index of the government's justifications for the war. As Slotkin observed in *Gunfighter Nation*: 'What is interesting about the film is not its misrepresentation of the war-as-fought but the accuracy with which it reproduces and compounds the official misunderstanding and falsification of the conflict.'[95]

The film begins with a lesson in politics at Fort Bragg in North Carolina where a convenient banner reminds the audience of John F. Kennedy's commitment to the Green Berets. The film's opening scenes establish the Green Berets as intelligent professionals who understand the situation in Vietnam because they, unlike their detractors, have been there. Muldoon, played by Aldo Ray, announces their credentials: 'I'm Master Sergeant Muldoon and this is Sergeant McGee. Between us we have three tours of duty in South Vietnam which makes us experts.'[96]

McGee, played by Raymond St. Jacques, tells a group of visitors to Fort Bragg that the South Vietnamese 'need us and … want us' and that, to appreciate their situation, Americans have to imagine a scenario in which:

> every mayor in every city would be murdered, every teacher that you'd ever known would be tortured and killed, every professor you ever heard of, every governor, every senator, every member of the House of Representatives and their combined families – all would be tortured and killed and a like number kidnapped.

Even in the face of such terror, McGee continues, 'there's always some little fellow out there' who will fight back.[97] Muldoon then lists the origins of the 'captured weaponry' that he drops in front of Beckworth: 'Chinese Communist … Russian Communist … Czech Communist'. What is being resisted in South Vietnam, he concludes, is 'Communist domination of the world'.[98] This summarised the arguments the American people had been given in favour of intervention: that the North Vietnamese were agents of international Communism seeking to crush their neighbours by the cruellest means; that South Vietnam was one of the dominoes and that its people were deserving and desirous of help as they tried to build a democracy.

Despite the Green Berets' expert status, Beckworth is unconvinced. Having gone to Vietnam to see for himself he quickly learns that the Communists are a sly and vicious enemy and that American soldiers deserve support rather than criticism. In Dodge City Viet Cong infiltration leads to the death of a Special Forces Captain who had been due to go home the next day. Objecting to the slapping of a suspected infiltrator, Beckworth is given proof of the man's guilt, a looted lighter inscribed: 'Congratulations, Green Beret – Love Joanne.' It had belonged to a Special Forces medic who was killed returning from a local village where he had been delivering a baby. Having reminded the audience of the medical aid provided by the Green Berets, Wayne adds that the medic was found mutilated and beheaded. Later, after a Montagnard village has been assaulted by the Viet Cong, Wayne clinches Beckworth's conversion and underlines the nature of America's enemies:

> Pretty hard to talk to anyone about this country until they've come over here and seen it. The last village that I visited they didn't kill the chief, they tied him to a tree and brought his teenage daughters out in front of him and disembowelled them and then forty of them abused

his wife and then they took a steel rod and broke every bone in her body. Somewhere during the process she died.[99]

America's strengths are also stressed. When a detachment of Seabees arrives to help Wayne prepare for the defence of Dodge City, the young lieutenant in charge responds to Wayne's request to move the jungle back by saying: 'Say the word sir and I'll move it all the way to China.'[100] Such notions of America's technological power do not prevent Wayne's Special Forces from demonstrating their individual ingenuity in the face of superior odds and in the film's climax a Viet Cong General is cleverly kidnapped by a small unit of men led by Wayne.

American troops arriving in South Vietnam were told: 'we are here to help save this valiant little country, and with it all of South-East Asia, from Communist aggression and oppression.'[101] In the final scene the Vietnamese orphan Hamchunk represents the 'valiant little country' and Wayne stands for America. He breaks the news that Peterson, who has been looking after Hamchunk, has been killed:

> *Wayne:* You always knew it could happen, didn't you?
> *Hamchunk:* But I didn't want it to.
> *Wayne:* None of us did.
> *Hamchunk:* Was ... my Peterson brave?
> *Wayne:* He was very brave. Are you going to be?
> *Hamchunk:* I'll try.
> *Wayne:* I know you will and I'm sure that your Peterson would want you to have that. (Handing Hamchunk Peterson's green beret.)
> *Hamchunk:* What will happen to me now?
> *Wayne:* You let me worry about that Green Beret, you're what this is all about.[102]

As Wayne and Hamchunk disappear into the sunset, unfortunately setting over the South China Sea which is to the east, the credits roll and words from the 'The Ballad of the Green Berets' repeat the moral for those who might have missed it: 'he has died for those oppressed'.[103] Out of date and probably ignored by its intended audience, Wayne's propaganda serves a useful purpose today, demonstrating the nature of the arguments the American government wanted to present to its people in support of its war in Vietnam.

Determined to assert the heroism of the Green Berets, Robin Moore and John Wayne produced versions of the war that are highly flawed but historically valuable for reasons neither writer nor actor/director might have imagined: as reflections of the attitudes of Americans; as evidence of the appeal that the Special Forces and the mythology surrounding them continued to have, despite an increasingly peripheral role in Vietnam; and, individually, as indications of some of the views of a small group of soldiers in Vietnam and the avowed views of the American government in Washington. The next chapter, however, considers a text that was created with the far more conscious intention of enabling Americans to understand an aspect of their nation's history.

Notes

1. *Time*, 11 May 1962.
2. 'The Men in the Green Berets', *Time*, 2 March 1962.
3. Shelby L. Stanton cites the assigned strength of the 1st Special Forces Group in South Vietnam at the end of June 1962 as 213 officers and 778 enlisted men, in Stanton, *Green Berets at War: U.S. Army Special Forces in Southeast Asia, 1956–1975* (New York: Ivy Books, 1985), p. 180.
4. William Prochnau, *Once Upon a Distant War* (New York: Vintage Books, 1996), p. 41.
5. Eric James Schroeder, *Vietnam, We've All Been There: Interviews with American Writers* (Westport, CT: Praeger, 1992), p. 49.
6. Stanton, *Green Berets at War*, p. xiii.
7. Ibid. p. xiii.
8. The figure of 2,000 is cited in Francis J. Kelly, *The Green Berets in Vietnam, 1961–1971* (New York: Brassey's, [1985] 1991), p. 7.
9. Ibid. p. 10.
10. Christian G. Appy, *Working-Class War: American Combat Soldiers and Vietnam* (Chapel Hill: University of North Carolina Press, 1993), p. 66.
11. William J. Lederer and Eugene Burdick, *The Ugly American* (New York: W. W. Norton, 1958), p. 7.
12. Ibid. p. 284.
13. *New York Times*, 23 January 1959.
14. The full text of Kennedy's inaugural address can be found in *Public Papers of the Presidents: John F. Kennedy, 1961–1963*, 3 vols (Washington, DC: Government Printing Office, 1962–4), vol. 1, p. 1.
15. Richard Reeves, *President Kennedy: Profile of Power* (London: Papermac, 1994), p. 69.
16. Kennedy's message is cited in Robin Moore, *The Green Berets* (New York: Crown, 1965), p. 8.
17. Stanton, *Green Berets at War*, p. 42.
18. The figure of 991 is cited in ibid. p. 55.
19. *Public Papers of the Presidents: John F. Kennedy*, vol. 2, p. 453.
20. Loren Baritz, *Backfire: A History of How American Culture Led Us Into Vietnam and Made Us Fight The Way We Did* (Baltimore: The Johns Hopkins University Press, [1985] 1998), p. 241; General Wheeler's comments, made in November 1962, are cited in Arthur M. Schlesinger, Jr, *Robert Kennedy and his Times* (Boston: Houghton Mifflin, 1978), vol. 2, p. 740.

21. Reeves, *President Kennedy*, p. 307.

22. Guenter Lewy, *America in Vietnam* (New York: Oxford University Press, 1978), p. 85.

23. Halberstam's description is cited in Jeff Shesol, *Mutual Contempt: Lyndon Johnson, Robert Kennedy, and the Feud that Defined a Decade* (New York: W. W. Norton, 1997), p. 254.

24. 'The American Guerrillas', *Time*, 10 March 1961.

25. 'The Men in the Green Berets', *Time*, 2 March 1962.

26. 'The American Guerrillas', *Time*; 'The Men in the Green Berets', *Time*.

27. John Hellmann, *American Myth and the Legacy of Vietnam* (New York: Columbia University Press, 1986), pp. 47–8.

28. Stanton, *Green Berets at War*, p. 5.

29. Ibid. p. 43.

30. Kelly, *The Green Berets in Vietnam*, p. 175.

31. Colonel McKean's comments are cited in ibid. p. 86.

32. Hellmann, *American Myth and the Legacy of Vietnam*, p. 53.

33. Emile Capouya, Review of *The Green Berets*, *Commonweal*, 6 August 1965; Donald Ringnalda, *Fighting and Writing the Vietnam War* (Jackson: University Press of Mississippi, 1994), p. 22.

34. Robin Moore, *The Green Berets* (New York: Crown, 1965), p. 2.

35. These figures are cited in William L. Lunch and Peter Sperlich, 'American Public Opinion and the War in Vietnam', *Western Political Quarterly*, March 1979.

36. Moore, *The Green Berets*, p. 18.

37. Ibid. p. 26.

38. Murdock speaking in *Rambo: First Blood Part II*, directed by George P. Cosmatos (Anabasis Investments, 1985).

39. Moore, *The Green Berets*, pp. 162–3.

40. Ibid. p. 163.

41. Ibid. p. 142.

42. Ibid. p. 17.

43. Jim Neilson, *Warring Fictions: Cultural Politics and the Vietnam War* (Jackson: University Press of Mississippi, 1998), p. 104.

44. Moore, *The Green Berets*, p. 121 and p. 57.

45. Ibid. p. 69; p. 252.

46. Ibid. p. 237.

47. Ibid. pp. 240–1.

48. Ibid. p. 79.

49. Ibid. p. 104.

50. Ibid. p. 155.

51. Ibid. p. 128.

52. Ibid. p. 140.

53. General Paul Harkins cited in Stanley Karnow, *Vietnam: A History* (London: Guild Publishing, [1983] 1985), p. 258.

54. Halberstam David, *The Making of a Quagmire* (London: The Bodley Head, 1965), p. 166 and p. 170.

55. Vann's story is told in *The Making of a Quagmire* and at greater length in Neil Sheehan, *A Bright Shining Lie: John Paul Vann and America in Vietnam* (New York: Vintage Books, 1989).

56. Prochnau, *Once Upon a Distant War*, p. 22.

57. Moore, *The Green Berets*, p. 1.
58. Ibid. p. 7.
59. 'One Man's War', *Time*, 25 June 1965.
60. Stanton, *Green Berets at War*, p. 342.
61. Richard Slotkin, *Gunfighter Nation: The Myth of the Frontier in Twentieth-Century America* (Norman: University of Oklahoma Press, [1992] 1998), p. 745 (note).
62. George C. Herring, *America's Longest War: The United States and Vietnam, 1950– 1975*, 3rd edn (New York: McGraw Hill, 1996), p. 86.
63. Ibid. p. 86; James William Gibson, amongst others, has noted that in Laos the CIA 'maintain[ed] its secret Army operations after the 1962 Geneva Accords.' Gibson, *The Perfect War: Technowar in Vietnam* (New York: The Atlantic Monthly Press, [1986] 2000), p. 388.
64. Al Santoli, *To Bear Any Burden: The Vietnam War and its Aftermath in the Words of Americans and Southeast Asians* (London: Abacus, [1985] 1986), pp. 98–9.
65. Stanton, *Green Berets at War*, p. 182.
66. Ibid. p. 82.
67. Santoli, *To Bear Any Burden*, pp. 99–100.
68. Gloria Emerson, *Winners & Losers: Battles, Retreats, Gains, Losses, and Ruins from the Vietnam War* (New York: W. W. Norton, [1976] 1992), p. 267.
69. Moore, *The Green Berets*, p. 164.
70. Ibid. p. 169.
71. Ibid. p. 211.
72. Ibid. p. 210.
73. Kelly, *The Green Berets in Vietnam*, p. 172.
74. Stanton, *Green Berets at War*, p. 195.
75. Moore, *The Green Berets*, pp. 209–13.
76. Capouya, *Commonweal*, 6 August 1965.
77. Richard Schickel, 'Duke Talks Through His Green Beret', *Life*, 19 July 1968.
78. The interview is cited in Julian Smith, *Looking Away: Hollywood and Vietnam* (New York: Charles Scribner, 1975), p. 135.
79. Joseph Evans, 'The Logic of the Battlefield', *Wall Street Journal*, 23 February 1968.
80. Mark Baker, *Nam: The Vietnam War in the Words of the Men and Women Who Fought There* (London: Abacus, 1982), p. 221.
81. Renata Adler, *New York Times*, 20 June 1968.
82. Lawrence H. Suid, *Guts and Glory: Great American War Movies* (Reading, MA: Addison-Wesley, 1978), p. 234.
83. Hellmann, *American Myth and the Legacy of Vietnam*, p. 93.
84. Lieutenant Colonel Michael Kirby speaking in *The Green Berets*, directed by John Wayne and Ray Kellogg (Batjac Productions and Warner Bros., 1968).
85. Michael Wayne cited in Suid, *Guts and Glory*, p. 233.
86. The Green Berets' comments are cited in ibid. p. 233.
87. Garry Wills, *John Wayne: The Politics of Celebrity* (London: Faber and Faber, 1997), p. 12.
88. Richard Slotkin, *Gunfighter Nation*, p. 473.
89. William Manchester, *American Caesar: Douglas MacArthur 1880–1964* (Boston: Little, Brown and Co., 1978), p. 515.
90. Joan Didion, *Slouching Towards Bethlehem* (London: Flamingo, 1993), p. 30.
91. Richard Schickel, 'Duke Packs a Mean Punch', *Life*, 4 August 1967.
92. Wayne's letter is cited in Suid, *Guts and Glory*, p. 222.

93. Valenti's advice is cited in ibid. p. 221.
94. Ibid. p. 223. This paragraph is based upon the detailed account of the film's production history which Suid provides in pp. 222–9.
95. Richard Slotkin, *Gunfighter Nation*, p. 523; Gilbert Adair offered a similar argument in Adair, *Hollywood's Vietnam: From The Green Berets to Apocalypse Now* (New York: Proteus, 1981), pp. 35–52.
96. Muldoon speaking in *The Green Berets*.
97. McGee speaking in ibid.
98. Muldoon speaking in ibid.
99. Wayne speaking as Kirby in ibid.
100. Lieutenant Jamieson speaking in ibid.
101. Part of 'an indoctrination lecture of thirty … pages' these lines are part of a longer extract cited in Martha Gellhorn, *The Face of War* (London: Granta, 1993), p. 249.
102. Wayne speaking as Kirby in *The Green Berets*.
103. Played over closing credits of ibid.

CHAPTER 3

Cinematic History:
The Case of *JFK*

In December 1991 Warner Brothers released *JFK*, a film by Oliver Stone. It provoked violent debate. Although the most immediate controversy surrounded the ideas Stone communicated about the shooting of President Kennedy and the claim that Kennedy's assassination was part of a conspiracy to escalate the war in Vietnam, the film provided stimulation to another, less sensational dispute, concerning the nature of the relationship between film and history. Defending his film against what were sometimes virulent attacks, Stone, who has referred to himself as a 'cinematic historian', estimated that more than 'fifty or so million Americans' would watch his film and be rewarded with 'a little more information on their history'.[1] Film critic David Thomson, on the other hand, has described *JFK* as: 'loony irresponsibility of a kind that ill equips its maker to defend the claims of history.'[2] What sort of 'information' Stone's film, or indeed any feature film, can give audiences about their history is one subject of this chapter. The other, for which a crucial episode in *JFK* provides a starting point, is the question of responsibility for the escalation of America's military involvement in Vietnam during the 1960s and the means by which this question can best be answered.

It may seem perverse to focus an examination of the contribution that cinema may make to an understanding of historical events upon a film which has been widely criticised for its manipulations of historical evidence. Strange also to concentrate upon a work by a director whose willingness to engage in debate about his films has been accompanied by a tendency to contradict himself. Stone's attitude towards history, for example, has hardly been consistent. His observation 'So, what is history? Who the fuck knows?' was quoted in *Esquire* in November 1991. A month later he proclaimed in the *New York Times* that history was 'too important to leave to newsmen.'[3] Nevertheless, Stone and his film, which Robert A. Rosenstone described in 1995 as 'among the most important works of American history ever to appear on the screen', have prompted public discussion in a way that few history books could.[4] *JFK* is an important text for study because of the directness with which it handles a critical period in the history of America's war in Vietnam, the intensity of its impact as film and its popularity. In the first two weeks of January 1992, *JFK* grossed 30.8 million dollars and Norman Mailer, writing in *Vanity Fair* in February 1992, predicted that: '[*JFK*] is going to be accepted as fact by a new generation of moviegoers.'[5] If that, indeed, has happened, what has a viewing of *JFK* communicated to audiences about America's war in Vietnam?

Stone's account of the assassination features a conspiracy involving leaders of the American 'military-industrial complex' intent upon clearing Lyndon Johnson's path to the presidency in order that the war in Vietnam could be prosecuted with greater vigour.[6] Kennedy's assassination was, according to Stone, a necessary stage in that process because Kennedy was intending to withdraw Americans from Vietnam if he was re-elected in 1964. Stone perceived his story, which he co-wrote with Zachary Sklar, as 'more of a "whydunit" than a "whodunit"' and the explanation of why Kennedy was killed is presented in a key scene featuring Kevin Costner and Donald Sutherland.[7] Costner played the film's protagonist, Jim Garrison, the district attorney from New Orleans whose book *On the Trail of the Assassins*, published in 1988, had described his own efforts to prove that Kennedy's assassination was the result of a conspiracy. Sutherland played X, a character partly based on an ex-Air Force colonel called L. Fletcher Prouty who had worked as an aide to the Joint Chiefs of Staff during Kennedy's presidency. Garrison's book was an important source for Stone, and Prouty, whose ideas about Kennedy and Johnson's policies on Vietnam had influenced the director, was employed as a technical adviser during the making of *JFK*.

The scene in which Garrison meets X in front of the Lincoln Memorial in Washington DC is highly characteristic of the rest of the film in its mixing of colour and black and white shots. The colour shots which tell Garrison's story frequently cut to documentary footage in black and white, black and white stills and hypothetical re-enactments in black and white which are intended to illustrate Stone's version of the truth. Whilst it is not difficult to distinguish between the different types of black and white shot, the pace of the cutting and the suggestiveness with which spoken narrative and documentary image are married together make it harder for the viewer to retain a critical distance from the messages which are being communicated. The director's manipulation of dramatic effect is additionally persuasive. For example, in the encounter between

Garrison and X, which was fabricated by Stone, X gives the impression of having highly privileged and accurate information, telling Garrison that 'everything I'm going to tell you is classified top secret', and consequently 'precautions' have had to be taken in the arrangement of their meeting. X's encouragement also seems to verify Garrison's inquiries: 'you're close, you're closer than you think'. More importantly, however, X clarifies Stone's 'central issue' – the killing of Kennedy in order to escalate the war in Vietnam – by referring to primary sources as evidence for his explanation.[8]

Having claimed an experience of 'black-ops' stretching back to World War II and commented on the resentment caused by Kennedy's refusal to invade Cuba, X's narrative turns to Vietnam:

> So, 1963, I spend much of September, '63 working on a Kennedy plan for getting all US personnel out of Vietnam by the end of 1965. This plan was one of the strongest, most important papers issued from the Kennedy White House, this National Security Action Memo 263 ordered home the first 1,000 troops for Christmas.[9]

The introduction of portentous music as the words 'most important papers' are spoken by X contributes a further sense of their significance. Earlier in *JFK*, Stone had prepared the audience for the idea that Kennedy wanted to extricate America from Vietnam with an extract from a television interview. With a caption indicating the date to be 2 September 1963, Stone had shown the president informing interviewer Walter Cronkite: 'in the final analysis it's their war'.[10] Thus, Stone's self-description as a 'cinematic historian' seems borne out by the initial stage of his argument, which is supported by reference to a primary source, the National Security Action Memorandum (NSAM), and oral testimony, the president's words to Cronkite, as well as sustaining reinforcement from a number of dramatic and cinematic techniques: the implication of privileged information; the setting in the heart of Washington DC which links X and Garrison with the more positive aspects of American presidential history; the addition of music which highlights moments of particular significance in X's explanation; and close-ups on Costner and Sutherland which suggest their sincerity. The casting of Costner ensured additional impact when *JFK* was released. Costner had already developed a reputation for playing the parts of honest men who would not be corrupted, in films like *The Untouchables* (1987) and *Dances With Wolves* (1990), and Stone believed that his star had 'a sort of fundamental decency to him, and integrity'. Costner's acceptance of what X had to tell him was intended to set a powerful example for audiences.[11]

Seated on a park bench with the Washington Monument behind him, X remarks that after Kennedy's assassination, 'Vietnam started for real', and delivers Stone's theory that the details of the assassination are of secondary importance: 'That's the real question, isn't it? Why? The how and the who is just scenery for the public ... [which] prevents them from asking the most important question ... why?' X answers his own question: 'Kennedy wanted to end the cold war in his second term ... he set out to withdraw from Vietnam'.[12] The response of the 'military-industrial complex' to Kennedy's determination to avoid war is presented by Stone with a variety of techniques. As X suggests the nature of the conspiracy which led to Kennedy's death, his spoken narrative is accompanied, and sometimes interrupted, by black and white still photographs of Kennedy, soundless black and white documentary footage of Lyndon Johnson, Secretary of Defense Robert McNamara and the Joint Chiefs of Staff and, again in black and white, acted scenes representing meetings between Johnson, military men and civilians before and after the assassination. Although Stone has denied that his film asserts Johnson's involvement in the conspiracy, the images of Johnson which accompany parts of X's narrative imply the connection.[13]

As X builds his argument that a conspiracy, about which 'everybody in the loop' knows, sought to prevent Kennedy from fulfilling his plans, an actor representing Johnson (Tom Howard) takes the leading role in a meeting of military men and civilians:

> Well, just don't let McNamara start sticking his damn nose in this thing. Every time he goes over to Saigon on some fuckin' fact finding mission he comes back and just scares the shit out of the President. Now I want Max Taylor on him night and day like a fly on shit. Now you control McNamara and you control Kennedy.[14]

Here, Johnson's contempt for McNamara and President Kennedy, who is portrayed by the Johnson character as repeatedly frightened by the news from Vietnam, is clear. So, too, is the authority with which he issues instructions for Maxwell Taylor, the Chairman of the Joint Chiefs during the majority of Kennedy's administration. However, the most powerful message is communicated in the scene which follows immediately upon Johnson's plan for the manipulation of the president. An anonymous general receives a telephone call asking him to prepare a

President Johnson listening to a tape sent to him
by his son-in-law, Captain Charles Robb, who was
serving in Vietnam in 1968 (LBJ Library Photo by
Jack Kightlinger).

plan for the assassination. The link between Johnson and the conspiracy
has been made by the juxtaposition of the scenes. When X's narrative
continues, he refers to the 'military firing squad' which killed Kennedy
and observes that 'everyone in the power structure who knows anything
has a plausible deniability'. As the phrase 'who knows anything' is spoken,
documentary footage displays a smiling Johnson. More images of Johnson
accompany the summary of this second stage of X's argument: 'the per-
petrators must be on the winning side and never subject to prosecution
for anything by anyone. That is a coup d'état.'[15] Although Stone offers
no historical evidence for Johnson's complicity in the conspiracy to kill

Kennedy, the episode's structure and the matching of speech and image in *JFK* demonstrate the capacity of film to convey a message in a persuasive although unsupported form.

Stone concludes the argument presented by X with another reference to documentation, thus bracketing the unsubstantiated implication of Johnson's guilt with two examples of the way in which his film seeks to offer evidence for its propositions. X recalls that the day after Kennedy's funeral: 'Lyndon Johnson signs National Security Memo 273 which essentially reverses Kennedy's new withdrawal policy and gives a green light to covert action against North Vietnam which provoked the Gulf of Tonkin incident ... In that document lay the Vietnam War.'[16] These words are accompanied by black and white shots of the actor representing Johnson, now the president, signing a document identified as NSAM 273. The document's importance is emphasised in several ways: the camera rests for a moment upon its heading, 'Top Secret', which again implies that the audience is being given privileged information, and its signing is prefaced by a statement indicating the new president's determination with regard to the war in Vietnam: 'Gentlemen, I want you to know I'm not going to let Vietnam go like China did. I'm personally committed. And I'm not going to take one soldier out of there until they know we mean business in Asia'.[17] Spoken to an apparently approving group of shadowy men in suits and military uniforms, the speech implies that the succession of Johnson to the presidency resulted in the change of policy, asserted in NSAM 273, which had been sought by the men who conspired to kill Kennedy. The final line spoken by Johnson in this hypothetical re-enactment, 'Just get me elected. I'll give you your damned war', seems to confirm Johnson's willingness to strike a deal with the 'military-industrial complex'.[18] Indeed the line was based on a comment attributed to Johnson by General Harold K. Johnson, who was Army Chief of Staff when Johnson became president.[19] However, it is X's closing sentence, 'In that document lay the Vietnam War', which receives the most striking treatment from the director. As music fades, the pace slackens for a moment with a long pause between the words 'document' and 'lay', a pause filled by a sound effect suggestive of a bullet hitting its target and ending with a cut from a shot of the document to the face of X, the agent of revelation for both Garrison and the audience. Hence, the shooting of Kennedy is linked, via a variety of cinematic devices and historical sources, to the signing of NSAM 273 and the beginning of the 'real' war in Vietnam.

The setting of the conversation between Garrison and X, a rainy day amidst the presidential memorials of Washington, is initially gloomy. As the two men emerge from the dark tunnel of trees through which they have been walking, the rain has stopped and there is more light. The two men sit on a bench in an open space around which two young girls briefly play. The contrasts, of gloom with comparative light, of the innocent gaiety of the playing girls with the villainy which X has been explaining to Garrison, are conventional cinematic images. And when, at the scene's conclusion, X strides purposefully away, climbing a slope (or a grassy knoll) behind the bench, Stone perhaps sought to symbolise the determination of those who seek the truth about Kennedy's assassination. To what extent, however, has light been shed upon history? How much real, rather than reel, villainy uncovered? Has Stone's claim to have created a cinematic history, supporting his craft as a film maker by 'letting history speak for itself', any justification?[20]

What *JFK* has to say about the history of the Vietnam War cannot be judged against the same criteria that one would use for judging a book about history. It is necessary to consider how 'good' cinematic history might differ from 'good' history before one can assess a film maker who describes himself as a 'cinematic historian' engaged in an attempt to 'reinterpret the history of our times'.[21] *JFK* is a particularly helpful text for this sort of analysis because of Stone's willingness to talk and write about his film. Although there may be important differences between the way a work is perceived by an audience and the messages its creator hoped to communicate, it is useful to consider an artist's, or a historian's, expressed intentions and the extent to which the work has fulfilled them. For example, the contradictory statements which Stone has made about his purposes in *JFK* may demonstrate an uncertainty at the heart of the film's conception which may or may not be detectable in the film itself. On the other hand, if Stone had consistently stated that *JFK* was simply a thriller which used the Kennedy assassination and the Garrison investigation as a starting point, criticism would have concentrated on the film's strengths and weaknesses as cinema rather than as history.

A further advantage is that Stone's control of the film from its inception, through its writing and its shooting, and to the point of its final edit was sufficiently close that *JFK* can be accurately described as Oliver Stone's film, rather than as a joint enterprise in which writer, director, producer, photographer and editor have each made distinctive contributions.

Stone's publication of an annotated script, entitled *JFK: The Book of the Film*, to accompany his film demonstrated a consciousness that the nature of film precludes the sort of detailed reference to sources that written history can offer. As Bob Katz observed in a review of *JFK*: 'Hollywood has never been the land of footnotes'.[22] The annotated script also reveals the extent to which the demands of film making impinged upon historical precision in Stone's film. The most powerful pressure upon a Hollywood director is to make a film that audiences will consider watchable. To that end, historical events in *JFK* were compressed, characters combined into composites, scenes invented or adapted for dramatic effect or narrative clarity and a sense of closure provided with Garrison's account of the assassination in the final courtroom scene. Individual agency, the actions and speeches of characters such as Garrison and X, were stressed. The figures of Kennedy and Johnson were presented as the prime movers of events because film works more effectively with individuals and their motivations than it does with impersonal forces like the imperatives of the cold war or, indeed, the military-industrial complex.

At the most basic level, the actors pretended to be who they were not and Stone used a variety of artistic techniques to create an illusion of the past. Pierre Sorlin, in one of the earliest attempts to theorise about the relationships between film and history, was aware of the role that imagination played in film making when he wrote in 1980 that a historical film:

is not an historical work: even if it appears to show the truth, it in no way claims to reproduce the past accurately. So ... when professional historians wonder about the mistakes made in an historical film, they are worrying about a meaningless question ... Historical films are all fictional.[23]

Something similar, however, might be said about a written version of an event in the past. Having done their research, historians select language in order to describe the past as accurately as they can, accepting that they cannot 'reproduce' it and, even, accepting the existence of more than one interpretation of a set of facts. A film maker can adopt the same principle in using the language of film to approach historical material, whilst accepting that some departure from the facts may contribute towards the telling of other truths. For example, it may be appropriate for a director to invent the details of a scene in order to communicate the ideas or attitudes of a historical figure for which there is sound documentary evidence.

A striking difference between writing about history and film about history is, however, the size of the audience, which is one reason why it is so important to consider the ways in which film makers treat history and to assess the reliability of their research. The consequence of Stone's claim to be offering more than fifty million Americans 'a little more information on their history' is an acceptance of some responsibility for the quality of that information.

Good cinematic history, then, whilst accepting the limitations of the medium in terms of the presentation of evidence and the necessity of editing or adapting material, can also pursue historical accuracy as an objective. It will resist the temptation to manipulate the facts for purely dramatic effect. It may offer a particular version of the past, but, ideally, it will recognise the difficulties involved in the historical process and prompt the audience, as Stone hoped, to 'leave the theater ready to think about things ... and rethink them'.[24] As Rosenstone noted, there is a tendency for 'the huge images on the screen and wraparound sounds ... to overwhelm us, swamp our senses and destroy attempts to remain ... critical.'[25] Being overwhelmed by a film is, of course, one of the most satisfying experiences the cinema has to offer – given the choice between drama and data, most people will opt for the first, as Shakespeare knew. Nevertheless, the cinematic historian must be prepared to sacrifice the dramatic moment in the interests of offering an interpretation firmly based upon the available facts, and to risk inspiring scepticism in the audience rather than catharsis.

Experimenting with the techniques with which film can recreate rather than reproduce the past may also be the concern of the cinematic historian, although the form which Stone chose has prompted much criticism. Hayden White, who defended *JFK* as 'perfectly respectable' in his essay 'The Modernist Event', summarised the objections to a film which:

> seemed to blur the distinction between fact and fiction by treating an historical *event* as if there were no limits to what could legitimately be said about it, thereby bringing under question the very principle of objectivity as the basis for which one might discriminate between truth on the one side and myth, ideology, illusion on the other.[26]

For White it was exactly this blurring which strengthened Stone's film because it highlighted that 'what is at issue here is not the facts of the matter regarding such events but the possible meanings that such facts can be construed as bearing.'[27] In White's view, by directing his full battery of cinematic techniques at the national traumas of the assassination of Kennedy and the Vietnam War, Stone addressed events of such complexity that the story told in *JFK* is, firstly, as meaningful as other narratives might be and, secondly, communicated in a form which stresses the uncertain nature of the truth.

It was Stone's original intention to model *JFK* upon Akira Kurosawa's film *Rashomon* (1951), in which audiences are presented with four contradictory accounts of the same event and left to draw their own conclusions. It is significant, however, that he retreated from this design. Perhaps such a project would have required a structure of such complexity and a film of such length that many viewers would have been intimidated. Whatever the reason for Stone's change of mind, it altered the very nature of his film. Despite references to *Rashomon* in defence of *JFK*, Stone's film does not problematise the notion of truth. Instead, it presented a single narrative which is clarified in the scene between Garrison and X and in the climactic courtroom scene in which Garrison provides his account of the assassination. Stone has sometimes downplayed the extent to which *JFK* is the truth, saying, 'I don't have all the facts', but this is not communicated in the film.[28] As Dana Polan observed: 'In [*JFK*] the flashbacks are put forward as unequivocal and unchallengeable bits of verity. Through Garrison's perception and ours a totalized and radiant Truth is to be built up out of these bits.'[29] While X confesses that some of the details he offers about the 'how and the who' of Kennedy's killing are guesswork, his answer to 'the most important question ... why?' is delivered with no trace of uncertainty and the form in which Stone communicated, rather than questioning the 'principle of objectivity', tended to convince the audience of the historical accuracy of his ideas.

Unfortunately, as the following pages will reveal, those ideas rely upon a highly selective use of evidence and simplify what is complicated and ambiguous. By reducing the question of responsibility for the escalation of the war to a question of personalities, Stone opted for drama rather than history. Closer scrutiny of the primary and secondary sources suggests that rather than 'letting history speak for itself', as Stone claimed, or exploring 'the possible meanings that such facts can be construed as bearing', as White claimed, *JFK* illustrates the dangers of jumping to conclusions.

The specifics of Stone's ideas about Kennedy's intentions in Vietnam were the consequence of his collaboration with John M. Newman, a historian whose research into the Kennedy administration's handling of events in South Vietnam, *JFK and Vietnam*, was published in 1992. Newman made his perspective clear in the documentary film *Beyond 'JFK': The Question of Conspiracy*:

> I don't think there's any doubt that JFK was pulling out of Vietnam when he ... was killed ... [B]ecause the most fundamental tenet of his policy was no combat troops and we know that Johnson put in combat troops, I feel it is safe to say that the assassination led to the escalation of the war.[30]

JFK and Vietnam was a highly detailed version of this argument, with the additional strand that the withdrawal plan was to be kept secret until after the presidential election of 1964 in order to avoid the political fall-out of such a decision. The secrecy, according to Newman, explains the lack of documentary evidence in support of this claim. However, he cited the memory of Kenneth O'Donnell, a Kennedy aide, that Kennedy had told Senator Mansfield, who by 1963 was urging complete withdrawal from Vietnam, that he agreed with him, 'But I can't do it until 1965 after I'm re-elected.'[31] NSAM 263, signed by President Kennedy on 11 October 1963, and NSAM 273, signed by President Johnson on 26 November 1963, are of central importance in Newman's demonstration of the different attitudes towards Vietnam of the two presidents, hence Stone's references to these two documents in *JFK*.

NSAM 263, which Stone does not show in *JFK*, is a single-sided document of three short paragraphs. Top secret at the time of its signing, it is a confirmation of the president's approval of the military recommendations proposed in a report on the situation in South Vietnam attributed to Robert McNamara and Maxwell Taylor. The only detail is to be found in the second paragraph which stated: 'The President ... directed that no formal announcement be made of the implementation of plans to withdraw 1,000 U.S. military personnel by the end of 1963.'[32] It is important to note that a summary of the McNamara-Taylor report had already been released by Kennedy's press secretary, Pierre Salinger, on 2 October 1963. The summary included a prediction that:

> the major part of the U.S. military tasks can be completed by the end of 1965 ... by the end of this year, the U.S. program for training Vietnamese should have progressed to the point where 1,000 U.S. military personnel ... can be withdrawn.[33]

Consequently, the notion of withdrawing advisors had been floated. Kennedy, however, was careful to ensure that his name was not attached to the suggestion and in Saigon, American Ambassador Henry Cabot Lodge privately dismissed the idea in the report as 'just politics', rather than the beginning of an American withdrawal.[34]

Historians have speculated about the thinking behind the withdrawal plan and about Kennedy's reasons for withholding formal announcement of what, for Newman (and X), was the first stage of the complete withdrawal of American advisors from South Vietnam. Newman argued that the most important reason for the President's reticence was that 'Kennedy had not yet decided how *he* was going to publicly justify his withdrawal plan', although he hoped to present it as a consequence of an improving military situation in South Vietnam.[35] *JFK and Vietnam* includes a painstaking attempt to show that Kennedy was not engaged in political sign language and that he was determined to begin the process of extricating America from Vietnam. However, Stanley Karnow has commented that the 1,000-man withdrawal was intended to pressurise South Vietnamese president Diem into following American advice: 'a way of prodding Diem into behaving more leniently', with the implication that Kennedy had withheld formal announcement of the withdrawal plan in order to retain the possibility of cancelling it if it seemed appropriate.[36] George C. Herring has observed that a token withdrawal was suggested to Kennedy as a political tactic which would 'reassure the American public' that America was not drifting into a land war in Asia, and undermine the Communist argument that 'the United States was running the war'. Herring also thought that, rather than pressurising Diem, such a withdrawal was intended to 'reassure the South Vietnamese'. Nevertheless, like Karnow, he felt that Kennedy was eager to keep his options open, pointing out that Kennedy had instructed McNamara: 'to begin planning for overt military actions against Vietnam *and* for a phased withdrawal of U.S. troops from South Vietnam'.[37] And Robert D. Schulzinger has muddied the waters further with the unsourced speculation that McNamara and Taylor: 'proposed that the President remove a one-thousand-man construction battalion once it finished its work at the end of 1963. Kennedy agreed to do so but stipulated that an additional thousand men were to be sent as replacements.'[38]

Despite their different perspectives, each of these historians displayed an awareness that decisions taken by Kennedy in October 1963 were coloured by the prospect of new leaders in South Vietnam, although

Newman is somewhat reluctant to deal with Kennedy's involvement in the military coup which toppled Diem's administration on 1 November 1963. Only half a dozen of the 460 pages of *JFK and Vietnam* are devoted to an episode which was of decisive importance in the history of America's relationship with South Vietnam. As Robert McNamara pointed out in his memoir, *In Retrospect*, there were six different governments in the first year of Johnson's presidency. Thus: 'whatever [Kennedy's] thoughts may have been before Diem's death, they might have changed as the effect of that event on the political dynamics in South Vietnam became more apparent.'[39]

The planning of the coup had been carefully monitored by the Kennedy administration which, anxious to avoid conspiring with the plotters, still hankered after a measure of control over their actions. Thus the instruction that Ambassador Lodge received from the White House on the day before the coup reveals a mixture of messages:

> We do not accept as a basis for U.S. policy that we have no power to delay or discourage a coup ... U.S. authorities will reject appeals for direct intervention from either side ... But once a coup under responsible leadership has begun ... it is in the interests of the U.S. government that it should succeed.[40]

In other words, we should not take any direct action but we should maintain control over events. This will include encouraging a coup, if it would be in our interests, and discouraging it if it seems likely that the alternative would be worse than Diem. The instruction to Lodge suggests the dilemma which haunted Kennedy's attempts to handle affairs in Vietnam: desperate for improvement, convinced that American solutions would be superior to those of the Vietnamese, the American president remained uncomfortably conscious that a choice had to be made between greater American influence, which incurred a moral, political, economic and military debt, and stepping back from the problems in Vietnam, which would result in a loss of control.

Newman's observation that Kennedy ensured that the McNamara–Taylor report did not include a recommendation for a coup because 'such an act would only force the United States into assuming more responsibility for South Vietnam's fate' shows a sound grasp of what Kennedy wished to avoid.[41] Frustration with Diem, however, and hopes of a more pliable South Vietnamese leadership were enough to tilt Kennedy towards provocation. One of the economic pressures suggested in the McNamara-Taylor report, which Richard Reeves has described as 'Diem's death warrant', included a recommendation to cancel the funding for the LLDB force which had been adopted by Diem as his presidential guard.[42] By agreeing the cut, Kennedy sent the same message to Diem and his opponents: Diem could no longer rely upon American support. As Robert Kennedy observed in a 1964 oral history interview, his brother wanted 'somebody that can win the war.'[43]

With all of this going on, it is not surprising that at a news conference in Washington on the afternoon before the coup Kennedy was carefully keeping his options open about the 1,000-man withdrawal: 'Secretary McNamara and General Taylor ... announced that we would expect to withdraw a thousand men from South Vietnam before the end of the year ... If we are able to do that, that would be our schedule.'[44]

It would be absurd to blame Stone for failing to refer to each of the possible interpretations of NSAM 263 in *JFK*. Film cannot deal with the minutiae of such arguments. Nevertheless, his failure to acknowledge the uncertainties surrounding the significance of NSAM 263 was seriously misleading. Robert Brent Toplin has presented the defence that:

> Stone challenged viewers to transcend the particular arguments about Kennedy's posture towards Vietnam (such as what, specifically, was intended by memorandum 263) and to consider a broad question of how history might have been different if the tragedy of 22 November 1963 had not intervened.[45]

However, Stone's position on NSAM 263 did not urge the transcending of a particular argument. X's words about the memorandum are unambiguous: 'This plan was one of the strongest, most important papers issued from the Kennedy White House, this National Security Action Memo 263 ordered home the first 1,000 troops for Christmas.' Stone's decision to refer to the document by name rather than to show it on screen was borne of an unwillingness to lessen the force of his particular argument that NSAM 263 was Kennedy's plan to withdraw from Vietnam. Had the camera rested upon the second paragraph of the document, alert viewers might have detected the faint sound of a can of worms being opened.

In *Beyond 'JFK'* Newman admitted:

> By 1963 Kennedy had a problem — that problem was his re-election. You have to reconcile this public record and the public record itself is

ambiguous because Kennedy makes statements – the Cronkite one – which appear to be 'well, it's their war, they'll have to fight it' and there are these many public statements that indicate we should stay the course.[46]

In the Cronkite statement, a televised interview broadcast on 2 September 1963 in which Kennedy answered questions put by Walter Cronkite for the *CBS Evening News*, Kennedy had heaped pressure upon the South Vietnamese government to institute reforms:

> I don't think that unless a greater effort is made by the government to win popular support that the war can be won out there. In the final analysis, it is their war. They are the ones who have to win it or lose it ... We can give them equipment, we can send our men out there as advisors, but they have to win it, the people of Vietnam ...[47]

As Newman observed in *JFK and Vietnam*: 'These remarks are usually cited in the perennial debate over whether Kennedy would have committed U.S. combat troops to the war later, as Lyndon Johnson did.'[48] Newman argued that Kennedy's remarks were intended to prepare the way for an acceptance that the war might be lost and for the South Vietnamese leadership to be saddled with the blame for such a defeat. Stone had shown Kennedy saying: 'in the final analysis it's their war', to make the rather simpler point that Kennedy was ready to leave the Vietnamese to decide their own fate.

Newman was honest enough to admit that Kennedy made 'many' public statements indicating his belief that America should not withdraw from Vietnam, although he did not offer any examples in his appearance in *Beyond 'JFK'*. In fact, Kennedy had told Walter Cronkite: 'I don't agree with those who say we should withdraw', that withdrawal would be 'a great mistake' and that those who suggested it were 'wholly wrong', in the same interview to which Newman referred.[49] Later in the month Kennedy made similar comments, telling television interviewer David Brinkley on the 9th: 'What I am concerned about is that Americans will get impatient and say because they don't like events in Southeast Asia or they don't like the government in Saigon, that we should withdraw ... I think we should stay', and declaring at a press conference on the 12th: 'We are not there to see a war lost'.[50] On the morning of his death, Kennedy told a crowd in Fort Worth: 'Without the United States, South Vietnam would collapse', and the speech which he intended to give in

Dallas included an insistence that America 'dare not weary of the task' in South-east Asia.[51] As Michael Lind observed of Kennedy's public position on South-east Asia in *Vietnam: The Necessary War*, 'The historical record on this point is clear': the president regularly stated his opposition to withdrawal.[52]

In *JFK and Vietnam* Newman explains Kennedy's repeated assurances that he would not abandon the South Vietnamese by arguing that the president was lulling his opponents into the belief that he would stay the course in Vietnam in order that his electoral chances in 1964 would not be damaged. Having said in his inaugural speech, 'In the long history of the world only a few generations have been granted the role of defending freedom in its hour of maximum danger. I do not shrink from this responsibility. I welcome it', Kennedy was scarcely in a position to make a public reversal on the issue.[53] Moreover, it seems likely that Kennedy's inaugural remarks represented sincerely held beliefs. Nigel Hamilton, one of Kennedy's biographers, has referred to 'the one moral crusade that stirred his soul: the defense of freedom.' Kennedy's determination to resist the Communists, argued Hamilton: 'was and would remain the first and only fundamental plank in [his] political philosophy'.[54] Thus, Newman's argument presents several difficulties. Even if one accepts that Kennedy's refusal to commit American troops, rather than American advisors, to South Vietnam had become a firm principle, if one sets aside the moral question of a president lying about his intentions in order to get elected, one is left pondering the selectivity with which Newman handles the evidence regarding the withdrawal plan. If whatever Kennedy said in contradiction of Newman's belief that the president had such a plan was a deliberate lie and whatever he said in support of withdrawal, which wasn't much, was a moment of truth, it is hard to imagine a piece of evidence which would convince Newman that his theory was wrong. A further weakness is Newman's tendency to interpret Kennedy's actions as part of a master plan when there is significant evidence that Kennedy was often confused about what to do in Vietnam. He said different things to different people (or, in the case of the Cronkite interview, different things to the same person) and, as his eagerness to keep his options open in the weeks before the coup demonstrated, was uncertain about what American policy should be. Curiously, although this uncertainty is not reflected in *JFK*, Stone expressed his consciousness of it in a contribution he made to *Beyond 'JFK'*, suggesting that:

[Kennedy] was making tentative steps in one direction, tentative steps in the other direction. I think he was a very beleaguered man and ambivalent about how to deal with this cold-war machine that had been in place since World War II.[55]

Kennedy's last instruction regarding Vietnam, the commissioning of a further study 'of every possible option we've got', may illustrate that ambivalence and his feeling that he was trapped.[56] It was hardly the act of a president who had already made a decision to withdraw.

As David Halberstam observed in *The Best and the Brightest*, an account of how American policy makers struggled with the problems in South Vietnam during the 1960s, Kennedy 'markedly escalated the rhetoric and the rationale for being [in Vietnam]', during his presidency. President Johnson inherited the consequences of this escalation, having 'to deal not so much with Kennedy's inner doubts so carefully and cautiously expressed, but with his public statements, all supportive of the importance and significance of Vietnam.'[57] Newman's determination to confer upon Kennedy the credit for planning a complete withdrawal and upon Johnson the opprobrium of instituting a reversal of that policy does not recognise the predicament of the new president. Not only did Johnson have the additional difficulty of operating in a political climate made even more tense by Kennedy's assassination and the change of government in South Vietnam, but as Herring has observed: 'JFK bequeathed to his successor a problem eminently more dangerous than the one he had inherited.'[58]

America had been financially involved in Vietnamese affairs since March 1950, when President Truman agreed a grant of fifteen million dollars in military aid to support French efforts to regain control of their colony. They had been militarily involved since February 1955, when, under President Eisenhower, responsibility for the training of the South Vietnamese Army had been accepted by America's military leaders. Eisenhower, however, had restricted the number of American advisers to approximately 700. By the time Johnson took over from Kennedy, the number of Americans in uniform in South Vietnam had risen to over 16,000 and many of the new personnel, soldiers and airmen were engaged in combat.[59]

President Johnson recorded a number of justifications for his continuing commitment to South Vietnam in his presidential memoir, *The Vantage Point*. The reasoning may be flawed but it provides an interesting demonstration of the dilemmas Johnson apparently believed himself to confront:

> It seemed likely that all of Southeast Asia would pass under Communist control ... The evidence before me as President confirmed the previous assessments of President Eisenhower and President Kennedy.
> Second, I knew our people well enough to realize that if we walked away from Vietnam ... there would follow a divisive and destructive debate in our country. This had happened when the Communists took power in China ... We had a solemn treaty commitment to Southeast Asia. We had the word of three Presidents that the United States would not permit this aggression to succeed ...
> Third, our allies, not just in Asia but throughout the world would conclude that our word was worth little or nothing ...
> Fourth, [the Soviets and Chinese] would move to exploit the disarray in the United States and in the alliances of the Free World ...[60]

Johnson was aware, as Kennedy was, of his vulnerability to attack from the American right should he be perceived as acting weakly in the face of Communist aggression. Richard Reeves' perception that 'politically [Kennedy] could not afford to look weak militarily' was just as applicable to his successor.[61] Johnson also feared that any failure of nerve on his part would be contrasted with the determination of previous presidents, that the 'loss' of South Vietnam to Communism would be compared to the loss of China during Truman's presidency, and that 'divisive and destructive debate' would wreck his chances of achieving the reforms that would secure his reputation as a great president. The tape of a telephone conversation with McNamara in July 1965 reinforces the image of a reluctant president: 'we know ourselves, in our own conscience, that when we asked for [the Tonkin Gulf] resolution, we had no intention of committing this many ground troops. We're doing so now, and we know it's going to be bad.'[62]

This was certainly not the Johnson that Stone depicted. In *JFK* Johnson was shown embracing the opportunity to escalate the war in Vietnam, rather than as a president confounded by forces he felt unable to control. Stone followed Newman's example in portraying NSAM 273 as the turning point in American policy towards Vietnam. According to Newman: 'The dam broke when NSAM–273 was re-written four days after Kennedy's assassination.'[63] According to X, Johnson's signing of NSAM 273: 'essentially reverses Kennedy's new withdrawal policy and gives a green light to covert action against North Vietnam which provoked the Gulf of Tonkin incident ... In that document lay the Vietnam War.' However, a closer look at the historical record indicates not only that Newman and Stone are guilty, once again, of simplification, but also the ease with which documentary evidence can sometimes be manipulated to suit a particular theory.

Newman's reference to the re-writing of NSAM 273 requires explanation. Two days before Kennedy's death, a day long conference had been held in Honolulu to discuss, once again, a way forward in South Vietnam. McNamara, Henry Cabot Lodge, Secretary of State Dean Rusk, military leaders and senior Kennedy aides, including McGeorge Bundy, had met to hear what turned out to be surprisingly pessimistic briefings about conditions in South Vietnam in the aftermath of the coup. It was Bundy's job to communicate the conference's recommendations to the president in the form of a draft NSAM. Kennedy was never to see the draft which Bundy produced. Instead, after discussion with the new president, the draft was revised into the document which became NSAM 273. The final document, which Stone provided a brief glimpse of in *JFK*, consists of ten paragraphs. A comparison of two treatments of its opening paragraph offers a striking demonstration of the caution with which one must approach explanations of documents.

In *Robert Kennedy and his Times*, published in 1978, Arthur M. Schlesinger, Jr argued that John Kennedy was intending to withdraw American advisors by the end of 1965 and that Johnson's signing of NSAM 273 four days after Kennedy's assassination revealed a wholly different approach by the new president. Schlesinger, apparently unaware that much of NSAM 273 had been drafted by McGeorge Bundy the day before Kennedy's death, quoted the first point in the Memorandum and included his own emphases to support his argument: 'It *remains* the *central objective* of the United States in South Vietnam to assist the people and Government of that country to *win* their contest against the *externally directed* and supported communist conspiracy.' Here, Schlesinger explained, was a false claim that the policy expressed in the Memorandum represented continuity. Here too was a 'total commitment Kennedy had always refused' and 'a diagnosis of the conflict' which Kennedy did not entirely share.[64]

Fourteen years later, in *JFK and Vietnam*, Newman chose the same paragraph and the same technique to provide evidence of a contradictory position. Aware that the Memorandum had been drafted by Bundy for Kennedy and that the opening paragraph had appeared unchanged in the version signed by Johnson, Newman added emphases to demonstrate that it 'reiterated the essence of Kennedy's policy', a determination to establish the war as the responsibility of the Vietnamese: 'It remains the central object of the United States in South Vietnam to *assist* the people and government of that country to win *their* contest against the externally directed and supported Communist conspiracy'.[65]

It is ironic that Schlesinger and Newman had the same goal: Kennedy's exculpation. Nevertheless, their manipulation of the same piece of evidence raises the question: how many other meanings may be wrested from this paragraph, or others, by the selective use of emphasis? A case of 'Beware historians bearing emphases', apparently, but also another warning of the dangers of building complex theories upon too selective an interpretation of the evidence.[66]

In *JFK and Vietnam* Newman observed that the 'truly important change' appearing in the final form of NSAM 273 was: 'the authorization for plans to widen the war against North Vietnam.'[67] He connected, as X did in *JFK*, this change to the Gulf of Tonkin incident, which led to the first American bombing of North Vietnam and to a Congressional resolution, passed on 7 August 1964, enabling the president to 'take all necessary measures ... to prevent further aggression', a resolution widely accepted as signalling an American willingness to prosecute the war unilaterally.[68] In the original draft Bundy had referred to 'action against North Vietnam' and 'a detailed plan for the development of additional Government of Vietnam resources ... [in order] to achieve a wholly new level of effectiveness in this field of action'.[69] In its final form, however, the paragraph dealing with action against North Vietnam was different, omitting reference to Government of Vietnam resources and thereby allowing the possibility of direct American involvement in such activities.

The argument that this represented a change in policy and that one of the consequences was the sending of American ships on surveillance missions along the North Vietnamese coastline, an action that resulted in the Gulf of Tonkin incident, is valid. It is another matter to suggest, as Newman does, that this is evidence of a second master plan, of Johnson carefully clearing a path to escalation. Even less convincing is X's assertion that NSAM 273 reversed Kennedy's 'new withdrawal policy' and initiated covert action against North Vietnam as an act of provocation. Had provocation of the North Vietnamese been Johnson's objective he would presumably have responded to the first North Vietnamese attack upon American destroyers in the Gulf of Tonkin, which took place on 2

August, rather than waiting for reports of a second attack two days later. Moreover, to suggest that NSAM 273 initiated covert action against North Vietnam is to ignore covert action by South Vietnamese forces already approved by Kennedy, to which Newman referred in *JFK and Vietnam*.[70] And, of course, the status of the 'new withdrawal policy' had remained unconfirmed by Kennedy. If the *Pentagon Papers* described as 'essentially an accounting exercise' the processing of the 1,000-man withdrawal which was confirmed by NSAM 273, there is no evidence to indicate that it would have been any different under Kennedy.[71] The sentence in NSAM 273 which dealt with the withdrawal, 'The objectives of the United States with respect to the withdrawal of U.S. military personnel remain as stated in the White House statement of October 2, 1963', was the same as it had been in Bundy's original draft.[72] Once again, Newman's approach to the evidence, like Stone's, seems highly selective, focusing upon those details which support his theory and neglecting the bulk of the evidence which, in the case of NSAM 273, suggest continuity rather than change.

Other historians have perceived Johnson's initial attitude towards South Vietnam in this light. In *Dereliction of Duty*, published in 1997, H. R. McMaster described Johnson as: 'Preoccupied with the election and committed to taking only the minimum action necessary to keep South Vietnam from going Communist'.[73] Karnow, writing about *JFK*, commented that the Johnson administration: 'With slight modifications … perpetuated the Kennedy policy.'[74] And, as Herring has argued, to concentrate upon the attitudes of individuals, even presidents, probably misses the point:

> U.S. involvement in Vietnam was not primarily a result of errors of judgment or of the personality quirks of the policy makers … It was a logical, if not inevitable outgrowth of a world view and a policy – the policy of containment – which Americans in and out of government accepted without serious question for more than two decades.[75]

The willingness to identify the dynamics of historical change with the actions of individuals may have been what attracted Stone to Newman's theories. Stone's simplification of the complexities of American involvement in Vietnam – Kennedy as a fallen hero and Johnson as the villain – bears a startling similarity to the Manichean dynamic of his earlier film, *Platoon* (1986), in which the good Sergeant Elias is destroyed by the evil Sergeant Barnes. As drama *JFK* has most of the ingredients for success.

However, as cinematic history concerned with the reasons for the escalation of America's military efforts in Vietnam it missed an opportunity. By 'letting history speak for itself' Stone might have made a film which demonstrated some of the ambiguities and uncertainties surrounding the attitudes of Kennedy and Johnson towards Vietnam, a film which signalled the possibility of alternative explanations and the significance of forces other than the personal determinations of America's presidents. Instead, he used the power of film to encourage his audience to overlook the weakness of his research.

The analysis presented in this chapter is intended to sound two warnings. The first is about the dangers involved in uncritical acceptance of theories which claim to accommodate the confused and various documentary record which is available to the historian who researches the history of Kennedy and Johnson's thinking about Vietnam. This is not to dismiss the importance of the documentary record, but to suggest that sustainable explanations of the causes of the escalation of America's war in Vietnam are more likely to be found in consideration of the pressures which moulded America's foreign policy in the 1960s than in speculations concerning the secret intentions of America's presidents.

The second warning concerns Oliver Stone's *JFK*. A. J. P. Taylor's remonstrance about the dangers of film is appropriate because *JFK* is misleading, and particularly because Stone seems to be using some of the tools of the historian's trade as well as the persuasive power of film in building support for his argument. Of course, it is one thing to establish the weaknesses of *JFK* as cinematic history, and another to assess the extent to which the ideas expressed in *JFK* actually influenced those who watched it. There is no reliable method of measuring the impact of Stone's explanation of the assassination or the war's escalation. Many will have dismissed *JFK* as 'just a film', while others will have been convinced of the existence of a conspiracy anyway. And whilst the proportion of those newly convinced of the truth of Stone's account may be large, it is likely that the benefits of the controversy stimulated by *JFK* and his defence of it have outweighed the damage done by the inadequacies of his history. Reaction to the film focused pressure upon the American government to release confidential documents about the assassination and, by arousing popular interest in the questions surrounding Kennedy's assassination and the origins of the Vietnam War, Stone administered an important corrective to the mood President Bush had sought to inspire after American success in the Gulf War earlier in 1991. Bush's boast that 'we've kicked the Vietnam Syndrome once and for all' was an attempt to close discussion of America's mistakes in Vietnam and *JFK* helped to ensure that some of the questions raised by the war in Vietnam remained in the public consciousness.

Whilst noting the dangers of film, Taylor commented that film could be 'very useful' as an 'instrument for historical study', and analysis of Stone's film, as well as revealing its faults, does highlight some of the possibilities of cinematic history.[76] Roger Donaldson's *Thirteen Days*, released in 2000, a film which used the documentary record with some integrity to depict the Cuban Missile Crisis from the perspective of the Kennedy administration, suggested that Hollywood might be interested in pursuing such possibilities. Whether such interest will survive the failure of *Thirteen Days* at the American box office is another matter. It did not recoup half of the eighty million dollars it cost to make. Of *JFK* it must be concluded that it is more useful to historians as a reflection of a cultural and political mood at the start of the 1990s – a scepticism about the nature of government and an anxiety to protect Kennedy's presidential reputation – than as a demonstration that America's war in Vietnam was the fault of Lyndon Johnson.

Notes

1. Oliver Stone's self-description as a 'cinematic historian' was cited in George Lardner, Jr, 'On the Set: Dallas in Wonderland', *Washington Post*, 19 May 1991; Stone's estimate of *JFK*'s potential was given in a speech to the National Press Club in January 1992. Cited in Norman Kagan, *The Cinema of Oliver Stone* (Oxford: Roundhouse, 1995), p. 207.

2. David Thomson, *A Biographical Dictionary of Film* (London: Deutsch, 1994), p. 719.

3. Stone cited in *Esquire*, 116, no. 5, November 1991; Oliver Stone, 'Who is Rewriting History?', *New York Times*, 20 December 1991.

4. Robert A. Rosenstone, *Visions of the Past: The Challenge of Film to our Idea of History* (Cambridge, MA: Harvard University Press, 1996), p. 131.

5. Norman Mailer, 'Footfalls in the Crypt', *Vanity Fair*, February 1992. Cited in Kagan, *The Cinema of Oliver Stone*, p. 202.

6. The opening of *JFK* (Warner Bros., 1991) includes documentary footage of President Eisenhower referring to the dangers posed by the 'military-industrial complex' in his farewell address to the nation in January 1961. *JFK: The Director's Cut* has been used as the source for this analysis.

7. Stone cited in Kagan, *The Cinema of Oliver Stone*, p. 183.

8. X speaking in *JFK*; Stone described the question of 'what threat to power did [Kennedy] represent' as the 'central issue' of the assassination in *Beyond 'JFK': The Question of Conspiracy*, directed by Danny Schecter with Barbara Kopple (Embassy International Pictures, 1992).

9. X speaking in *JFK*.

10. Another example of Stone's use of documentary footage in *JFK*.

11. Cited in Kagan, *The Cinema of Oliver Stone*, p. 188. Stone added that Costner reminded him of James Stewart and Gary Cooper, other actors whose screen presence suggested reliability.

12. X speaking in *JFK*.

13. Stone regarded Johnson's involvement in a conspiracy as a possibility but insisted that 'I never made that assertion' in *JFK*. Cited in Robert Brent Toplin, *History by Hollywood: The Use and Abuse of the American Past* (Chicago: University of Illinois Press, 1996), p. 68.

14. Although the character is not named at this stage in the film, his accent, style of speech, size and posture, as well as the content of his remarks, firmly suggest Johnson. Shortly afterwards, the same character is portrayed as the new President and the final credits indicate that the part of 'L.B.J.' was played by Tom Howard, although the voice was that of another actor, John William Galt.

15. X speaking in *JFK*.

16. Ibid.

17. Words spoken by Galt, as LBJ, in *JFK*.

18. Ibid.

19. Cited in Stanley Karnow, 'JFK'. Printed in Mark C. Carnes (ed.), *Past Imperfect: History According to the Movies* (New York: Owl Books, 1996), p. 273. Karnow added, however, that Stone 'lifted the story out of context' in *JFK*. The remark was certainly not made on the occasion of the signing of NSAM 273.

20. Oliver Stone, *JFK: The Book of the Film* (New York: Applause Books, 1992), p. 353.

21. Stone cited in Toplin, *History by Hollywood*, p. 69.

22. Bob Katz cited in Janet Staiger, 'Cinematic Shots: The Narration of Violence', in Vivian Sobchak (ed.), *The Persistence of History: Cinema, Television and the Modern Event* (New York: Routledge, 1996), p. 42.

23. Pierre Sorlin, 'How to Look at an "Historical" Film'. Reprinted in Marcia Landy (ed.), *The Historical Film: History and Memory in Media* (London: The Athlone Press, 2001), pp. 37–8.

24. Stone cited in *Esquire*, 116, no. 5, November 1991.

25. Rosenstone, *Visions of the Past*, p. 27.

26. Hayden White, 'The Modernist Event', in Sobchak (ed.), *The Persistence of History*, p. 22 and p. 19.

27. Ibid. p. 21.

28. For example, Stone's comments cited in Toplin, *History by Hollywood*, p. 67.

29. Dana Polan, 'The Professors of History', in Sobchak (ed.), *The Persistence of History*, p. 239.

30. John M. Newman speaking in *Beyond 'JFK'*.

31. The words attributed to President Kennedy are cited in John M. Newman, *JFK and Vietnam: Deception, Intrigue and the Struggle for Power* (New York: Warner, 1992), p. 322.

32. NSAM 263, http://www.fas.org/irp/offdocs/nsam-jfk/nsam–263.htm, accessed 9 September 2001.

33. The extract from the summary is cited in Richard Reeves, *President Kennedy: Profile of Power* (London: Papermac, 1994), p. 614.

34. Lodge cited in ibid. p. 615.

35. Newman, *JFK and Vietnam*, p. 410.
36. Karnow, 'JFK', in *Past Imperfect*, p. 272.
37. George C. Herring, *America's Longest War: The United States and Vietnam, 1950–1975*, 3rd edn (New York: McGraw Hill, 1996), pp. 104–5.
38. Robert D. Schulzinger, *A Time for War: The United States and Vietnam, 1941–1975*, (New York: Oxford University Press, 1998), p. 122.
39. Robert S. McNamara, *In Retrospect: The Tragedy and Lessons of Vietnam* (NewYork: Times Books, 1995), p. 101; pp. 95–6.
40. The instruction is cited in Reeves, *President Kennedy*, p. 643.
41. Newman, *JFK and Vietnam*, p. 401.
42. Reeves, *President Kennedy*, p. 615.
43. Robert Kennedy cited in Michael Lind, *Vietnam: The Necessary War – A Re-interpretation of America's Most Disastrous Military Conflict* (New York: The Free Press, 1999), p. 197.
44. President Kennedy cited in Newman, *JFK and Vietnam*, p. 425.
45. Toplin, *History by Hollywood*, pp. 57–8.
46. Newman speaking in *Beyond 'JFK'*.
47. President Kennedy speaking in an interview with Walter Cronkite on the *CBS Evening News*, broadcast on 2 September 1963.
48. Newman, *JFK and Vietnam*, p. 365.
49. President Kennedy speaking in Cronkite interview.
50. President Kennedy cited in Lind, *Vietnam: The Necessary War*, p. 197 and in Karnow, 'JFK', p. 272.
51. President Kennedy cited in Lind, *Vietnam: The Necessary War*, p. 197.
52. Ibid. p. 196.
53. *Public Papers of the Presidents: John F. Kennedy, 1961–1963* (Washington, DC: Government Printing Office, 1962–4), vol. 1, p. 1.
54. Nigel Hamilton, *JFK: Reckless Youth* (New York: Random House, 1992), pp. 792–3.
55. Stone speaking in *Beyond 'JFK'*.
56. Reeves, *President Kennedy*, p. 660.
57. David Halberstam, *The Best and the Brightest* (Greenwich, CT: Fawcett Crest, 1973), p. 366.
58. Herring, *America's Longest War*, p. 119.
59. Arthur M. Schlesinger, Jr offered exact figures in *Robert Kennedy and his Times* (Boston: Houghton Mifflin, 1978), vol. 2, p. 756: 'When Kennedy became President, there were 685 American military advisers in Vietnam. In October 1963 there were 16,732.' Others have been more tentative. The approximate figure of 700 is taken from Ronald H. Spector, *Advice and Support: The Early Years of the U.S. Army in Vietnam, 1941–1960* (New York: The Free Press, 1985), p. 291; Reeves suggested a figure of 17,000 for 1963 in *President Kennedy*, p. 614. The imprecision of the figures springs from American unwillingness to admit the extent to which the Geneva Accords of 1954, which limited the size of military advisory efforts in North and South Vietnam, were being breached. Whether Schlesinger's figures are entirely accurate or not, the essential point is that under Kennedy there was, as Schlesinger noted, 'a formidable escalation'.
60. Lyndon Baines Johnson, *The Vantage Point* (New York: Holt, Rinehart and Winston, 1971), pp. 151–2.
61. Reeves, *President Kennedy*, p. 604.
62. Telephone conversation between Johnson and McNamara, 2 July 1965. Printed in

Michael Beschloss (ed.), *Reaching for Glory: Lyndon Johnson's Secret White House Tapes, 1964–1965* (New York: Simon and Schuster, 2001), p. 382.

63. Newman, *JFK and Vietnam*, p. 447.
64. Arthur M. Schlesinger, Jr, *Robert Kennedy and his Times*, vol. 2, p. 759.
65. Newman, *JFK and Vietnam*, p. 439. Other than the emphases, the slight differences in the texts of the Memorandum cited by Schlesinger and Newman are the consequence of each using a different source.
66. H. R. McMaster has applied his own emphases to the same paragraph in NSAM 273. Although mounting a similar argument to Newman's, that the paragraph stressed South Vietnamese responsibility, McMaster used emphases slightly differently: 'the American objective was to "assist the people of *that* country win *their* contest against the … Communist conspiracy."' McMaster, *Dereliction of Duty: Lyndon Johnson, Robert McNamara, The Joint Chiefs of Staff and the Lies that Led to Vietnam* (New York: Harper Perennial, 1998), p. 64.
67. Newman, *JFK and Vietnam*, p. 448.
68. Gareth Porter (ed.), *Vietnam* (New York: Earl M. Coleman Enterprises, 1979), vol. 2, p. 307.
69. The original draft is cited in Newman, *JFK and Vietnam*, p. 440.
70. For example, Newman's reference to 'the dropping of South Vietnamese commandos into the North that Kennedy had approved.' *JFK and Vietnam*, p. 446.
71. The lines from the *Pentagon Papers* are cited in Newman, *JFK and Vietnam*, p. 433.
72. NSAM 273 http://www.lbjlib.utexas.edu/johnson/archives.hom/NSAMs/nsam 273.asp, accessed 9 September 2001.
73. McMaster, *Dereliction of Duty*, p. 84.
74. Karnow, 'JFK' in *Past Imperfect*, p. 272.
75. Herring, *America's Longest War*, p. xi.
76. A. J. P. Taylor cited in Nicholas Pronay, 'The Moving Picture and Historical Research', *Journal of Contemporary History*, July 1983.

CHAPTER 4

Battles

Shakespeare's Cleopatra welcomed her lover Antony back from success on the battlefield with the words: 'Lord of lords, / O infinite virtue, com'st thou smiling from / The world's great snare uncaught?'[1] Few of the Americans who fought in Vietnam took part in the sort of monumental battle which Shakespeare and more recent writers have envisaged in their portrayals of warfare. Indeed, fighting was the primary role of only about a quarter of the 3.14 million Americans who served in Vietnam and there was considerable variety in the experiences of the men who were charged with killing the enemy.[2] For some, the enemy was the elusive guerrilla and tours of duty consisted of frustrating humps through exhausting terrain, the boredom punctuated by the snares provided by sniper, mine or booby trap. Others, for example those who fought in the Ia Drang or A Shau Valleys or at Khe Sanh or in Hue City during the Tet Offensive, found more conventional engagements with the regulars of the North Vietnamese Army, the sort of fighting that veterans of World War II or Korea might have recognised. Support troops also lived in danger, however. Scorned by the men in the combat units as REMFs, an acronym for Rear Echelon Mother Fuckers, those in the rear could be killed or wounded, as the Tet Offensive demonstrated. A survey in 1980 showed that at least 'Seventy-seven percent of those who served in Vietnam *saw* Americans wounded or killed'.[3] Different in many ways from other wars, America's war in Vietnam was characteristic in the respect that combat was its 'essential, defining feature', a feature which a significant majority of the Americans who served there encountered in various forms.

Representations of the fighting done by Americans in Vietnam appear in most of the novels, memoirs, histories, journalism and films stimulated by the war. Some have sought to make sense of combat, to explain its nature in the most explicit detail, others to demonstrate that only veterans can fully appreciate its horror and chaos. Still others have adopted

American soldiers carry a wounded comrade out of combat (Rex/SIPA).

techniques intended to disorientate the reader or viewer, to suggest the confusion of those who have participated in battle. Being under fire in Vietnam was, as in any war, both central to the experience and difficult to communicate to others.

Two of the most intense battles in which Americans participated were at Khe Sanh in early 1968, when 6,000 Marines were surrounded by at least two divisions of North Vietnamese regulars consisting of more than 15,000 men, and in the A Shau Valley in May 1969, when elements of the 101st Airborne Division had to fight for ten days to dislodge soldiers of the North Vietnamese 29th Infantry from the summit of Hill 937.[4] The Airborne's objective became known as Hamburger Hill because of the number of Americans killed or wounded in securing it. Both battles caused controversy as well as stimulating writing or film which sought, in different ways, to depict what American soldiers had endured.

Khe Sanh was in the north-western corner of South Vietnam near the Laotian border. It was vulnerable to attack because of its isolation but General Westmoreland, the commander of American forces in Vietnam, had been convinced of its importance as the western point of his defences south of the Demilitarized Zone (DMZ) and as a base from which to monitor, or even attack, North Vietnamese movements of men and supplies down the Ho Chi Minh trail in Laos. As NLF forces prepared for and mounted the Tet Offensive in the major cities and towns of the remainder of the country in the last days of January 1968, America's political and military leaders became convinced that the enemy's real target was the Marine force which had been cut off at Khe Sanh. The NVA was subjecting the combat base to daily shelling which, along with the poor weather, was threatening to prevent the Marines receiving the air supply upon which they depended. Trenches were being dug towards the American perimeter and determined attacks had been launched against Marine positions on nearby hills. The North Vietnamese, some believed, wanted to repeat the Viet Minh's success against the French at Dien Bien Phu in 1954. Then, the capture of a lonely town defended by thousands of French troops had been decisive and the French had withdrawn from Vietnam. President Johnson was so concerned about the Marines at Khe Sanh that he was given 'a written guarantee from the nation's highest-ranking military men' that the base would be held.[5] Khe Sanh also seized the attention of the American public, *Time* magazine observing on 16 February that: 'No single battle of the Vietnam War has held Washington – and the nation – in such complete thrall'.[6] Then, in early March, after the American Air Force had 'carried out the heaviest air raids in the history of warfare … dropping more than 100,000 tons of explosives on a five square mile battlefield', North Vietnamese forces departed.[7] They killed, if one accepts the figures of the American military, 205 Marines and lost 1,602 men themselves.[8] By the end of June the Americans had abandoned the base. Westmoreland claimed victory, calling Khe Sanh: 'one of the most damaging, one-sided defeats among many that the North Vietnamese incurred'. Others disagreed, believing that the North Vietnamese had not intended to capture Khe Sanh but that their actions had created 'a superb diversion for the Tet Offensive' as British military analyst Sir Robert Thompson suggested.[9]

Much has been written about Khe Sanh. Some of the contemporary journalism has been reprinted, of which John T. Wheeler's piece for Associated Press, 'Life in the V Ring', which appeared in the collection *Reporting Vietnam*, is a valuable example. The most widely known piece is probably the later 'Khe Sanh', an unconventional article by Michael Herr which became, in an extended version, the longest chapter in his 1977 novel *Dispatches*. There are also books devoted to the battle, amongst them *The End of the Line: The Siege of Khe Sanh*, published in 1982 by war correspondent Robert Pisor, and *Khe Sanh: Siege in the Clouds*, an oral history by Eric Hammel completed in 1989. For writers the battle was exceptional because, in a war in which Americans were usually the pursuers, the Marines at Khe Sanh were, as David Douglas Duncan observed in *Life* magazine, the 'tethered bullocks'.[10] It could also be argued, however, that Khe Sanh was symbolic of America's war in Vietnam, a costly, finally futile effort that became a source of controversies. Who won? Was there a parallel between Khe Sanh and Dien Bien Phu? Did the North Vietnamese even want the base? Was Westmoreland's decision to put the Marines at risk there a mistake? In their portrayals of the battle at Khe Sanh writers have been challenged by such questions as well as the more basic concern of what it was like for Americans in combat there.

Wheeler's 'Life in the V Ring', a story which appeared on 12 February 1968, depicts a day and night in the most heavily shelled sector of the base at Khe Sanh. Wheeler, who spent longer at the base than any other reporter, focused upon the danger and the bravery of the enlisted men. The story's opening puts the reader into the midst of the action: 'The first shell burst caught the Marines outside the bunker' and the repeated shouts of 'Corpsman' emphasise the danger. The 'random explosions' and the observation that only 'the artillery could fire back' are reminders that the enemy at Khe Sanh was usually invisible. The men 'are frightened but uncowed' although it 'is not uncommon' to see 'the 1,000 yard stare', a possible symptom of combat fatigue. Recording what he saw and heard Wheeler makes no reference to his own feelings, although he assumes a knowledge of the feelings of the Marines as they take cover, writing of how 'the small opening to the bunker seemed in their minds to grow to the size of a barn door.'

Presented chronologically, the account provides the names of units and individuals, sometimes adding their age and home town, as well as details about the way they pass the time and snippets of their conversation. Occasional statistics like the number of shells hitting the base during the night, the size of the shells being fired by the Americans and some reference to the number of casualties contribute to the impact of a story that is devoted, in conventional journalistic style, to the communication of facts. Wheeler does not state any opinions about the battle's larger significance although he does imply a scepticism about the war's purpose. He notes that the Marines, whom he has portrayed sympathetically, placed a 'hard emphasis' on the words of a popular song which they sang late that night: 'Where have all the soldiers gone? To the graveyard every one. When will they ever learn?' By placing these words in the penultimate paragraph the story leaves the reader with the distinct impression that the war is a mistake. Written in short sentences, short paragraphs and simple language with few literary flourishes, 'Life in the V Ring' is the attempt of a reporter to convey with some objectivity a glimpse of life at Khe Sanh. Its value lies in its concentration on the experience and attitudes of a few of the Marines, its limitation in the absence of any wider context for the events it describes.[11]

Herr's 'Khe Sanh' was published in *Esquire* in September 1969 and, like the book it became part of, it was based upon Herr's experiences. It is important to remember the kinship of 'Khe Sanh' to *Dispatches* in which, as Herr told Eric James Schroeder, 'I was not always bound by the facts' and which features 'talk ... that is invented.'[12] Going to Vietnam in late 1967, Herr had intended to write a monthly column about the war for *Esquire*, as well as collecting material for a book, but he had rapidly 'realized what a horrible idea' the monthly column was and dropped it.[13] Instead, his work became a preparation for what Herr 'always privately thought of as a novel'. *Dispatches* concentrates upon the way the war affected him but, as he has pointed out: 'The "I" in the book shouldn't be taken – at any rate always – as me'.[14] On the other hand, Herr had been stimulated to write about Vietnam because he was convinced that 'Vietnam was *the* story at the time ... and that it wasn't being told in any true way'.[15] One of the book's main concerns is to identify the elusive truths of America's war in Vietnam. Herr includes a scene in which a Marine demands that he should get the truth about the war back to America: 'His face was all but blank with exhaustion, but he had enough feeling left to say, "Okay, man, you go on, you go on out of here you cocksucker, but I mean it, you tell it! You tell it, man"', and he describes the refrain of other soldiers:

> And always, they would ask you with an emotion whose intensity would shock you to please tell it, because they really did have the

feeling that it wasn't being told for them, that they were going through all of this and that somehow no-one back in the world knew about it.[16]

Apparently determined to satisfy such pleas but convinced that, as he wrote in his penultimate chapter, 'This war could no more be covered by conventional journalism than it could be won by conventional fire-power', Herr opted to pursue the truths of the war using the techniques of a novelist rather than those of a reporter.[17]

He rejected conventional journalism for three reasons. The first was the unreliability of the 'facts' offered by official sources, a concern shared by many journalists. There had been suspicion about the information presented by the American and South Vietnamese authorities since the days of Kennedy and Diem and, after one of the first major battles of the war at LZ Albany in the Ia Drang Valley in November 1965, many reporters had refused to accept the official version of what had happened. Their reaction was described in *We Were Soldiers Once ... and Young* by Lt. Gen. Harold G. Moore and Joseph L. Galloway: 'The general's summary of what he understood had happened at Albany was greeted by roars of disbelief from the assembled reporters.'[18] Herr's belief that such reporters 'worked in the news media, for organisations that were ultim-ately reverential towards the institutions involved: the Office of the President, the Military, America at war and, most of all, the empty tech-nology that characterized Vietnam' provided the second reason.[19] In Herr's view, this meant that even when stories revealing the truth about the war were printed in their original form they were overwhelmed by material that was blindly supportive of the war effort. This hardly does justice to the impact of the reportage from Vietnam throughout the1960s and it was certainly not the perception of those who governed America. According to John Mecklin, a US press attaché in Saigon in the early 1960s: 'a major American policy was wrecked, in part, by unadorned reporting of what was going on.'[20]

The third reason for Herr's rejection of the conventional approach was the conviction that his expectations of war, based upon the false images offered by Hollywood and America's other media, were so persist-ent that 'unlearning' them was a process that required complete immer-sion in the war and time to learn anew from his experiences. The point about his unreadiness for the reality of war is made in several ways in *Dispatches*. In the first chapter there is an exchange between an experienced sergeant and the newly arrived narrator: '"This ain't the fucking movies over here, you know." [Said the sergeant.] I laughed ... and said that I knew but he knew that I didn't.'[21] Later in the book the narrator observes that even experience was no guarantee of clear perception: 'A lot of things had to be unlearned before you could learn anything at all, and even after you knew better you couldn't avoid the way things got mixed, the war itself with those parts of the war that were just like the movies'.[22] Specifically, he had to learn about death and how one resists its finality. He recalls that, early in his tour, he saw an American killed but refused to accept what he was seeing: 'he was dead, but not (I knew) really dead.'[23] To assimilate the reality of death required a frame of reference that only months in the war zone could bring.

Critics responded with enthusiasm to *Dispatches* and to the ideas that explanation of the war must avoid official dogma and the convenient preconceptions determined by cultural attitudes imbibed in America (attitudes like those Moore's *The Green Berets* had exhibited, for example). In a November 1977 issue of the *New York Times Book Review* C. D. B. Bryan called *Dispatches*: 'Quite simply ... the best book to have been written about the Vietnam War' and, in the following month's *New York Review of Books*, Roger Sale praised Herr's insistence that 'an uninitiated reader be comforted with no politics, no certain morality, no clear outline of history.'[24] There was also approval for Herr's suggestion that 'hiding low under the fact-figure crossfire there was a secret history' and a feeling that his writing about the war had revealed it. Herr's radically different approach, John Hellmann claimed in *American Myth and the Legacy of Vietnam*, took him 'through the woods that conventional journalists and historians will not enter in order to bring back essential information'.[25] Such information is not dependent upon facts. As Herr wrote in *Dispatches*: 'The press got all the facts (more or less), it got too many of them. But it never found a way to report meaningfully about death, which of course was really what it was all about.'[26] Instead of pursuing the facts about the war, Herr relied upon the intensity of his own experience and the stories he heard. By the end of the year the narrator: 'felt so plugged into all the stories and the images and the fear that even the dead started telling me stories ... no ideas, no emotions, no facts, no proper language, only clean information.'[27] Assessing the battles of the Ia Drang Valley in 'Khe Sanh', for example, Herr relies upon the war stories he has heard and the way: 'A few correspondents, a few soldiers ... still shuddered uncontrollably at what they remembered' as evidence of their horror. This creates a striking image of the awfulness of the fighting that took place in the Ia Drang, although it does not distinguish between the different battles there, of which one was an American victory.[28]

Such an approach makes Herr an awkward character for historians to handle. Frequently sharp in its insight into the war and convincing in its portrayal of what ordinary soldiers had to say about it, his writing 'was not always bound by the facts' and some of the 'talk ... is invented.' This has not stopped some historians from citing *Dispatches* as if it were an oral history. In *Working-Class War* Christian G. Appy used the words of soldiers who appear in *Dispatches* on more than one occasion, and in *Backfire* Loren Baritz claims a portion of Herr's narrative to be the words of a GI.[29] That some historians trust Herr so implicitly is testimony to the persuasiveness of his writing and the cleverness with which *Dispatches* is structured, its apparent formlessness an effective reflection of the randomness of his own experiences in Vietnam as he helicoptered from one story to another and of the confusion of a war zone. The structure also leads to deliberate ironies at the narrator's expense which imply the authenticity of these stories. The narrator's initial eagerness to distance himself from the work of killing is reflected in his response to a soldier's explanation of America's role in Vietnam: 'We're here to kill gooks. Period.' The narrator adds: 'Which wasn't at all true of me. I was there to watch.'[30] Soon, however, he is taking pride in another role and another perspective:

> one night ... I slid over to the wrong end of the story ... firing cover for a four-man reaction team trying to get back in ... I wasn't a reporter, I was a shooter ...
>
> In the morning there were about a dozen dead Vietnamese across the field there where we'd been firing ... I couldn't ever remember feeling so tired, so changed, so happy.[31]

Such a confession of the excitement involved for those who survive combat is an important contribution to an understanding of its nature. In a description of the experience of combat in 'Khe Sanh', Herr offers a further insight which stresses the multiplicity of sensations that it can generate and something of the illicitness of the appeal it can hold:

> It came back the same way every time, dreaded and welcome ... your senses working like strobes, free-falling all the way down to the essences and then flying out again in a rush to focus ... springing all

the joy and all the dread ever known … And every time, you were so
weary afterwards, so empty of everything but being alive … it was
like something else you had felt once before … the feeling you'd had
when you were much, much younger and undressing a girl for the
first time.[32]

On at least one point, however, the irony regarding the narrator's
perspective gives way to a claim which is less convincing. In 'Breathing
In', the first chapter, the narrator admits his inability to observe the war
dispassionately: 'Talk about impersonating an identity, about locking
into a role, about irony: I went to cover the war and the war covered me.'[33]
Later in the same chapter, however, he seeks to persuade the reader that
he could switch from one perspective to another when he chose.
Describing his relationship with the 'grunts' he explains: 'I stood as close
to them as I could without being one of them, and then I stood as far back
as I could without leaving the planet.'[34] One of the weaknesses of
Dispatches is Herr's tendency to romanticise about the 'grunts' and what
the war had given them which made them special. In 'Khe Sanh' he
suggests: 'they got savaged a lot and softened a lot, their secret brutalized
them and darkened them and very often it made them beautiful.'[35] Their
secret is one that the narrator lays claim to later in *Dispatches*: 'I was in
many ways brother to these poor, tired grunts, I knew what they knew
now'.[36] What the narrator knows, one of the pieces of 'essential information' which Herr brings 'through the woods that conventional journalists
and historians will not enter', is about the intensity with which death
confronts those who go into combat and how the act of killing: 'fixed
them so that they could never, never again speak lightly about the Worst
Thing in the World.'[37] As a novelist Herr is free to make such an assertion about America's 'grunts'. The reader must decide whether it reflects
the understanding of a significant number of soldiers or Herr's compulsion to invest their role, and his sharing of it, with a romance which
Robin Moore might have appreciated.

Written in the first person, 'Khe Sanh' begins with the story of a
young Marine who has spent five months at the combat base. The story
emphasises the unreliability of official discourse and the suffering of the
individual soldier, two of the most persistent ideas in the novel. The
Marine's tour of duty is up but he cannot bring himself to depart. This is
not simply because of the danger of boarding a plane out of Khe Sanh,
although Herr describes the airstrip there as 'the worst place in the

world', but because he is 'suffering from shell shock'. Herr notes that this is called 'acute environmental reaction', an example of how military language in Vietnam is so convoluted that 'it's often impossible to know even remotely the thing being described'.[38] The account, which has no closure because the narrator is not sure if the Marine ever left the base, includes a brief sketch of the history of the 26th Marine regiment at Khe Sanh. This is done from the perspective of the Marine, who 'remembered' the pastoral nature of the regiment's early days at Khe Sanh 'when there was time to play in the streams below the plateau of the base, when all anybody ever talked about were the six shades of green that touched the surrounding hills' and contrasts it to their recent experience under fire when 'he and his friends … began taking pills called Diarrhea-Aid to keep their walks to exposed latrines at a minimum.' The consciousness of this description, the contrast highlighted by a pair of similes which explain how the Marines 'had lived like human beings … instead of like animals' and the subtle use of 'touched' suggest that Herr has not recorded the words of a shell-shocked Marine on the day of his departure from Khe Sanh but provided his own literary embellishments to what he has been told.[39] It is apparently an unintended irony that, having criticised officialdom for manipulating language to create an alternative reality, Herr does something very similar.

The content of the opening section of 'Khe Sanh' is characteristic of Herr's work in several ways. The tale of the Marine is a starting point for a range of comment by the narrator including discussion of the American leadership's 'obsession' with Khe Sanh juxtaposed with the deaths of the Marine's friends there; the psychological impact of combat upon the young who have the 'look of extreme fatigue or even a glancing madness'; the trauma of boarding a plane to fly out and how 'There was no feeling in the world as good as being airborne out of Khe Sanh.'[40] The higher levels of command provoke the narrator's rage throughout *Dispatches*. Their 'obsession' with Khe Sanh leads to 'mindless optimism, the kind that rejected facts and killed grunts wholesale.' Listening to such talk 'it was all you could do to keep from seizing one greying crew-cut head or another and jamming it deep into the nearest tactical map.'[41] A return to Milton J. Bates' analogy of the different sorts of knowledge possessed by the 'man in the valley' and the 'man on the hilltop' aids interpretation here. It is the experience of the 'man in the valley', the ordinary 'grunt', which attracts the narrator's sympathy in *Dispatches*. It is from his perspective that events are often viewed and his knowledge that is esteemed and communicated, usually very convincingly. Conversely, the 'man on the hilltop' is presented as dangerous in *Dispatches* because his knowledge is not based upon the 'facts' and leads to American deaths. Interestingly, elsewhere in *Dispatches* the narrator suggests the unhelpfulness of the 'facts' as a means of grasping the reality of the war. Apparently, then, Herr's objection is not to facts but to official data which mislead or facts which have not been appropriately valued, either of which lead to false views of the war. This is a reasonable concern which historians would share but Herr, having upbraided those on 'the hilltop' for their failure to recognise the importance of the facts, permits himself considerable freedom in his choice of alternative means of getting at the 'truth'.

The notion of supporting evidence, for example, is replaced in *Dispatches* by other criteria. How people look is often a decisive indicator in Herr's work. The most extreme example of this and a demonstration of how far Herr has travelled from the approach of the conventional journalist is a comment made about a soldier in the chapter entitled 'Colleagues': 'we knew that he was telling the truth. You only had to look at his face to see that he really knew what he was talking about'.[42] Similarly, in 'Khe Sanh', it is the look of the Marine which Herr dwells upon as the grounds for speculations about his psychiatric condition, even attributing to the Marine that special 'knowledge' about combat on the strength of a smile which said, 'I'll tell you why I'm smiling, but it will make you crazy.'[43]

The narrator's comments reveal the range of feelings his experience at Khe Sanh stimulated. Having told the reader that the airstrip was the 'the worst place in the world', after a few hours on Hill 861 with the 1st Battalion of the 9th Marine Regiment he was convinced that: 'Anything was better than this.'[44] On the other hand: 'There was no feeling in the world as good as being airborne out of Khe Sanh.' The focus on the extremes of emotion to be found in the battle zone, and the parallel with his description of combat, is useful. In fact, the 1st of the 9th served not on Hill 861 but on a hill called the Rock Quarry.[45] Herr's error of detail does not diminish the importance of his insight but it does remind the reader that Herr's rejection of conventional journalism came at a cost.

Subsequent sections of 'Khe Sanh' sketch a wider context: the geography and history of the area; the appropriateness of the parallels with Dien Bien Phu; American objectives and, in the extra sections of the chapter on 'Khe Sanh' in *Dispatches*, a description of the Marine commanders involved and an account of the 'relief' of Khe Sanh by the AirCav. All of this is mixed with stories which develop Herr's depiction of the perspective of the 'man in the valley', stories which are ranked as more important than anything the American commanders might offer. 'In fact', comments the narrator in 'Colleagues', 'my concerns were so rarefied that I had to ask other correspondents what they ever found to ask Westmoreland' and other 'highly placed' officials.[46]

Herr shares Appy's conviction in *Working-Class War* that 'the experiences and stories of veterans represent what Michel Foucault has described as "disqualified" or "illegitimate" forms of knowledge. The task ahead is to recover and interpret that knowledge.'[47] The importance of the ordinary soldier's view of war and Herr's version of the language and attitudes of the ordinary soldier, alongside the narrator's self-analysis, make 'Khe Sanh' and *Dispatches* so interesting. Whether Herr could claim to have recovered and interpreted this 'disqualified' knowledge is another question. Only some of the stories he tells have been recovered. Others, which may still be illuminating, have been created and the interpretations which he bases upon his 'information' are highly partial. It is significant that a 'Postscript' in *Dispatches* announces the death of Mayhew, one of the Marines whom the narrator had met at Khe Sanh. For Herr, Mayhew's death and the added sadness that, only weeks afterwards, two of the men in his company cannot even remember his name, symbolise America's war. His comments about the battle at Khe Sanh do not resolve any of the controversies which surround it because his perspective is so close to that of the Marines who fought it. Nevertheless, as Robert Pisor commented in *The End of the Line*, Herr: 'captured the mad pace and contradictions of the Vietnam war. [He] writes with his nerve ends, and his book is an important contribution to understanding the war.'[48]

Pisor's own writing about Khe Sanh is less evocative but the variety of perspectives in *The End of the Line* encourages the reader to develop a broader grasp of what occurred. Pisor was a correspondent for the *Detroit News* in Vietnam during 1967 and 1968 and his book exhibits a continuing faith in the reporter's ability to ferret out the facts. He questions the wisdom of America's strategy at Khe Sanh and in Vietnam, challenges the official casualty figures and records the frustrations of men who took part in the fighting. References to primary and secondary sources support chapters which describe the events leading up to the battle, probe the thinking of Westmoreland, Giap and President Johnson, give accounts of the fights for the hills around the Combat Base and portray 'Life in the V Ring', a title borrowed from Wheeler. He also explains the battle's significance in the history of combat, pointing out that 'the first sustained use of B–52 strategic bombers for close-in support of ground troops' took place at Khe Sanh and that the 'field commander had begun preparations for the tactical use of nuclear weapons'.[49]

At times his diction is unnecessarily elaborate. In the first chapter he writes: 'Captain Dabney had become the conductor of a great orchestra of death. From a shell hole, with a backpack radio for a baton, he cued a score of the big guns at the Khe Sanh Combat Base', a contrived metaphor which compares poorly with the excitement of Herr's use of language'.[50] Another of the differences between the two works is highlighted by Pisor's inclusion of maps. At the beginning of *Dispatches* Herr writes: '*It was late '67 now, even the most detailed maps didn't reveal much anymore; reading them was like trying to read the faces of the Vietnamese and that was like trying to read the wind*'.[51] For Herr maps are part of the 'fact-figure crossfire' but for Pisor they are an important aid to the reader's understanding of the battle. Whereas Herr excludes some sources of information as potentially dangerous, preferring his own perhaps flawed perceptions and the war stories of people he trusted as the basis of his intense vision of the war, Pisor's portrayal of the battle at Khe Sanh is a collection of material which allows the reader to sift a wider range of evidence.

Eric Hammel's oral history, *Khe Sanh: Siege in the Clouds*, offers a further range. In addition to the oral testimony of men who served at the combat base, on the outlying hills and in the command and support structures, it includes extracts from the 26th Marines Command Chronology and After Action Reports, medal citations and, once again, maps. By organising the material in several ways, according to chronology, action and topic, and providing a glossary, Hammel achieves a thorough and accessible account of the battle from a variety of perspectives. Several of the insights in *Dispatches* are underlined by the factual record here, not least the tendency to see the world of combat through the lens of Hollywood. Remembering the air strikes on the surrounding hills, a sergeant comments, 'It looked like a war movie' and a lance corporal recalls, 'All the movies I watched as a kid – the John Wayne movies – all that bullshit went out the window at Khe Sanh.'[52] A concrete example of the unreliability of official figures is also given by a captain who describes the persistent requests of his superiors for the number of enemy killed when his men fired through the fog at a group of NVA soldiers: 'they kept bugging and bugging. Finally my exec ... said ... "it could ... have been an 82mm mortar section [which] has twenty-one men in it" ... just to get them off our backs.' Hammel's next entry is an extract from the 26th Marines Command Chronology: '21 NVA KIA (confirmed)'.[53]

If the testimony of participants in Hammel's account is sometimes stilted, especially when that testimony has been written rather than spoken, there are also occasions when a contribution condenses an essential feature of warfare.[54] A corpsman describes being caught under fire and how: 'When I got back, one of the other corpsmen told me about what he had seen going on out there. He could see it from where he was inside the base, but I was right in the middle of it and hadn't seen a damned thing.'[55] Hammel's book is organised on the principle that the understanding of combat demands more than one perspective. It ends, like Pisor's, with a chapter which stresses the different opinions prompted by the battle at Khe Sanh. Two strands in these opinions are worthy of note. They are summarised by a 2nd lieutenant who observes:

> I still feel a certain bitterness about Khe Sanh. Not the actual fighting or being there. I'm very proud of that and of the Marines I served with there. I guess I'm still bitter about the whole Vietnam experience. It seems that it was such a waste, and to me, Khe Sanh is the classic example of that waste.[56]

The mixture of feelings expressed here is evidence that the combat experience in Vietnam was different in an important way from the experience of America's soldiers in other wars. The sensation of being under fire and the feeling of pride in one's comrades could be shared with the veterans of earlier wars but those who fought in Vietnam had to confront the realisation, sometimes even as they took part in combat, that their efforts may be without point.

On 10 May 1969, as America's military leaders considered the abandonment of the base at Khe Sanh, Operation Apache Snow began in the A Shau Valley. On 11 May a company of the 3rd battalion of the 101st Airborne encountered the enemy on Dong Ap Bia, a hill near the Laotian border. Three battalions of the 101st and an ARVN battalion were eventually committed to the battle for the hill which was not taken until 20 May. In *America in Vietnam* Guenter Lewy listed the ordnance expended during the assault: 'the Air Force flew 272 attack sorties, dropping more than one million pounds of bombs, including 152,000 pounds of napalm. Artillery fired 21,732 rounds.' It was claimed that over 500 enemy soldiers were killed in the fighting. After searching what had become known as 'Hamburger Hill' and destroying enemy defences, Allied forces left. Later the North Vietnamese reoccupied the hill. Senator Edward Kennedy called the action, in which 56 Americans were killed and 420 wounded, 'madness', and Major General Melvin Zais, commander of the 101st, admitted that 'Hill 937, as a particular piece of terrain, was of no tactical significance ... However ... the enemy had to be engaged where he was found if the mission was to be accomplished.'[57]

Eighteen years later British director John Irvin portrayed the taking of Hamburger Hill in a film written by Vietnam veteran James Carabatsos. Released by RKO in 1987, *Hamburger Hill* has no stars and focuses upon the progress of fourteen of the men who try, day after day, to master the hill. It is 'starkly realistic' and the winning of the hill becomes a 'symbol of the impotence and futility of the whole war' as Albert Auster and Leonard Quart have observed.[58] Obscured by two films of the same period which enjoyed greater success at the box office, Oliver Stone's *Platoon* and Stanley Kubrick's *Full Metal Jacket*, *Hamburger Hill* deserves attention because of its concentration upon the combat experience. Analysis of its message is clarified by comparison with a well-known film which also involved American soldiers taking a heavily defended peak, Allan Dwan's *Sands of Iwo Jima*.

Irvin's film shows the psychological as well as the physical effects of combat to stress the particular pressures under which American soldiers fought in May 1969. The twelve men who make up 3rd Squad are divided by experience, by race, by outlook and, finally, by their luck – only three of them reach the summit of the hill. They share a need to rely upon each other in combat and a conviction that they are the victims of an unsympathetic command. 'Same old shit, man. Man in the bird wants to play war', says one.[59] As casualties mount, the anti-war movement becomes a further focus of their discontent.

It has been argued by Judy Lee Kinney that *Hamburger Hill*, like *Platoon*, fails to treat 'war as a political fact, an endeavour organized by men, amenable to men's control if the desire is there.'[60] Irvin's concern in *Hamburger Hill* was less ambitious, to show the way in which ordinary soldiers reacted to combat in 1969. As responsibility for fighting the war began to be handed over to the South Vietnamese and President Nixon prepared to announce the first US troop withdrawals, the soldiers' feeling that the war was, indeed, out of their control is represented by the 'man in the bird' who 'wants to play war'. The commander is one of their antagonists, a disembodied voice irately urging them to greater efforts in a task whose meaning escapes them. There are other enmities, too. Blacks and whites fight with each other and the FNGs (Fucking New Guys) are treated with suspicion because their incompetence might get the more experienced men killed. The media and those who stay at home also attract the men's hostility. Comments in the film about the anti-war movement have provoked criticism, Joanna Bourke complaining that:

> the poignant opening scenes of the Vietnam Veterans' memorial in Washington were utilised simply to justify the actions of the good servicemen, the dropping of napalm was portrayed as purely aesthetic, and the real enemies were the effete men at home and anti-war protestors.[61]

This misses the point that the prejudice of the soldiers in the film about 'the effete men at home and anti-war protestors' is an accurate reflection of the feelings of many of the soldiers in combat in 1969. As Appy pointed out in *Working-Class War*: 'Recruits were encouraged to believe that all protesters supported the Viet Cong and that the antiwar movement cheered when American troops got wiped out in Vietnam.'[62]

Bourke's description of the 'poignant opening scenes' as a justification of the men's actions is also questionable. Rather than a justification, the film's opening shots, which pan so rapidly across the names of the American dead upon the memorial in Washington that it is impossible to read any of them, suggest only the anonymity of the dead. Indeed, on one viewing it is hard to register and remember the names of many of the characters in the film and the leafless trees surrounding the memorial provide no suggestion of a symbolic rebirth. This seems to represent the men's sense that the winning of the hill was a pointless endeavour for which there was no reward. Even the notion that they are fighting for each other is presented as something to be manipulated. As Frantz (Dylan McDermott), the squad leader, bitterly considers the death of the point man McDaniel, Sergeant Worcester (Steven Weber) tells him that McDaniel fought and died: 'for you and for 3rd Squad ... don't you give him anything less'.[63] Worcester, however, only seems to make the comment to encourage Frantz back into the fighting.

The ending of *Hamburger Hill* provides a sharp contrast with a famous scene from an earlier war film. Made in 1949, *Sands of Iwo Jima* starred John Wayne as a Marine sergeant leading his men against the Japanese entrenched on the island of Iwo Jima during World War II. Its portrayal of men at war, convinced of the rightness of their cause, was very familiar to Americans in Vietnam. Indications of the film's continuing influence have been provided by Marines at Fort Pendleton in 1961, half of whom 'gave Wayne movies (principally *Sands*) as their reason' for enlisting and by Marine recruiters who claimed that even in the late 1970s enlistment rose when *Sands of Iwo Jima* was revived on television.[64] Wayne's final line summarised the success on Iwo Jima: 'I never felt so good in my life.'[65] Although the fighting cost the Americans 26,000 casualties and there was some criticism that American commanders had wasted the lives of thousands of men, Iwo Jima is remembered as a glorious victory. Whilst peaceful deaths, purposeful action and cool heroism under fire characterise the combat in *Sands of Iwo Jima*, the men in *Hamburger Hill* are killed and mutilated in what Kinney described as a 'frequently stunning depiction of combat'.[66] There is no time, as there is in the earlier film, to pray with the dying. Instead of ending with the raising of an American flag while the Marine Hymn plays on the soundtrack, the final images in *Hamburger Hill* are of a wasteland, the soundtrack almost empty.

Only Frantz, Washburn (Don Cheadle) and Beletsky (Tim Quill) reach the summit of the hill. It is almost bare, a blasted tree reminding the audience of the trees around the Wall in the film's opening shots. The only sounds are the whistling of the wind and the occasional sob of a casualty. The audience is denied the words muttered to Frantz by Beletsky and thus excluded from the world of the veteran. The three men look down the hill rather than up to a flag and the only words audible are those of the commander in the helicopter above who seeks to communicate with those on the ground. As the film ends, the repeated demands from the safety of the helicopter are ignored, symbolising the men's rejection of the 'man in the bird'. Looking down the hill, Beletsky sheds a single tear which might have been caused by the wind. The ending of *Hamburger Hill* offers no consolations and 'the world's great snare' is revealed as a cause of waste and nothing more. In this regard and in its accurate portrayal of the feelings of American soldiers as they went into battle Irvin's film serves an important purpose. Senator Kennedy's description of the 'madness' of the battle for Hamburger Hill is borne out by the film.

Notes

1. William Shakespeare, *Antony and Cleopatra* (London: Methuen, 1965), p. 160.
2. The figure of 3.14 million is taken from Robert Jay Lifton, *Home From The War: Learning From Vietnam Veterans* (Boston: Beacon Press [1973] 1992), p. ix; Ronald H. Spector estimated that: 'By 1968 service, support, and headquarters troops made up at least 70–80% of all U.S. military personnel in Vietnam.' Spector, *After Tet: The*

Bloodiest Year in Vietnam (New York: The Free Press, 1993), p. 260.

3. The survey, entitled *Myths and Realities: A Study of Attitudes Towards Vietnam Era Veterans*, is cited by Myra MacPherson, *Long Time Passing: Vietnam and the Haunted Generation* (London: Sceptre Books, [1984] 1988), p. 738 (note).

4. There is considerable disagreement about the size of the enemy force at Khe Sanh. Michael Herr, for example, claims 'five full divisions of North Vietnamese regulars' and refers elsewhere to an enemy force '20,000 to 40,000 strong'. Herr, *Dispatches* (London: Picador, 1977), p. 82 and p. 95. The more conservative figures are General Westmoreland's, cited in Robert Pisor, *The End of the Line: The Siege of Khe Sanh* (New York: W. W. Norton, [1982] 2002), p. 265.

5. Pisor, *The End of the Line*, p. 138.

6. 'The General's Biggest Battle', *Time*, 16 February 1968.

7. George C. Herring, *America's Longest War: The United States and Vietnam, 1950–1975*, 3rd edn (New York: McGraw Hill, 1996), p. 205.

8. Pisor gives the military's figure for Marine deaths and adds: '205 is a completely false number'. He offers the figure of 475, a personal estimate by Marine chaplain Reverend Ray W. Stubbe, as an alternative. Not only Marines died. Other Americans, including Green Berets and Air Force personnel, and soldiers of the ARVN and civilian irregular forces perished. Meanwhile, the number of North Vietnamese killed generates even greater argument. Pisor cites Westmoreland's suggestion, based on estimates made by his staff, that 'the North Vietnamese lost 10,000 to 15,000 men' in the siege. Stubbe estimated that up to 5,000 Montagnard civilians were also killed during the battle. Most of these, presumably, were the victims of American bombs. Pisor, *The End of the Line*, pp. 258–61.

9. Westmoreland and Thompson are cited in Pisor, *The End of the Line*, pp. 265–6.

10. David Douglas Duncan, 'Khe Sanh', *Life*, 23 January 1968.

11. John T. Wheeler, 'Life in the V Ring', Associated Press wire copy, 12 February 1968. Reprinted in *Reporting Vietnam: American Journalism 1959–1975* (New York: The Library of America, 2000), pp. 327–31.

12. Eric James Schroeder, *Vietnam, We've All Been There: Interviews with American Writers* (Westport, CT: Praeger, 1992), p. 45 and p. 43.

13. Ibid. p. 33.

14. Ibid. pp. 34–5.

15. Ibid. p. 33.

16. Herr, *Dispatches*, p. 45 and p. 167.

17. Ibid. p. 175.

18. Reporters' attempts to tell the truth about the war in the early 1960s is the subject of William Prochnau's *Once Upon a Distant War* (New York: Vintage Books, 1996); Lt. Gen. Harold G. Moore and Joseph L. Galloway, *We Were Soldiers Once … and Young* (London: Corgi Books, [1992] 2002), p. 360.

19. Herr, *Dispatches*, p. 171.

20. John Mecklin cited in Paul Fussell (ed.), *The Bloody Game* (London: Scribner's, 1991), p. 656

21. Herr, *Dispatches*, p. 25.

22. Ibid. p. 169.

23. Ibid. p. 138.

24. C. D. B. Bryan, *New York Times Book Review*, 20 November 1977; Roger Sale, *New York Review of Books*, 8 December 1977.

25. John Hellmann, *American Myth and the Legacy of Vietnam* (New York: Columbia University Press, 1986), p. 154.
26. Herr, *Dispatches*, p. 173.
27. Ibid. p. 32.
28. Ibid. p. 80. Although American forces suffered a defeat at LZ Albany, an earlier battle at LZ X Ray resulted in a hard-fought American victory.
29. Christian G. Appy, *Working-Class War: American Combat Soldiers and Vietnam* (Chapel Hill: University of North Carolina Press, 1993), pp. 228–9; Loren Baritz, *Backfire: A History of How American Culture Led Us Into Vietnam and Made Us Fight The Way We Did* (Baltimore: The Johns Hopkins University Press, [1985] 1998), p. 24.
30. Herr, *Dispatches*, p. 24.
31. Ibid. p. 60.
32. Ibid. pp. 111–12
33. Ibid. p. 24.
34. Ibid. p. 59.
35. Ibid. p. 87.
36. Ibid. p. 166.
37. Ibid. p. 87.
38. Ibid. pp. 76–8.
39. Ibid. p. 74.
40. Ibid. pp. 74–7.
41. Ibid. p. 119.
42. Ibid. p. 176.
43. Ibid. p. 75.
44. Ibid. p. 101.
45. A reading of Hammel's book makes Herr's error clear. Eric Hammel, *Khe Sanh: Siege in the Clouds* (Pacifica, CA: Pacifica Press, 1989).
46. Herr, *Dispatches*, p. 174.
47. Appy, *Working-Class War*, p. 10.
48. Pisor, *The End of the Line*, p. 286.
49. Ibid. p. 231.
50. Ibid. p. 31.
51. Herr, *Dispatches*, p. 11. The italics are in the original.
52. Hammel, *Khe Sanh*, p. 83 and p. 331.
53. Ibid. pp. 100–1.
54. In the extracts from Ernest Spencer's *Welcome to Vietnam, Macho Man*, for example. Especially, ibid. pp. 129–34.
55. Hammel, *Khe Sanh*, p. 382.
56. Ibid. p. 458.
57. The description of the battle, figures, Senator Kennedy's comment and the text of Zais' 'clarification of the record' are all taken from Guenter Lewy, *America in Vietnam* (New York: Oxford University Press, 1978), pp. 144–5.
58. Albert Auster and Leonard Quart, *How the War was Remembered: Hollywood and Vietnam* (New York: Praeger, 1988), p. 146.
59. Motown (Michael Patrick Boatman) speaking in *Hamburger Hill*, directed by John Irvin (RKO, 1987).
60. Judy Lee Kinney, '*Gardens of Stone, Platoon* and *Hamburger Hill*: Ritual and Remembrance', in Michael Anderegg (ed.), *Inventing Vietnam: The War in Film and*

Television (Philadelphia: Temple University Press, 1991), p. 163.

61. Joanna Bourke, *An Intimate History of Killing: Face-to-Face Killing in Twentieth-Century Warfare* (London: Granta Books, 1999), p. 19.

62. Appy, *Working-Class War*, p. 106.

63. Worcester speaking in *Hamburger Hill*.

64. Garry Wills, *John Wayne: The Politics of Celebrity* (London: Faber and Faber, 1997), p. 337; Lawrence H. Suid, *Guts and Glory: Great American War Movies* (Reading, MA: Addison-Wesley, 1978), p. 100.

65. John Wayne speaking as Sergeant Stryker in *Sands of Iwo Jima*, directed by Allan Dwan (Republic, 1949).

66. Kinney, '*Gardens of Stone*', p. 160.

CHAPTER 5

Villains

On 2 April 1969 Ronald Ridenhour, a Vietnam veteran, posted copies of a letter he had written to a selection of America's political and military leaders, including President Nixon, Secretary of Defense Melvin Laird and the Chairman of the Joint Chiefs of Staff, General Earle Wheeler. The letter contained information that Ridenhour had gleaned from other veterans about 'something rather dark and bloody' which had occurred 'sometime in March, 1968 in a village called "Pinkville" in the Republic of Viet Nam.' In the penultimate paragraph of his letter Ridenhour admitted: 'Exactly what did, in fact occur in the village of "Pinkville" in March, 1968 I do not know for certain, but I am convinced that it was something very black indeed.'[1] Ridenhour's allegations were sufficiently shocking and detailed to provoke a reaction at the highest level in the US Army. Chief of Staff William Westmoreland ordered the Army's Office of the Inspector General to conduct an inquiry. The officer charged with the responsibility of a preliminary investigation of Ridenhour's claims, Colonel William V. Wilson, was initially sceptical. Within weeks, however, interviews with soldiers identified in Ridenhour's letter had convinced the colonel that on 16 March 1968 a 'massacre had been committed' by American troops in a sub-hamlet in South Vietnam's Quang Ngai province.[2] The sub-hamlet was identified on American maps as My Lai 4 and was part of an area known to American troops as 'Pinkville'. Soldiers admitted to Wilson that, while serving with Task Force Barker, a strike force attached to the Americal Division, they and other members of Charlie Company had participated in the murder of hundreds of unarmed South Vietnamese civilians. Wilson also gathered evidence that complaints about the events in My Lai 4 had been dismissed by senior officers in the Americal Division in the weeks following the massacre.

Wilson's work was the preliminary to two further Army investigations, each conducted behind closed doors, which discovered that Ridenhour's fears of something 'very black indeed' were more than justified. The

Army's Criminal Investigation Division (CID), which concentrated on discovering the nature and extent of the crimes committed by American soldiers on 16 March, 'concluded that there was sufficient evidence to charge thirty men with major crimes.'[3] The official military inquiry into the cover-up of the massacre, led by Lieutenant General William Peers, also identified thirty men who, it was believed:

> had known of the killing of noncombatants and other serious offences committed during the ... operation but had not made official reports, had suppressed relevant information, had failed to order investigations, or had not followed up on the investigations that were made.[4]

The Peers Report, which was completed between 26 November 1969 and 14 March 1970, was the product of considerable industry. In order to assess the extent of the cover-up, Peers and his military and civilian assistants made painstaking attempts to reconstruct what had happened in My Lai 4 and the surrounding area on 16 March, and during the days which led up to and followed the massacre. As well as visiting the site of the massacre and interviewing Vietnamese survivors, the testimony of 403 witnesses was taken and included in Volume III of the final report. This volume alone consists of approximately 20,000 pages. The fourth and final volume contains the statements of approximately 100 men interviewed by the CID. During the two investigations, which were run separately but co-operatively, evidence was found that a second massacre had occurred on 16 March over a mile away from My Lai 4. Members of Task Force Barker's Bravo Company, Peers concluded, had been responsible for the killing of approximately ninety noncombatants at a sub-hamlet identified on American maps as My Khe 4.

News of the massacre at My Lai 4, and particularly of the role played by Second Lieutenant William Calley, Jr, leader of Charlie Company's 1st Platoon, had started to seep out before Peers even began his work. A story by Wayne Greenshaw appeared in the *Alabama Journal* on the afternoon of 12 November 1969 which identified Calley as an officer 'suspected of wiping out an entire South Vietnamese village by killing 91 people – men, women and children.'[5] The following day a story by Seymour Hersh appeared in thirty newspapers across America giving details of the Army's charge that Calley: 'deliberately murdered at least 109 Vietnamese civilians during a search and destroy mission in March 1968, in a Viet Cong stronghold known as "Pinkville".'[6] One week after the Hersh story the *Cleveland Plain Dealer* published photographs of the carnage at My Lai 4 which had been taken by Ronald Haeberle, an Army photographer who had watched Charlie Company at work. It was not, however, until veteran Paul Meadlo appeared live on a CBS evening news programme on 24 November to describe how he and other members of Charlie Company had killed about 370 people in My Lai 4 that the American people began to grasp the full horror of what had happened. Meadlo described the victims: 'begging and saying, "No. No." And their mothers were hugging their children, but they kept on firing. Well, we kept on firing.'[7] By the time *Life* magazine purchased Haeberle's photographs and printed some of them in colour on 12 December alongside an eyewitness account of the massacre, the events at My Lai 4 had become major news in America and around the world.

In *Gunfighter Nation: The Myth of the Frontier in Twentieth-Century America* Richard Slotkin suggested that:

> More that any other single event, the revelation [of the massacre at My Lai 4] transformed the terms of ideological and political debate on the war, lending authority to the idea that American society was in the grip of a 'madness' whose sources might be endemic to our 'national character'.[8]

Slotkin also pointed out that the revelations about My Lai 4 came in the wake of the assassinations of Martin Luther King and Robert Kennedy, the violence at the Democratic Party Convention in Chicago, the Manson murders and increasing casualties in Vietnam. Consequently, news of the massacre reinforced the belief held by some that Americans were 'trapped in an irrationally rising tide of violence' which shed doubt on the goodness of the American character.[9] Certainly, Americans continued to be fascinated by the My Lai story. After Calley's subsequent conviction for murder in April 1971, a Harris Poll 'revealed that an incredible 91% of its respondents had followed the trial closely.' It is important to note, though, that they could not agree on their attitude towards what had happened at My Lai 4. Of those polled, '36% disagreed with the verdict, 35% agreed, and 29% were undecided.'[10]

Initial reactions to the story had been similarly mixed. Many people had shared Ronald Ridenhour's instinctive response: 'I just couldn't believe that … so many young American men participated in such an act of barbarism.'[11] The Governor of Alabama had spoken for many when he said: 'I can't believe an American serviceman would purposely shoot any civilian'.[12] Even after Meadlo's confession and the publication of

Haeberle's photographs in *Life*, an article in the *National Review* expressed scepticism, 'Whether atrocities were committed at Songmy [sic] we do not as yet know', and a poll published in the *Minneapolis Tribune* shortly before Christmas 1969 showed that 49 per cent of a sample of 600: 'believed that the reports of mass murder at My Lai were false.'[13]

For others, the rightness of America's war in Vietnam and, indeed, America's status in the world, had been thrown into doubt, as Slotkin was to observe. *Time* magazine commented that the massacre: 'humiliated the U.S. and called in question the U.S. mission in Vietnam in a way that all the antiwar protesters could never have done.'[14] Some weeks later, however, a poll reported in a January 1970 issue of *Time* showed that 65 per cent of respondents thought that incidents like My Lai were 'bound to happen in a war' and the magazine noted that 'Americans are not particularly disturbed by the disclosure that U.S. troops apparently massacred several hundred South Vietnamese civilians at My Lai.'[15] Calley received significant support from veterans and other Americans. Audie Murphy, Hollywood star and the most decorated American of World War II, made speeches on his behalf.[16] A song celebrating his bravery entitled 'The Battle of Lt. Calley' sold a million copies, car bumpers sported 'Free Calley' stickers and President Nixon claimed that after Calley's sentencing: 'More than 5,000 telegrams arrived at the White House, running 100 to 1 in favor of clemency.'[17] Two months later a poll showed that 59 per cent of respondents disapproved of the trial. Of these, 45 per cent believed it to be wrong to 'send a man to fight in Vietnam and then put him on trial for doing his duty'.[18] How soldiers in Vietnam reacted to news of the massacre is a matter of some dispute but evidence suggests a similarly divided reaction. Daniel Ellsberg, a critic of the war, accepted that 'virtually every soldier in Vietnam' recognised that 'My Lai was beyond the bounds of permissible behaviour.'[19] At Khe Sanh, however, a sign reading: '"A" TROOP, 1st CAV, SALUTES LT. WILLIAM CALLEY' was raised when he was found guilty and, as Joanna Bourke has noted: 'Senior officers bombarded him with supportive letters'.[20]

Amidst the welter of opinions expressed in the months following the breaking of the news about the massacre, Peers and his staff sought to reconstruct events which had occurred more than a year and a half before. They experienced difficulties which would have been familiar to historians. Even the location of the two massacres was a source of confusions. The reference to 'Pinkville' in Ridenhour's letter was the simplest of these. American soldiers casually referred to a part of Quang Ngai as

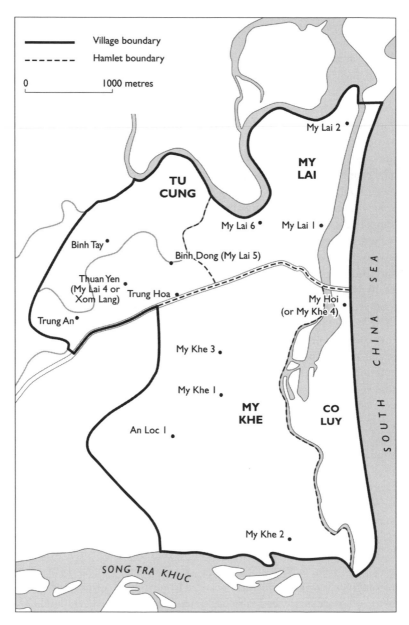

Map of Son My

'Pinkville' because the province of Quang Ngai had a history of support for the Viet Minh and the NLF and because on American maps a particularly dense area of population in one part of Son My village had been indicated by pink shading. Hence the term 'Pinkville' became a convenient, if imprecise, description of a geographical area which was considered hostile. However, on a more official level, the Americans often renamed Vietnamese settlements and used these names on their own maps. Meanwhile, the Vietnamese sometimes referred to their own communities by names other than those which appeared on Vietnamese maps, maps which had been designed by the French. On these maps the village of Son My was made up of four hamlets, each of which was sub-divided into smaller sub-hamlets. The larger hamlets were called Tu Cung, My Lai, Co Luy and My Khe. Within Tu Cung were five sub-hamlets, one of which was known locally as Xom Lang and identified on Vietnamese maps as Thuan Yen. It was this sub-hamlet that American maps referred to as My Lai 4, although it was not within the hamlet of My Lai. A similar disparity resulted in difficulties in establishing the site of the second massacre. Known as My Khe 4 by the Americans, the sub-hamlet assaulted by elements of Bravo Company was called My Hoi by the Vietnamese and was part of the hamlet of Co Luy rather than part of the hamlet of My Khe. As well as causing confusion, American relabelling of the geography of South Vietnam and the determination of the local communities to stick to their own nomenclature was symptomatic of the insularity of the two peoples, an insularity which was particularly marked in Quang Ngai. As an American soldier serving in the province had told reporter Jonathan Schell in 1967: 'even when a Vietnamese guy speaks perfect English *I* don't know what the hell he's talking about'.[21]

Peers' difficulties were not restricted to negotiating the gap between American and Vietnamese perceptions. On the American side official reports were missing or hopelessly inaccurate. Asked to recall the details of a traumatic experience soldiers did not always provide reliable testimony. Some were determined to conceal their actions or confused about what had happened. Some might have unwittingly repressed the more harrowing features of their involvement or sincerely told stories about the day which mingled memory and imagination. Witnesses contradicted each other or stated that they could not remember. Nevertheless, the Peers Report which was presented to the Secretary of the Army on 14 March 1970 was explicit in its assertion that American soldiers had committed war crimes. Admitting that some facts, including the number of victims, remained unknown and that some questions remained un-answered, its description of the massacres and the cover-up was unam-biguous.

A summary of the Report stated that:

> US Army troops of TF Barker … massacred a large number of non-combatants in two hamlets of Son My Village … The precise number of Vietnamese killed cannot be determined but was at least 175 and may exceed 400 …
>
> A part of the crimes visited on the inhabitants of Son My Village included individual and group acts of murder, rape, sodomy, maim-ing and assault on noncombatants …
>
> At every command level within the Americal Division, actions were taken both wittingly and unwittingly, which effectively sup-pressed information concerning the war crimes committed at Son My Village.[22]

Having established that American soldiers had committed war crimes if not their precise extent, the investigators of the CID and the Peers Inquiry might have hoped that their efforts would result in the punishment of the guilty. Despite the evidence of criminality, however, only one man, Calley, was convicted. Sentenced to life at hard labour on 31 March 1971, Calley spent only three days behind bars before President Nixon ordered that he be kept under house arrest until the results of an appeal were known. On 9 November 1974 he was released on parole. Of the others whom the CID had evidence against, charges were taken forward in only twelve cases. Each of these actions resulted in acquittal or a dismissal of the charges. In a personal account of the Inquiry's work entitled *The My Lai Inquiry*, published in 1979, Peers commented:

> To this day the matter that most greatly concerns me is that so many people in command positions – perhaps as many as fifty – had inform-ation that something most unusual had occurred during the My Lai operation and yet did nothing about it.[23]

Only Colonel Oran Henderson was tried for concealing evidence of the massacre. He, too, was acquitted.

The failure of American military justice was neither the fault of those who investigated the massacres nor proof of the impossibility of assign-ing guilt. Explanation of the judicial outcomes is simple. The Army was

Some of the dead at My Lai 4 (Rex photo by Ronald Haeberle).

reluctant to dwell publicly upon events which were so damaging to its reputation, especially during a period of continued conflict in Vietnam. Vocal sectors of the public were against the punishment of American soldiers who had, it was argued, done their duty. Additionally, some of the accused had left the Army and the procedures for taking legal action in either military or civilian courts against civilians who had committed offences while in uniform were unwieldy and uncertain. The legal situation was further complicated, perhaps deliberately, by the concurrent investigation into the massacre conducted by a sub-committee of the House Armed Services Committee which had created difficulties regarding the admissibility in military court of evidence already given to the congressional sub-committee.

While Americans continued to fight in Vietnam, political sympathies rather than detailed understanding tended to define attitudes towards the events at Son My. Two theories had been developed to account for what had happened. One held that the massacre was an aberration, a consequence of frustration, poor leadership and madness. This was the conclusion of the sub-committee of the House Armed Services Committee which, in July 1970, published a report of its own investigation into the massacre at My Lai 4:

What obviously happened at My Lai was wrong ... In fact, it was so wrong and so foreign to the normal character and actions of our military forces as to immediately raise a question as to the legal sanity at the time of those men involved.[24]

The notion of insanity was a curiously comforting one for the war's defenders. They could console themselves with the thought that 'normal' American soldiers would never have acted in this way. Others took the position that the massacre was the product of military policies which, as Senator George McGovern argued: 'put these men in a situation where it was inevitable that sooner or later events of this kind would take place.'[25] This argument, which attracted the support of those who were against the war, shifted the responsibility from the soldiers who wielded the weapons and placed it instead on the shoulders of those who put them in My Lai 4.

Each of these views has its weaknesses. Peers concluded that 'there was little to distinguish' the men of either Bravo or Charlie Company, 'from other rifle companies' and their experiences prior to the massacres were hardly exceptional.[26] Suffering casualties to a largely invisible enemy was a common frustration. As Myra MacPherson has pointed out: 'More than 90 per cent of the Americal Division's combat injuries and deaths in early 1968 resulted from booby traps and land mines.'[27] Calley might have been, as Ridenhour put it, 'a fifteen-watt bulb' but he was not the only inadequate platoon leader in Vietnam and psychiatrists who examined him during his trial 'found no psychiatric disease and were certain [Calley] knew the difference between right and wrong.'[28] His superior, Captain Ernest Medina, was described by Peers as 'a strong, effective leader who took care of his men.'[29] And if the massacre at My Lai 4 was an aberration, was that also an explanation for the separate massacre at My Khe 4 on the same day? The theory that such events were inevitable also had its flaw. Why did some of the men at My Lai 4 refuse to kill? Why did some rape and mutilate as well as kill? If it was inevitable that military policies would lead to such outcomes, why did they occur, and on such a scale, at My Lai 4 and My Khe 4, rather than anywhere else? Or did, as some suggested, other atrocities remain undiscovered?

After American withdrawal from Vietnam, memories of the massacres and of the court cases faded from the public consciousness. Then, in 1974, the release of the first and third volumes of the Peers Report offered researchers the opportunity to develop a more complete understanding.

Unfortunately, historians have not always made the most of Peers' work
and mistakes of detail have been common. In *America's Longest War*
George C. Herring referred to the 'murder of more than 200 civilians' at
My Lai by 'an American company under the command of Lieutenant
William Calley', apparently unaware that Calley was a platoon leader
and that Charlie Company had been led by Captain Ernest Medina.[30]
Stanley Karnow's *Vietnam: A History* initially numbered the Vietnamese
dead at My Lai as 'more than three hundred' but later in the same book
the figure became 'a hundred Vietnamese peasants'.[31] Guenter Lewy's
America in Vietnam described the killing of 'all the inhabitants' of My Lai
4, a figure of 175–200.[32] And Joanna Bourke stated in *An Intimate History
of Killing* that Charlie Company had 'slaughtered around 500 unarmed
civilians' at Son My.[33] Of these writers none made specific mention of a
second, separate massacre by Bravo Company. That each found Peers'
estimate of the number of dead too broad to repeat is more comprehensible than the errors of detail. Such errors are, however, examples of
historical carelessness rather than demonstrations of the slippery nature
of truth. The first volume of the Peers Report provides a detailed and
convincing account of much of what happened at Son My. Yet one
question remained unanswered by Peers, one which had been at the heart
of much of the debate about the massacres at Son My when the story was
at its height: why had American soldiers murdered hundreds of Vietnamese civilians?

Even those who have admitted to murdering noncombatants at Son
My have found it hard to explain their actions. *Four Hours in My Lai*, a
documentary film directed by Kevin Sim, illustrates the sort of difficulty
faced by Peers and his investigators. First shown in 1989, *Four Hours in
My Lai* features an interview with Varnado Simpson who confessed to
'killing about 25 people' at My Lai 4.[34] Asked why, Simpson could only
respond, 'I just went' and suggest that his military training had program-
med him to behave as he did.[35] Although his training might have been a
factor, it scarcely explains why he killed women and children at My Lai 4
while others did not. A similar example occurs in the book, also entitled
Four Hours in My Lai, which Sim wrote with Michael Bilton. According
to testimony given to the CID by Herbert Carter of Company C, radio
operator Fred Widmer shot as many as fifteen people, including a mother
and her baby, at My Lai 4. Recalling one of the killings twenty years
later, Widmer was at a loss to explain it: 'when you look back at things
that happened, things that transpired, things you did, you say: Why?

Why did I do that? That is not me. Something happened to me.'[36] It is hard to find the language to represent highly charged emotional reactions even if one wishes to and the feeling amongst the soldiers at My Lai 4 that they were acting in a way which defied explanation was apparently widespread. As a soldier who had witnessed the massacre told Seymour Hersh: 'The people didn't know what they were dying for and the guys didn't know why they were shooting them.'[37]

The eighth chapter of Volume I of the Peers Report identified 'Significant Factors Which Contributed to the Son My Tragedy'.[38] The Report noted the ambiguous nature of the orders given to the men of Bravo and Charlie Companies (although witnesses disagreed about the precise nature of those orders and, as the post-World War II Nuremberg Trials had demonstrated, the following of orders does not excuse criminal acts); the way in which the men of Charlie Company 'were given the impression that the only people left in the area would be the enemy', an idea which might have been reinforced by the designation of the area as a free fire zone by South Vietnamese government officials; the racist attitudes of many of the men toward the Vietnamese; the bitterness caused by the loss of comrades to booby traps and mines; and, in the case of Charlie Company, a sense of frustration at previous failures to find and punish an enemy who were at times indistinguishable from the civilian population.[39] Training deficiencies, inadequate organisation and poor leadership which, for example, had permitted previous mistreatment of Vietnamese civilians by members of Charlie Company to go unchallenged, exacerbated a situation in which the men of Charlie Company were psychologically prepared for the opportunity for revenge and 'not told of any restrictions of any kind'.[40]

Peers was, nevertheless, careful to note that his explanation of the causes of the massacres at Son My was neither 'exhaustive' nor 'definitive'. Prefacing the eighth chapter is the admission that: 'Undoubtedly, there were facts and circumstances beyond those dealt with in this chapter which could be said to have had a major influence'.[41] In *The My Lai Inquiry* Peers observed that, whilst 'The Inquiry recognised that it had neither the time nor the talent to do an in-depth study of why the My Lai tragedy occurred … Knowing the "why" might help prevent any future such occurrence.'[42] The pursuit of a more complete answer to the question 'why' has subsequently engaged historians, psychiatrists, novelists and film makers. Exploration of those other 'facts and circumstances' has tended to focus upon two lines of investigation: firstly, the broader issue of the nature of the war which America fought in South Vietnam and, particularly, in the province of Quang Ngai and, secondly, the psychology of the men involved.

In his introduction to *Facing My Lai: Moving Beyond the Massacre*, published in 1998, David L. Anderson suggested the helpfulness of considering three types of cause for the massacre at My Lai 4, which 'might be characterized as individual, group, and general'.[43] Peers, whose original task had been to examine the cover-up of the massacre at My Lai 4, focused on the first and second of these: the soldiers who perpetrated the massacres and the leaders immediately responsible for the performances of Bravo and Charlie Companies at company, brigade and divisional level. In other words, Peers concentrated on deciding how much culpability could be assigned to the individuals and groups involved. He was less willing to assess the importance of the more general factors, collectively described by Anderson as 'the American way of war in Vietnam.'[44] Criticism of the military policies with which the American Army prosecuted the war was not part of his remit.

The US Army was not prepared for the complex struggle it faced in South-east Asia during the 1960s. Designed for conventional warfare in Europe, it had been organised to achieve a maximum of destructiveness with minimal losses in manpower and to apply the advantages of technology and concentrated firepower against a clearly identifiable enemy in order to win territory. America's military leaders were deprived of such a clear objective in South Vietnam, however. Winning land was rarely of value to the Americans and they were repeatedly frustrated by the elusiveness of their enemies. In particular, NLF forces regularly slipped away from combat to be absorbed by the civilian population or the landscape, re-emerging later to fight somewhere else. So, the Americans adopted an alternative criterion of military progress although they continued to search for opportunities to apply their destructive might. The number of enemy dead, referred to as the body count, replaced the winning of territory as an index of success and the concepts of the free fire zone and the search and destroy mission were introduced to permit the use of that concentrated firepower which was the hallmark of the American Army.

Body count provided a tangible measure of achievement to report to Washington and, therefore, pressure was applied at each level of the military command structure to record higher body counts. It is hard to feel surprise at the outcome. Inflated reports of the number of enemy soldiers killed helped to obscure the difficulty of finding them. Dead

Vietnamese civilians were counted as enemies. Most American soldiers became aware of an unwritten rule: 'If it's dead and Vietnamese, it's VC.'[45] Superiors co-operated by making little comment about the disparity between the number of bodies and the number of weapons captured. Their enemies were simply credited with enormous cunning at spiriting away the weapons of their dead comrades. Racism sanctioned the 'mere gook syndrome', which translated into the belief that the lives of the Vietnamese were of negligible importance, and helped to render any 'civilian death acceptable'.[46]

Amongst the nightmarish details about the massacre at My Lai 4 which emerged in the newspapers and on the television in late 1969 was the uncomfortable fact that, back in March 1968, Task Force Barker had been commended for its performance in and around My Lai. A press release written by Sergeant Jay Roberts, an Army reporter who had been present during the massacre at My Lai 4, had described the killing of '128 enemy in a running battle' and cited the assessment of Task Force Commander, Lieutenant Colonel Frank Barker, that: 'The combat assault went like clockwork'.[47] The *New York Times* had repeated the military's success story in an account published on 17 March 1968 which referred to the killing of 128 NVA soldiers at My Lai.[48] General Westmoreland, commander of American forces in Vietnam at the time of the massacres, had sent his customary message of congratulation for a job that seemed to have been well done. And the official version of the My Lai operation, Barker's Combat Action Report dated 28 March 1968, had made no reference to the killing of noncombatants. Barker had claimed enemy losses of 128 killed in action and summarised the operation as 'well planned, well executed and successful'.[49] The gap between the original portrayal of a disciplined American victory at My Lai and the reality is a dramatic example of the misuse of the criterion of body count. The Peers Report, however, whilst it recognised the 'unfavorable attitude' towards the Vietnamese of some of the men at My Lai 4, did not suggest that this attitude might have been connected with the policy of body count.[50]

As Peers noted, the village of Son My had, on previous occasions, been designated as a free fire zone by officials of the South Vietnamese government. Such a designation simplified a complicated war by assuming that an area was exclusively inhabited by enemy soldiers. America's technological superiority could be pounded home with bombs and shells and the victims added to the total of dead enemies. Search and destroy missions also contributed to what psychiatrist Robert Jay Lifton has

described as an 'atrocity-producing situation'.[51] Intended to remove the
support structures upon which the NLF depended, the effect of search
and destroy was to remove entire communities. Quang Ngai was a
particular target because of its long and proud history of support for the
Viet Minh and the NLF. According to journalist Jonathan Schell, in the
two years prior to August 1967: 'the Marines, the Army, the Korean
Marines, and the ARVN had destroyed approximately seventy per cent
of the villages in the province'.[52]

The particularly destructive form of the 'American way of war in
Vietnam' in Quang Ngai provided the context in which Bravo and
Charlie Companies worked. The argument that a military strategy which
featured search and destroy missions, free fire zones and the counting of
dead bodies as an index of success was a general cause of the massacres is
persuasive. It does not follow, however, that such a strategy rendered the
massacres of civilians at Son My inevitable or that it can fully explain
why American soldiers acted as they did. For what Peers described as a
'more definitive rationale' for the events at Son My it is the behaviour of
the individuals which holds the key.[53]

Second Lieutenant Robert C. Ransom served in Quang Ngai during
March and April of 1968. After a month he wrote home to his parents:

> we have lost 4 killed and about 30 wounded. We have not seen a single
> verified dink the whole time ... I've developed hate for the Vietnamese
> because they come around selling Cokes and beer to us and then run
> back and tell the VC how many we are, where our positions are ...
> [the platoon leader] said that ... the people in the village ... were laugh-
> ing at him because they knew we had been hit. I felt like turning my
> machine guns on the village to kill every man, woman and child in it.[54]

The hatred Ransom expressed was of a similar order to that evidently
experienced by members of Charlie Company. That Ransom did not
apparently succumb to the temptation for revenge highlights the most
complex aspect of the study of the massacres: the psychological processes
that led some to perpetrate atrocities. What caused individuals at My Lai
4 and My Khe 4 to cross the line between rage and murder when others
who took part in the 'American way of war' did not? As Tim O'Brien,
who served as an infantryman in Quang Ngai in 1969, put it:

> What about those of us who went through exactly what Charlie Com-
> pany went through? I went through exactly what they went through

in the same place, and we weren't killing babies. I experienced the
same frustrations, but I didn't cross that line ... between rage and
frustration on the one hand and murder on the other. Although I
experienced exactly what those people experienced in the same place,
we didn't cross the line. The question then becomes why[?] ... That's
the abiding mystery.[55]

That O'Brien was wrong to state that his experience was 'exactly' the
same as that of the men of Charlie Company is clear. Presumably he did
not have to watch his comrades engage in multiple murder and resist
pressure from his peers or orders from his superiors to join in. Nevertheless, O'Brien's comments raise the critical question: why did soldiers
of Charlie Company and Bravo Company cross the line?

Some believe that such a question may be unanswerable. The 'abiding
mystery' of Son My has its precedents. The notion that some human
experience is beyond not only reason but also the capacity of language to
describe has often been suggested in relation to the Holocaust. George
Steiner, for example, argued that: 'The world of Auschwitz lies outside
speech as it lies outside reason.'[56] Whilst the massacres at Son My were
on a comparatively tiny scale, Joanna Bourke adopted a similar approach
to Steiner's when she observed that: 'The horror of acts such as those
carried out by ... Charlie Company ... resists rational analysis.'[57] Some
of those who perpetrated the murders at My Lai 4, like Simpson and
Widmer, have claimed an inability to explain their own actions. Whether
the difficulty is one of reason or language (and it is hardly easy to separate
the two), conventional historical inquiry has added little to Peers' efforts
to understand the behaviour of the soldiers at Son My.[58]

In a study of the processes that led the German civilians of Reserve
Police Battalion 101 to slaughter approximately 38,000 Jews during
World War II, Christopher R. Browning observed that: 'The behaviour
of any human being is, of course, a very complex phenomenon, and the
historian who attempts to explain it is indulging in a certain arrogance.'[59]
To focus on the behaviour of those human beings whose actions are so
awful as to challenge language's ability to represent them compounds the
difficulty. So, can explanation by the makers of films or writers of literature suggest different routes to an understanding of events such as the
massacres in Son My? Perhaps, to return to Bates' distinction between
the 'man in the valley' and the 'man on the hilltop', clues to the motivations of 'the man in the valley' whose finger was on the trigger may be

offered by those who imaginatively adopt the perspective from the valley, who try to go 'inside' the head of the individual soldier. Oliver Stone's film *Platoon* and the novel *In the Lake of the Woods* by Tim O'Brien, published in 1994, have attempted to explore the motivations of American soldiers responsible for the killing and mistreatment of Vietnamese noncombatants. The remainder of this chapter seeks to answer the question: can the film maker or the novelist clarify the nature of the line between 'rage and frustration ... and murder'?

Platoon is loosely based on the experiences of its director as an infantryman in Vietnam in 1967 and 1968. It includes a harrowing episode in which American soldiers, angered by the death of comrades, terrorise a Vietnamese village. Stone shows the killing of several villagers: most shocking are the bludgeoning to death of a young man in a hut and, in a separate incident, the shooting of a woman who complains about the killing of the villagers' animals. The behaviour of the film's central character, Chris (Charlie Sheen), the psychopathic Bunny (Kevin Dillon) and the evil Sergeant Barnes (Tom Berenger) is observed in detail to suggest a combination of the motivations which may lead to massacre.

Dragging the young man, who has only one leg, from a bunker in which he and an older woman have been hiding, Chris is enraged by his victim's fear and his inability to understand what Chris is shouting at him. When his comrade Francis (Corey Glover) points out that the villagers are scared, Chris shouts: 'Oh they're scared ... What about me, man? ... I'm sick of this fuckin' shit' and demands of the villagers: 'Who the fuck do you think we're fighting for?'[60] Within seconds of telling the young man, 'I wasn't going to hurt you', Chris is screaming, 'Dance, motherfucker' and firing madly at the ground on which his prisoner desperately hops.[61] He has been encouraged by Bunny, who is shortly to crush the young man's skull with his rifle butt, but Chris' misinterpretation of his victim's terrified expression as a smile has also acted as a trigger. The complex of emotions which film is able to communicate in a few seconds enables Stone to offer a far more immediate depiction of Chris' loss of control than language alone might. A series of tight close-ups suggests that Chris is tense, frightened, resentful and convinced that he is unappreciated and misunderstood. The audience is already aware of his inexperience and his eagerness to revenge the deaths of his comrades. Unable to communicate with his victim, his automatic weapon provides a convenient tool for the expression of his frustrations. Having terrified the two villagers, however, he weeps in horror at his own actions, as Paul

Meadlo did as he shot people in My Lai 4.[62] It is hard for an audience to dissociate itself entirely from his behaviour because it has shared his traumatic introduction to combat in Vietnam and empathised with many of his reactions. Although Stone quickly allows Chris to redeem himself when he prevents some of his comrades from raping a Vietnamese girl, this is only partly to retain the audience's sympathy for his protagonist. It is hypocritical for Chris to remind his comrades that their victim is a 'fuckin' human being' but Stone's point is that soldiers behave inconsistently.[63] After the platoon burns the village and wholesale massacre has been narrowly averted some of the soldiers look after Vietnamese children. The scene strikes the same note as a soldier's description of events after the massacre at My Lai 4. Some of those who had done the shooting: 'were giving the kids food – you know, just like nothing ever happened.'[64]

Bunny's actions invoke a simpler response from the audience. As Chris turns away in tears Bunny accuses him of cowardice and demonstrates his own 'courage' by battering the young man to death, the camera showing the descending blows from the perspective of the victim. His exhortation to the others in the hut, 'Let's do this whole fuckin' village' is ignored but not condemned. Like the men who refused to fire in My Lai 4 but failed to stop others, Bunny's comrades watch but do not challenge his violence, which seems the product of madness. He justifies himself with the fantasy that the woman in the hut has masterminded Viet Cong activity in the area and is fascinated by the physical consequences of the assault he has launched. 'Holy shit! Did you see that fuckin' head come apart?' he asks, without a trace of compassion for his victim. Later Bunny does exhibit momentary doubts about 'some of the things we've done'.[65] However, in a world in which 'you get to do what you want', he remains consumed by what World War II veteran J. Glenn Gray described as a 'delight in destroying'.[66] In *The Warriors: Reflections on Men in Battle*, Gray commented that this passion: 'has an ... ecstatic character. But in one sense only. Men feel overpowered by it, seized from without, and relatively helpless to change or control it.'[67] Naïve and vicious, Bunny seems out of control and beyond the comprehension of the audience who can only despise him. Stone's diagnosis of Bunny is limited to the truism that, in war, some enjoy killing.

When Sergeant Barnes kills he is motivated by his determination to achieve an objective. Apparently he kills the woman in the village in order to provide an appropriate context in which to secure an admission from the woman's husband that he is Viet Cong. Threatening to shoot the man's daughter has the same purpose. When he shoots Elias in a later scene it is to forestall Elias' attempt to bring him to justice for his earlier murder of the woman. Barnes, despite a disregard of conventional morality that is reminiscent of Calley, another man who was determined to get the job done, is less convincing than Chris or Bunny. His single-mindedness is necessary to sustain the symbolic conflict with the Christ-like Elias. Barnes must be completely evil and consequently, as Leo Cawley has observed, he is an 'all-too-symbolic lover of war' whose presence 'betrays the authenticity of the rest of the film.'[68] However, his abrupt killing of the woman, which shocks the rest of the platoon, prompts another soldier to repeat the idea: 'Let's do the whole fuckin' village.'[69] This time, the response is more positive. Only the force of Barnes' person-ality prevents several in the platoon from stumbling into mass murder. And had Barnes' objective included the shooting of all the villagers, Stone implies, only Elias would have tried to prevent him. Although the massacres at Son My were not Stone's particular concern in *Platoon*, the portrayals of Chris and Bunny and the readiness of some of the soldiers to copy Barnes' behaviour are powerful demonstrations of the different routes by which men may arrive at, or pass over, the threshold of atrocity.

It has been argued that making an event like the massacre at My Lai 4 the subject of a conventional narrative is to risk turning it into a story which simplifies and reduces, trivialising the horror of the experience by attempting to describe the indescribable and offering a closure which enables the event to be categorised and filed away. Hayden White has suggested that the particular techniques of modernism offer 'the only prospect for adequate representations of the kind of "unnatural" events – including the Holocaust – that mark our era'.[70] According to this view, modernist techniques which stress the unreliability of a single, realistic narrative could prompt the reader to question the principles on which any under-standing of such 'unnatural' events like the massacres at Son My is based and to resist accounts which misrepresent under the guise of offering a simple explanation. At first sight, the ambiguous structure and evasions of Tim O'Brien's *In the Lake of the Woods*, which takes the massacre at My Lai 4 as a context, seem to stimulate exactly this sort of questioning.

Winner of the Cooper Prize for Historical Fiction in 1995, *In the Lake of the Woods* presents several versions of events which led up to the disappearance of Kathy Wade and, later, her husband John Wade. A candidate for a Senatorial Primary in Minnesota, John Wade has been heavily defeated after his opponent discovered and publicised Wade's involvement in the massacre at My Lai 4. Having taken refuge from the humiliation of his defeat in a remote cottage on the shore of the Lake of the Woods, John awakes one morning to find Kathy gone. Later he discovers that a motor boat is missing as well. His recall of the events of the previous night incomplete, he seeks help, although there is plenty of evidence to indicate that he might have murdered his wife, dumped her body in the lake and sunk the missing boat. The police can find no trace of Kathy. At the novel's end Wade takes a boat out into the wilderness and disappears himself. The story is provided by an anonymous writer who claims to be, like O'Brien himself, a veteran of the Vietnam War who served in Quang Ngai. The narrator is as puzzled as the reader about the fate of the Wades and his uncertainty seduces the reader into a sifting of the available 'facts' in pursuit of a solution to the mystery of the disappearances.

The novel's structure is disconcerting. Sixteen chapters of narrative are interspersed with eight hypotheses about what might have happened to the Wades and seven chapters of evidence. However, each type of material is less straightforward than it appears. Whilst the novel is pre-faced with the disclaimer that 'it must be read as a work of fiction', distinguishing some chapters as hypotheses leads the reader to suppose that the narrative chapters are epistemologically different, that they can be relied upon more firmly. However, the narrative chapters frequently contain hypotheses. 'How He Went Away', for example, which provides an account of Wade's final disappearance, contains Wade's thoughts, feelings and actions as he makes his solitary way into the wilderness. On the other hand, the narrator sometimes assumes a greater omniscience. In the narrative chapter entitled 'How the Night Passed' the writer must be guessing at events to which there was a maximum of two witnesses, Wade and his wife. Wade, the reader is told, 'felt the pinch of depravity' before he picked up a kettle full of boiling water. The narrative continues: 'he was smiling but the smile was meaningless. He would not remember it.'[71] Here, not only does the narrator claim a knowledge of Wade's feelings, he also supposes a knowledge of something even Wade will not remember, usually the privilege of an omniscient narrator. When exactly the same lines appear in the twenty-seventh chapter, one of those headed 'Hypothesis', it strikes the reader that there is no firm line between the 'facts' of the story and the guesswork of the narrator, even though that guesswork sometimes masquerades as knowledge.[72]

The impact of the seven chapters of evidence is similar. In addition to accurate quotations from existing texts, including the Peers Report, the footnotes also contain invented testimony by some of the characters in the novel and intrusions by the narrator in which he comments upon the process of telling his story and his own reactions to the material. Instead of a reliable apparatus borne of the conventions of historical inquiry, the footnotes, Charles Baxter has argued: 'constitute a wild goose chase.'[73]

O'Brien's previous book *The Things They Carried* (1990) also questioned the authority and status of the storyteller. Stressing the perceptual problems of the soldier 'in the valley' in a chapter entitled 'How to Tell a True War Story', O'Brien's narrator observed: 'For the common soldier … the only certainty is overwhelming ambiguity.'[74] Acceptance of the ambiguities of individual perception, however, is not the same thing as accepting that all the facts of the war are lost in 'overwhelming ambiguity'. To suggest, as Steven Kaplan has, that *The Things They Carried* shows how: 'The only certain thing during the Vietnam War … was that nothing was certain', is to confuse two separate issues: 'to mystify the war by confusing its perceptual experience with its material fact', as Jim Neilson has put it.[75] The narrator of *The Things They Carried* is not rejecting the possibility of establishing material facts about America's war in Vietnam or of providing historical explanations. He is describing the perspective of the soldiers 'in the valley', for whom the experience of war was often shrouded in mystery and secrecy. O'Brien's comments about the confusion of his own war experiences support this distinction. Whilst he has said that 'Vietnam was a war that was essentially purposeless and aimless … in a literal sense. There was nothing to aim at physically, nothing to shoot', he does not accept that this removes the soldier's responsibility to be clear about the difference between right and wrong.[76] His response to the massacre at My Lai 4 is explicit: 'There were no mitigating circumstances. It was mass murder.'[77] He does not believe that the ambiguity of a soldier's perceptions implies that language's depictions of reality are always equivocal: 'Language has to mean something.'[78] How, then, can one explain O'Brien's apparent determination to overwhelm his portrayal of John Wade's actions with ambiguities?

When *In the Lake of the Woods* was published O'Brien reinforced the notion that the solution to the mystery of Kathy Wade's disappearance was intended to remain out of reach: 'My feeling is that John Wade didn't kill her. But that's just what I think. As an author I just have these hypotheses, I'm sort of neutral. But as a reader I have my own opinion.'[79] In an article published in 1994, however, H. Bruce Franklin argued that

In the Lake of the Woods: 'is not as indeterminate or unresolved as it may seem' and that 'enough details surface from the depths of [Wade's] memory – not his imagination – to allow readers to reconstruct the gruesome scene. Unless, O'Brien suggests, readers would rather indulge in elaborate fantasies of denial.'[80] According to this reading, John Wade poured boiling water into the eyes of his wife as she lay in bed, took her corpse out onto the lake in the missing boat and sank both of them. His actions were so horrible that Wade, who loved his wife, has pushed the event deep into his unconscious, although 'fragments of her screaming death agony, buried deep under layers of denial, later keep erupting from Wade's memory.'[81] In a similar way, readers of the novel recoil from what is the most obvious explanation and opt for a less horrible solution. Thus O'Brien's inclusion, as a piece of evidence, of Judith Herman's observation that 'The ordinary response to atrocities is to banish them from consciousness' becomes particularly telling.[82]

A close reading of *In the Lake of the Woods* offers support for Franklin's theory and suggests that O'Brien's claim of neutrality does not mean that a convincing solution to the mystery of Kathy's fate is out of reach. Although most of the references in the following analysis are taken from the novel's narrative chapters, some are taken from chapters headed 'Hypothesis'. This seems acceptable because the narrative chapters include so many hypotheses that the difference between narrative and hypothesis in the novel is neglible. And it should not be forgotten that this is a novel, not a 'real' mystery. O'Brien's most important idea is not about the fate of the fictional construct 'Kathy Wade' but about the capacity, individually and nationally, to deny atrocious acts. One of the ways in which denial becomes possible is by obscuring facts, in this case the killing of one person by another, behind suggestions that ambiguities of perception mean that reality becomes ambiguous too. Rather than a 'wild goose chase', the structure of *In the Lake of the Woods* provides false trails to tempt readers away from the horrible truth.

It is significant that Vinny Pearson, a Vietnam veteran, is convinced from the beginning of Wade's guilt. His willingness to accept that 'The fucker did something ugly' seems to be a consequence of his combat experience, his knowledge of the horrors of which a soldier is capable.[83] There are also persuasive parallels between the descriptions of Wade's actions at My Lai 4, actions which he denied to himself and to others, and the descriptions of Kathy's murder, which Wade also denies. The 'machine-gun wind' which 'seemed to pick him up and blow him from place to place' at My Lai 4 became a glide 'from spot to spot as if gravity were no longer a factor' in the cottage on the night of Kathy's death.[84] His comment about his experiences at My Lai 4 to Kathy's sister, that 'None of it ever seemed real in the first place', and his self-deception about his behaviour there, 'over time the impossibility itself would become the ... most profound memory. This could not have happened. Therefore it did not', is mirrored by his refusal to accept the possibility that he murdered Kathy: 'Unreal, John decided' and 'Impossible, of course.'[85] Other details emphasise the correspondence of the two events. After each, Wade is described as 'waist-deep', in the slime of an irrigation ditch at My Lai 4 and in the lake on the night of Kathy's disappearance.[86] And just as Calley is portrayed killing the grass before the massacre so Wade kills the plants in the cottage before his murder of Kathy.[87]

Compared with the events at My Lai 4, however, about which '[Wade] would feel only the faintest sense of culpability. The forgetting trick mostly worked', memories of Kathy's murder threaten to overwhelm him.[88] He feels an 'illicit little tug' at his memory and later 'he couldn't make the ugly pictures go away ... Ghosts and algae and bits of bone.'[89] As a consequence Wade takes refuge in ambiguity: 'The only explicable thing, he decided, was how thoroughly inexplicable it was. Secrets in general, depravity in particular,' just as he had done when Kathy questioned him about his participation in the massacre: 'Everything's true. Everything's not true.'[90] And in one of his final radio broadcasts from the boat in which he finally disappears Wade 'pooh-poohed the notion of human choice', as if to convince himself that anything he had done was outside of his control.[91]

O'Brien once said that he wanted his writing to be 'a way of jarring people into paying attention to things'.[92] *In the Lake of the Woods* requires the closest attention before it reveals its major concern, however. Rather than persuading the reader to doubt the reliability of narrative and understanding, it emphasises the importance of resisting attempts to escape the facts about the massacres at Son My, and the murder of Kathy Wade. Wade's perceptions may be confused but this does not alter his actions at My Lai 4 or in the cottage. His denial of his potential for evil and his abnegation of personal responsibility prevent Wade from understanding the origins of his behaviour: 'Why? he kept thinking, except there were no answers and never would be.'[93]

The narrator of *In the Lake of the Woods* does offer a partial explanation of why the massacre occurred, in a footnote:

I know what happened that day. I know how it happened. I know why. It was the sunlight. It was the wickedness ... Frustration ... Rage ... But it went beyond that. Something more mysterious ... The unknown, the unknowable. This is not to justify what occurred ... it's to bear witness to the mystery of evil.[94]

O'Brien has presented a similar opinion to an interviewer: 'No one knows what makes the blood sizzle to the point of pulling that trigger ... It's a mystery that's going to remain a mystery.'[95] His citation of Freud's opinion of biography as a piece of evidence in *In the Lake of the Woods* stresses his conviction that a writer cannot penetrate the darkness of another's mind: 'Whoever undertakes to write a biography binds himself to lying ... Truth is not accessible.'[96] Only a self-examination that was beyond Wade and those, like Simpson and Widmer, who murdered noncombatants at My Lai 4 offers any prospect of understanding what motivated their actions: 'We find truth inside, or not at all.'[97]

Stories about the killing of noncombatants continue to appear in the media. In 1999 it was reported that American soldiers had 'killed as many as 300 civilians at No Gun Ri in the opening weeks of the Korean War.'[98] In 2001 ex-Senator Robert Kerrey, a Vietnam veteran who ran for the presidency in 1992, admitted in *Time* that he and the men he led had massacred women and children in a village called Thanh Phong in the Mekong Delta. Whilst Kerrey maintained that the killings, which took place in February 1969, were accidental, one of his men disagreed. Gerald Klann said on television: 'We lined up, and we opened fire. We just slaughtered them.' *Time* reporters Johanna McGeary and Karen Tumulty concluded: 'It is still impossible to settle whose version is right and whose is wrong'. They also noted the difficulty faced by the men who had committed the killings: 'Memory plays tricks – and to ward off horror, we make our memories play tricks'.[99] Like the fictional John Wade, some of the men who fought in Vietnam were susceptible to self-deception, to forgetting or altering their part in murder. Film and literature can speculate about their psychology but neither has provided a more definitive explanation than the Peers Report of the 'mystery of evil' which descended upon the village of Son My in March 1968. Nevertheless, the work of Stone and O'Brien is an important reminder that in the world of combat, as O'Brien has pointed out: 'There's a sense of evil out there that one's trying to battle against, but always with a sense of futility ... you can't outrun it.'[100]

Notes

1. Ronald Ridenhour's letter is printed in James S. Olson and Randy Roberts (eds), *My Lai: A Brief History With Documents* (Boston: Bedford Books, 1998), pp. 148–51.

2. William Wilson, 'I Had Prayed to God That This Thing Was Fiction', *American Heritage*, February 1990.

3. Michael Bilton and Kevin Sim, *Four Hours in My Lai* (New York: Viking, 1992), p. 323.

4. Lt. Gen. W. R. Peers, *The My Lai Inquiry* (New York: W. W. Norton, 1979), p. 212.

5. Wayne Greenshaw, 'Ft. Benning Probes Vietnam Slayings', *Alabama Journal*, 12 November 1969.

6. The story is cited in Seymour M. Hersh, *My Lai 4: A Report on the Massacre and its Aftermath* (New York: Random House, 1970), p. 134.

7. Paul Meadlo cited in Fred Turner, *Echoes of Combat: The Vietnam War in American Memory* (New York: Anchor Books, 1996), p. 39.

8. Richard Slotkin, *Gunfighter Nation: The Myth of the Frontier in Twentieth-Century America* (Norman: University of Oklahoma Press, [1992] 1998), p. 581.

9. Ibid. p. 581.

10. David L. Anderson (ed.), *Facing My Lai: Moving Beyond the Massacre* (Lawrence: University Press of Kansas, 1998), p. 1. The results of a Gallup poll published in *Newsweek* on 12 April 1971 showed much greater support for Calley. Disapproval was registered by 79 per cent of those asked the question: 'Do you approve or disapprove of the court martial finding that Lieutenant Calley is guilty of premeditated murder?' Of those who disapproved, 71 per cent stated that it was because 'others besides Lieutenant Calley' shared responsibility for the crime. Interestingly, however, asked whether 'high government and military officials should be tried' for war crimes committed by Americans in Vietnam, only 32 per cent agreed, and this was despite the feeling of 50 per cent of respondents that incidents like My Lai were common in Vietnam. Study of opinion polls confirms, if nothing else, that Americans were mixed and mixed up in their responses to the events at My Lai 4.

11. Ridenhour's letter in Olson and Roberts, *My Lai*, p. 149. Westmoreland and Peers also claim to have been disbelieving at first. Westmoreland 'found it beyond belief that American soldiers … engaged in mass murder of unarmed South Vietnamese civilians.' William C. Westmoreland, *A Soldier Reports* (New York: Doubleday, 1976), p. 375. Peers 'found it hard to believe that an incident such as Ridenhour described not only could have happened but could have remained hidden for so long.' Peers, *The My Lai Inquiry*, p. 7.

12. Governor of Alabama cited in Joanna Bourke, *An Intimate History of Killing: Face-to-Face Killing in Twentieth-Century Warfare* (London: Granta Books, 1999), p. 193.

13. 'The Great Atrocity Hunt', *National Review*, 16 December 1969; the *Minneapolis Tribune* poll is cited in Hersh, *My Lai 4*, p. 153.

14. The comments in *Time* are cited in 'The Great Atrocity Hunt'.

15. 'The War: New Support for Nixon', *Time*, 12 January 1970.

16. Murphy's support of Calley is described in Julian Smith, *Looking Away: Hollywood and Vietnam* (New York: Scribner's, 1975), p. 76.

17. The record's sales are given in Bourke, *An Intimate History of Killing*, p. 194; Nixon referred to the telegrams in Richard Nixon, *RN: The Memoirs of Richard Nixon* (New York: Gossett and Dunlap, 1978), p. 450.

18. Poll cited in Bourke, *An Intimate History of Killing*, p. 195.
19. Ellsberg cited in Ronald H. Spector, *After Tet: The Bloodiest Year in Vietnam* (New York: The Free Press, 1993), pp. 205–6.
20. Bilton and Sim, *Four Hours in My Lai*, p. 338; Bourke, *An Intimate History of Killing*, p. 192.
21. Jonathan Schell, *The Military Half: An Account of Destruction in Quang Ngai and Quang Tin* (New York: Knopf, 1968), p. 42.
22. Joseph Goldstein, Burke Marshall and Jack Schwartz (eds), *The My Lai Massacre and Its Cover-up: Beyond the Reach of Law?* (New York: The Free Press, 1976), pp. 314–6. This book contains the complete text of Volume I of the Peers Report.
23. Peers, *The My Lai Inquiry*, p. 209.
24. Armed Services Investigating Subcommittee of the Committee on Armed Services, House of Representatives, *Investigation of the My Lai Incident* (Washington, DC: Government Printing Office, 1970), p. 53.
25. McGovern cited in Bilton and Sim, *Four Hours in My Lai*, p.13. Bilton and Sim also point out the division of opinion between those who believed the massacre at My Lai 4 to be an aberration and those, like McGovern, who believed such an event to be inevitable. Nearly twenty years later Neil Sheehan repeated the argument that the massacre was inevitable: 'The military leaders of the United States, and the civilian leaders who permitted the generals to wage war as they did, had made the massacre inevitable.' Sheehan, *A Bright Shining Lie: John Paul Vann and America in Vietnam* (New York: Vintage Books, 1989), p. 690.
26. Goldstein et al., *The My Lai Massacre*, pp. 82–4.
27. Myra MacPherson, *Long Time Passing: Vietnam and the Haunted Generation* (London: Sceptre Books, [1984] 1988), pp. 581–2.
28. Ridenhour's comment is cited in ibid. p. 585; Bilton and Sim, *Four Hours in My Lai*, p. 336.
29. Peers, *The My Lai Inquiry*, p. 233.
30. George C. Herring, *America's Longest War: The United States and Vietnam, 1950–1975*, 3rd edn (New York: McGraw Hill, 1996), p. 236. The responsibility for the massacre at My Lai 4 is wrongly ascribed to a platoon rather than a company of soldiers in Marilyn Young, *The Vietnam Wars 1945–1990* (New York: Harper Perennial, 1991), p. 243.
31. Stanley Karnow, *Vietnam: A History* (London: Guild Publishing, [1983] 1985), p. 24; p. 530. This discrepancy is pointed out in Christian G. Appy, *Working-Class War: American Combat Soldiers and Vietnam* (Chapel Hill: University of North Carolina Press, 1993), p. 339.
32. Guenter Lewy, *America in Vietnam* (New York: Oxford University Press, 1978), p. 326.
33. Bourke, *An Intimate History Of Killing*, p. 172.
34. *Four Hours in My Lai*, directed by Kevin Sim, was first shown in May 1989 as one of the *First Tuesday* series on ITV; Simpson's admission is in Bilton and Sim, *Four Hours in My Lai*, p. 7.
35. Simpson speaking in *Four Hours in My Lai*.
36. Carter's testimony regarding Widmer is printed in Olson and Roberts, *My La*i, pp. 80–1; Widmer's comments are in Bilton and Sim, *Four Hours in My Lai*, p. 80.
37. Herbert Carter cited in Hersh, *My Lai 4*, p. 187.
38. Goldstein et al., *The My Lai Massacre*, pp. 192–206.

39. Ibid. p. 206.

40. Ibid. p. 206.

41. Ibid. p. 192.

42. Peers, *The My Lai Inquiry*, p. 237.

43. Anderson, *Facing My Lai*, p. 7.

44. Ibid. p. 7. Anderson identified body count statistics, the strategy of search and destroy, and free fire zones as characteristic of the 'American way of war'.

45. Bilton and Sim, *Four Hours in My Lai*, p. 38. Or as a soldier who was present at the massacre at My Lai 4 put it: 'If it's dead it's VC. Because it's dead. If it's dead it had to be VC.' Cited in Robert Jay Lifton, *Home From The War: Learning From Vietnam Veterans* (Boston: Beacon Press, [1973] 1992), p. 64.

46. MacPherson, *Long Time Passing*, p. 59.

47. Roberts' press release is printed in Olson and Roberts, *My Lai*, p. 27.

48. *New York Times* cited in Appy, *Working-Class War*, p. 275.

49. Barker's Report is printed in Olson and Roberts, *My Lai*, pp. 28–32.

50. Goldstein et al., *The My Lai Massacre*, p.195.

51. Lifton, *Home From the War*, p. 65.

52. Schell, *The Military Half*, p. 10.

53. Peers, *The My Lai Inquiry*, p. 237.

54. Letter written home to his parents by 2Lt. Robert C. Ransom, Jr sometime during April 1968. Printed in Bernard Edelman (ed.), *Dear America: Letters Home From Vietnam* (New York: W. W. Norton, 1985), p. 181. A slightly different version of this letter appears in MacPherson, *Long Time Passing*, p. 481. MacPherson presented the final sentence in the quotation given above as the words of the platoon leader. Whomever the sentiment belonged to, it demonstrates the sort of hatred that American soldiers could feel for Vietnamese villagers in Quang Ngai.

55. O'Brien cited in Anderson, *Facing My Lai*, p. 174.

56. Steiner cited in Hayden White, 'The Modernist Event', in Vivian Sobchak (ed.), *The Persistence of History: Cinema, Television, and the Modern Event* (New York: Routledge, 1996), p. 30.

57. Bourke, *An Intimate History of Killing*, p. 175.

58. In *A Time for War: The United States and Vietnam, 1941–1975* Robert D. Schulzinger offers the unsourced speculation that the massacre at My Lai 4 was sparked because the villagers 'refused to talk'. Schulzinger, *A Time For War* (New York: Oxford University Press, [1997] 1998), p. 262. This (and his implication that Calley was the leader of Charlie Company) is not untypical of the carelessness with which historians have handled the massacres at Son My. Bilton and Sim's detailed account in *Four Hours in My Lai* is an honourable exception.

59. Christopher R. Browning, *Ordinary Men: Reserve Police Battalion 101 and the Final Solution in Poland* (London: Penguin, [1992] 2001), p. 188.

60. Chris speaking in *Platoon*, directed by Oliver Stone (Hemdale Film Corporation, 1986).

61. Ibid.

62. Robert E. Maples testified to the CID that: '[Meadlo] was one of those firing and he was crying at the same time.' Printed in Olson and Roberts, *My Lai*, p. 84.

63. Chris speaking in *Platoon*.

64. The soldier's words are cited in Robert Jay Lifton, *Home From The War*, p. 206.

65. Bunny speaking in *Platoon*.

66. Ibid; J Glenn Gray, *The Warriors: Reflections on Men in Battle* (Lincoln: University of Nebraska Press, [1959] 1998), p. 56.
67. Gray, *The Warriors*, p. 56.
68. Leo Cawley cited in Norman Kagan, *The Cinema of Oliver Stone* (Oxford: Round-house, 1995), p. 110.
69. Anonymous soldier speaking in *Platoon*.
70. White, 'The Modernist Event', p. 32.
71. Tim O'Brien, *In the Lake of the Woods* (London: Flamingo, [1994] 1995), p. 49.
72. The lines are repeated in ibid. p. 275.
73. Charles Baxter, 'Shame and Forgetting in the Information Age', in Charles Baxter (ed.), *The Business of Memory: The Art of Remembering in an Age of Forgetting* (Saint Paul: Graywolf Press, 1999), p. 156.
74. Tim O'Brien, *The Things They Carried* (London: Flamingo, [1990] 1991), p. 78.
75. Steven Kaplan, 'The Undying Uncertainty of the Narrator in Tim O'Brien's *The Things They Carried*', *Critique*, Autumn 1993; Jim Neilson, *Warring Fictions: Cultural Politics and the Vietnam War* (Jackson: University Press of Mississippi, 1998), p. 195.
76. O'Brien interviewed in Anderson, *Facing My Lai*, p. 173.
77. Ibid. p. 173.
78. Ibid. p. 175.
79. O'Brien cited in *Baltimore City Paper*, February 1994.
80. H. Bruce Franklin, 'Plausibility of Denial: Tim O'Brien, My Lai and America', *The Progressive*, December 1994.
81. Ibid.
82. O'Brien, *In the Lake of the Woods*, p. 140.
83. Ibid. p. 30.
84. Ibid. p. 63; p. 133.
85. Ibid. p. 189; p. 111; p. 276; p. 85. The quotation from page 276, for example, is from a chapter headed 'Hypothesis'.
86. Ibid. p. 36; p. 51.
87. Ibid. p. 104; p. 50.
88. Ibid. p. 111.
89. Ibid. p. 80; p. 94.
90. Ibid. p. 280; p. 56.
91. Ibid. pp. 286–7.
92. O'Brien interviewed in Eric James Schroeder, *Vietnam, We've All Been There: Interviews with American Writers* (Westport, CT: Praeger, 1992), p. 138.
93. O'Brien, *In the Lake of the Woods*, p. 276.
94. Ibid. p. 203.
95. O'Brien interviewed in Anderson, *Facing My Lai*, p. 174.
96. O'Brien, *In the Lake of the Woods*, p. 294.
97. Ibid. p. 298.
98. Mark Thompson, 'The Bridge at No Gun Ri', *Time*, 11 October 1999.
99. Johanna McGeary and Karen Tumulty, 'The Fog of War', *Time*, 7 May 2001. Klann's comments, made on *60 Minutes II*, are cited by McGeary and Tumulty.
100. O'Brien interviewed in Schroeder, *Vietnam, We've All Been There*, p. 140.

CHAPTER 6

Veterans

In an article considering the problems faced by America's returning war veterans, Franklin Fearing, Professor of Psychiatry at the University of California, wrote:

> The sudden removal of the bulwarks of comradeship precipitates the soldier into a world ... which seems harsh and uncompromising. His anxiety concerning his future in this world, and his lack of confidence in his capacity to cope with it on its own terms, is not easily admitted, even to himself. His defenses go up in the form of hostility and active aggression ... [H]alf-conscious guilt feelings ... may spring from the soldier's own sense of failure or inadequacy of performance in the war.

As the soldier attempts to adjust to civilian life, the professor continued, he is compelled to ask himself a 'basic question' about his service in the war: 'Was it worth it?'[1] Perhaps Fearing was aware that almost exactly this question was put to American soldiers in a government survey carried out from time to time during the war. Men were asked: 'Do you ever get the feeling that this war is not worth fighting?' Responding to the question shortly before the publication of Fearing's article, 29 per cent claimed that this thought never occurred to them, whilst 48 per cent experienced this feeling 'sometimes' or 'very often'.[2] Fearing's conclusion, that the answer to such a question 'may have devastating effects', was in line with fears already being raised, sometimes in sensational style, in the media: how many of the war's physical survivors were psychological casualties and how would men who had become killers behave as civilians?[3]

Amongst the magazine articles offering careful advice about how to treat the returning veteran, one entitled 'Do's and Don't's for Veterans' striking a characteristically concerned note, a widely quoted Army chaplain's description of the American soldier sharpened the anxiety of those expecting the return of a family member or a boyfriend:

He is not very clear in his own mind about why he fought ... he is not much interested in such matters ... His interests are chiefly three: 1) to find a woman and sleep with her; 2) to ... get stinking drunk; 3) to go home.[4]

Worse were the terrifying stories in the newspapers. 'Veteran Beheads Wife With Jungle Machete' and 'Ex-Marine Held In Rape Murder' were 'not atypical' of the headlines at the time, as Joseph C. Goulden observed. Indeed, what Goulden referred to as 'the War-Crazed Veteran theory' was, for a time, a media staple and the subject of much discussion across America.[5]

The 'War-Crazed' veterans considered by Fearing and Goulden had not fought in Vietnam, however. They had served in Europe and Asia during World War II, America's 'Good War'. Coming home, sometimes after years of absence, they had to cope with the physical or psychological consequences of their wars as well as sort out their futures and renegotiate their personal relationships. Like the Vietnam veteran who complained: 'One moment I was king and the next moment I'm the dregs of society', they learned that military prestige did not translate automatically into civilian status.[6] Furthermore they were not assured of a loving welcome from their wives, sometimes almost complete strangers whom they had married in the excitement of the days before their departure from America. In 1945 the number of divorces soared to 'thirty-one ... for every 100 marriages, double the prewar rate'.[7] As they tried to adjust to life at home they received a mixed reception from those Americans who had not gone to war. Fêted as heroes and victors, veterans were also suspected of a capacity for violent and uncontrolled behaviour. People believed them to be physical and mental wrecks but were convinced that they would snap up all the best jobs. Like the men returning from Vietnam, they could feel cut off from the world which they had thought about so longingly and reluctant to talk to anyone except other veterans about their experiences. Research showed that one in five Americans returning from World War II felt 'completely hostile to civilians'.[8]

Despite the similarity of some of the problems awaiting the veterans of the two wars on their return to America, veterans of the Vietnam War have usually perceived their experience as completely different. Tim O'Brien's explanation in 1974 of the attitude of Vietnam veterans towards the American Legion, an organisation which was dominated by the veterans of earlier wars, highlights the most important of the reasons for this:

The very words 'American Legion' make many of us shudder ... A place to go to ... wallow in pride and self congratulation. But we have no victories to celebrate till we die; we did not win; *our* war, it is said, was not a just war. We are loners. Loners and losers.[9]

Even though Vietnam veterans had to share the stigma of having taken part in an ultimately unpopular war, which resulted in America's first military defeat, it is difficult to generalise about what happened to them after their arrival home. Because of the restricted tour hundreds, and more often thousands, of Americans jetted back from Vietnam every month for more than a decade, each of them usually surrounded by unfamiliar faces. After this rapid and often isolating journey back to 'the World', the veteran's experience depended upon when it took place, what was at home and how meaningful each had found his or her tour of duty. Any reaction was also susceptible to alteration as the years passed, for reasons to do with individual psychology or because of the changing status of the war and the Vietnam veteran in the media.

Throughout the war there was the possibility that, because of the speed of the trip home, the terrifying excitement of a fire fight might be exchanged for a seat at the kitchen table with relatives within forty-eight hours. The formidable adjustment which that entailed was made harder by the sudden absence of the buddies who had sustained the soldier during the previous months. For some, though, the transition from war to peace was easier. For example, volunteers who returned earlier in the war, those who came back to parts of America in which the anti-war movement had made little progress and those who were granted a hero's welcome in a small town were protected from the sort of hostility which others encountered. Nevertheless, as the war ground on it became more likely that returnees would meet the silence or even abuse of those who were against the war. The traumatic experience described by this veteran in Mark Baker's oral history *Nam* may be apocryphal but it is also representative of what many began to fear:

The first day back, I had survived. I had made it.

I took a cab from the base to Berkeley ... I told the driver, 'I want to get out, I want to walk.'

'You want to walk? Here?' I was in full dress uniform with decorations, medals ...

Walking down the streets of Berkeley, I felt like the man from Mars visiting the earth. Everybody was looking at me. All kinds of comments. People spit [*sic*] at me. I was more scared walking down that street than I had been in Vietnam.[10]

Not every soldier had to go back to Berkeley, a hotbed of anti-war sentiment, but even those who negotiated the return to a more sympathetic hometown were hurt by the reception accorded to them at a national level. Myra MacPherson noted: 'In interview with hundreds of veterans – from the most successful to the least well-adjusted – I have yet to find one who did not suffer rage, anger, and frustration at the way the country received them.'[11] Both the Kennedy and Johnson administrations had tried to downplay the involvement of Americans in the war until, under Johnson, it became impossible to do so any longer because the anti-war movement had acquired such momentum. Even before they were doomed by the Tet Offensive, the president's attempts to win the media around to support of the war avoided the question of those Americans who had lost their lives. As Lawrence A. Tritle pointed out in *From Melos to My Lai*: 'Johnson spoke little publicly on the subject of American dead in Vietnam', thereby failing to assert the significance of their sacrifice.[12] Additionally, according to MacPherson: 'GIs returned when times were hard and jobs scarce', and to a GI Bill which 'was greatly inferior to that for World War II and Korean veterans.'[13] After Tet, Johnson's decision to sue for peace and the beginning of the four-year-long withdrawal of American forces under Nixon meant soldiers returned from Vietnam with the realisation that they had taken part in a war which America was not going to win. Coming home, those with experience of the war's final years found they had swapped one fractured world for another.

By the end of the decade a variety of tensions in Vietnam had escalated to the point of anarchy: between Americans and South Vietnamese; combat units and REMFs; blacks and whites; and between those who wanted to fight the enemy and those who were determined to avoid doing so. Whilst some Americans sought a discreet route to a safer war, conducting 'search and evade' operations with the connivance of sympathetic officers, others launched attacks on those officers and non-commissioned officers whose enthusiasm for combat was considered a danger. Known as 'fragging', killing by grenade was a popular form of attack because it left no fingerprints. The number of reported 'fraggings' aimed at either an officer or an NCO rose from 70 in 1969 to 154 in 1970 and 158 in 1971.[14] An article which appeared in the *Armed Forces Journal* in June 1971 by Robert Heinl, a colonel in the Marines, described the US Army in Vietnam as 'approaching collapse, with individual units avoiding or having refused combat, murdering their officers and noncommissioned officers, drug-ridden and dispirited where not near-mutinous', a state of affairs which, Heinl believed, represented the 'lowest state of military morale in the history of the country.'[15] At least one of the steps taken to reverse this decline in morale had made matters worse. Although the level of military activity was falling, American soldiers were given more medals. Intended as an encouragement, the award of 522,905 medals for bravery in 1970 resulted in their devaluation by the men who received them.[16]

Back in America, further division awaited the returnee, much of it related to the war. Amongst other grievances, civil rights leaders pointed to the injustice of a draft that had sent blacks and the poor to fight in Vietnam in disproportionate numbers. Events like the massacre at My Lai 4 or the shooting of thirteen students by the National Guard during an anti-war rally at Kent State University in Ohio polarised opinion. In April 1971 half a million Americans, some of whom had fought in Vietnam, took part in an anti-war demonstration in Washington. Reportage from Vietnam contributed to the idea that veterans had fought in a point-less war. Published in September 1971, an article in the *New York Times Magazine* by Donald Kirk entitled 'Who Wants To Be The Last American Killed in Vietnam?' featured an American soldier's assessment of the war in its final paragraph: 'Far as I'm concerned they can have this whole country. There ain't no reason for us bein' here. We was fightin' to win, that'd be one thing, but we're just wasting time.' Kirk concluded: 'It is a typical G.I. commentary – one I hear countless times around Military Region One – at the butt end of a bad war.'[17]

Before the war was over it was argued that Vietnam veterans were more likely to suffer adverse psychological reactions because they felt isolated by their reception in America and because they had not enjoyed the satisfaction of victory or the consciousness of having participated in a worthwhile national endeavour. Robert Jay Lifton's *Home From the War*, first published in 1973, dwelt upon the special nature of the Vietnam veteran. Lifton, a Professor of Psychiatry, noted that: 'Everyone who has contact with them seems to agree that they are different from the veterans of other wars', that a 'favorite word to describe them is "alienated"' and that Veterans Administration observers had identified their 'bitterness, distrust, and suspicion of those in positions of authority and responsi-bility.'[18] Accepting that the veterans of other wars often exhibited similar tendencies, Lifton insisted that 'these men give the impression of some-

Vietnam veterans at the memorial wall in Washington DC (Rex/SIPA).

thing more'. Citing research by historian Murray Polner which found that Vietnam veterans had the 'gnawing suspicion that "it was all for nothing"', Lifton identified the additional element in the men's alienation as their awareness that 'the central fact of the Vietnam War is that no one really believes in it.'[19]

In the preface to the 1992 edition of *Home From the War* Lifton concluded that: 'an impressive number of Vietnam veterans ... found meaning only in asserting the very meaninglessness of their war.'[20] Elsewhere in the preface, Lifton described the consequences of the Vietnam veterans' experience, referring to the 'astonishing psychological costs of the war' and to a 'definitive study' completed in 1990 by Richard A. Kulka and others which indicated the extent of the damage: 'At one time or another over 960,000 men and 1,900 women, between a quarter and a third of all who served in Vietnam' had suffered from post-traumatic stress disorder (PTSD) and others, about 350,000 of them, had experienced a partial form of PTSD.[21]

There is another view of the Vietnam veteran, however. The authors of a survey of 906 veterans in Illinois in 1974 concluded that 'these men are apparently coping well in mainstream America', although they accepted that men who had served in combat units were about twice as likely to experience psychological difficulties as veterans who had worked in the rear.[22] More recently, Lind argued in *Vietnam: The Necessary War* that America's psychiatric casualties in Vietnam were proportionately lower than in World War II or in Korea. He also observed that, compared to national averages, the unemployment rate of Vietnam veterans has, since 1974, been lower, the divorce rate no higher and the rate of suicide similar. Having cited the results of a poll taken in 1980 in which 'seventy-one percent of Vietnam veterans agreed with the statement, "Looking back, I am glad I served my country"', he concluded that Eric T. Dean, Jr, one of his sources, was correct to observe:

> The portrayal of the Vietnam vet as well-adjusted and untroubled by the war would have undermined [the] antiwar agenda, and hence evidence that Vietnam veterans were readjusting or had readjusted well to American society tended to be drowned out by excited and strident recriminations leveled against the U.S. government.[23]

Certainly, veterans of the war in Vietnam did not enjoy a positive image in the media during the early 1970s. According to a report in 1974, America's national newspapers had lost interest in Vietnam's veterans. MacPherson noted the response of one editor: 'Veterans are not sexy. Who cares?' She also pointed out that in 1946 there were over 500 articles about veterans in popular magazines. In 1972, while the Vietnam War was still going on, there were less than fifty.[24] The treatment of veterans on screen demonstrates the contrast between the images of the Vietnam veteran and the World War II veteran even more starkly.

Vietnam veterans made frequent appearances in films and television drama from the late 1960s onwards and, until the later 1970s, they usually meant trouble. As Julian Smith commented in 1975 in *Looking Away: Hollywood and Vietnam*: 'writers and producers have assumed the mass audience will accept the portrayal of veterans as constantly violent, given to handgrenade fraggings in hotel elevators and ... sniping from rooftops.'[25] On television, Vietnam often provided a convenient history for the men pursued by television detectives. Smith noted that, during January 1974 alone, episodes of *Colombo* and *Kojak* featured veterans as killers and in *Hawaii Five-O* another one blew himself up.[26] At the cinema, meanwhile, Tom Laughlin's *Born Losers* (1967) had initiated a spate of low-budget films in which Vietnam veterans were agents of retribution. Films like Al Adamson's *Satan's Sadists* (1969) and Lee Frost's *Chrome and Hot Leather* (1971) contributed to a sub-genre in which the villains were members of a motor cycle gang and the veterans notable for the enthusiasm with which they turned to violence. The hero of *Born Losers* reappeared in the eponymous *Billy Jack* in 1971. Directed once again by Laughlin, who also played the title role, the film grossed thirty million dollars and 'suggests in embryonic form all of the characteristics that were to become standard for the 1970s image of the returned Vietnam vet' as Albert Auster and Leonard Quart observed.[27] Billy Jack's image included significant details which would be inherited by Stallone's Rambo. A war hero and an ex-Green Beret with one native American parent, Billy Jack's status as a Vietnam veteran may not be emphasised in *Billy Jack* but the difficulty he has controlling himself is central to the film: 'I'm itching to kill somebody so it might as well be you', he tells one of the villains.[28] Established in *Born Losers* as a 'disillusioned war veteran', his appearance in the later film reinforces the message, as Auster and Quart put it, that: 'the veteran was returning alienated, angry, unsettled, and unable to adjust to post-war society'.[29] Asked by Bernard (David Roya), 'What are you? Nuts or something?', Billy Jack replies, 'Some people think so.'[30]

Other screen veterans did not receive the degree of sympathy accorded to Billy Jack's portrayal but most of them shared his propensity for violence. Provoked by the hostility they found in the ironically named Hope, in New Mexico, the four Green Berets returning from Vietnam in Richard Compton's *Welcome Home, Soldier Boys* (1972) reacted by destroying the town. Jack Falen, Dennis Hopper's veteran in Henry Jaglom's *Tracks* (1976), was depicted as a psychological victim of the war but the film ends, as Auster and Quart noted, 'with genuine menace' when he emerges, armed, from a grave, shouting: 'You want to know what it's like in Nam.'[31] Other screen veterans were simply frightening. In 1973 Don Siegel's *Charley Varrick* pitted Walter Matthau against a hitman who had honed his skills in Vietnam and, in John Frankenheimer's *Black Sunday* (1976), a veteran joined forces with the Palestine Liberation Organization in a bid to destroy a stadium full of spectators watching the Superbowl. Nominated for an Academy Award as Best Picture of 1976, Martin Scorsese's *Taxi Driver* featured Robert de Niro as Travis Bickle, a veteran apparently suffering from some form of post-traumatic stress. Insomniac, afflicted by headaches and unable to form relationships, the heavily armed Bickle prowled the streets of New York, plotted the assassination of a presidential candidate and, eventually, turned his guns on three men who ran a brothel.

Hollywood's reaction to the returning veterans of World War II had been very different, a reaction exemplified by William Wyler's *The Best Years of Our Lives*, winner of the Academy Award for Best Picture of 1946. The film traces the lives of three men, each of whom has particular problems in adjusting to civilian life. Homer (Harold Russell) has lost his arms, Fred (Dana Andrews) has nightmares in which he relives his traumatic experiences of combat and Al (Fredric March) drinks too much. In their relationships, too, they experience difficulties. Homer is reluctant to marry his fiancée because he fears that her only feeling for him is pity, Fred finds that a wartime romance has led to a marriage which was a mistake and Al struggles to relate to his teenage son. The film also shows the suspicion with which veterans were often met in the workplace.

When Homer is told by a customer in a drug store that he was 'deceived' into losing his hands, that Americans had 'fought the wrong people' during the war and that the 'unpleasant truth' is that Homer and his comrades were 'suckers', he is outraged. He confronts the man who has doubted the meaning of his sacrifice and Fred, who has been forced to accept a low-paid job in the drug store, punches the customer to the ground. Fred earns the audience's approbation when he quits his job, telling the manager of the drug store: 'This customer wasn't right' and his violence is presented as justified.[32] Homer's decision to stand by the sacrifice he has made rather than share the customer's cynicism is an important stage in his acceptance of his physical loss and his re-integration into the life of his community. The impact of the scene is even greater because Homer's part was taken by Russell, a non-professional actor who had lost both his hands during his military service. In *The Best Years of Our Lives* veterans' problems are recognised and then overcome. The film ends with Homer's marriage and the suggestion that Fred will be able to find happiness with Al's daughter.

A shift in Hollywood's treatment of the Vietnam War was signalled in 1978 by the presentation of Academy Awards to Michael Cimino's *The Deer Hunter* and Hal Ashby's *Coming Home*. Whilst Ashby's film depicted the impact of the war upon three characters to point a simple anti-war moral, Cimino attempted to show what the war had done to Americans on a broader canvas. Neither film offers the sort of optimism which marked the end of Wyler's film, although in *Coming Home* the love of a good woman (Jane Fonda) contributed to the transformation of Jon Voight's bitter, disabled veteran into an anti-war activist. The third character in the triangle, another veteran played by Bruce Dern, returned to America sickened by his experiences in Vietnam. His solution was to drown himself, an act which implied that the Vietnam veteran had only two choices, opposition to the war or suicidal despair. Ron Kovic's auto-biographical novel *Born on the Fourth of July*, published in 1976, and the film by Oliver Stone based upon it which appeared thirteen years later, demonstrate more powerfully than *Coming Home* how action protesting the war could become a way of responding with purpose to the futility of one's physical sacrifice. For the majority of veterans, of course, the choice was less dramatic.

Apparently more complex than *Coming Home*, *The Deer Hunter* bears superficial resemblances to Wyler's film. The lives of three soldiers are followed, immediately before, during and after their tours in Vietnam. Captured by the Viet Cong, the men are forced to play Russian roulette whilst their guards gamble upon the result. After their escape, Nick (Christopher Walken) remains in Vietnam, drug addicted and the victim of severe PTSD and Steven (John Savage) returns to America dependent upon a wheelchair. The Russian roulette metaphor is elaborated in the film's climax when Michael (Robert de Niro) returns to Saigon on the eve of its fall to the North Vietnamese to find Nick. The film, highly realistic in some ways, lurches into political allegory as it shows a French-man leading Michael to a gambling den where he must pay thousands of dollars to South Vietnamese entrepreneurs in order to risk his life in a game of Russian roulette which he hopes will shock the amnesiac Nick into recognising him. As South Vietnamese businessmen lay bets upon the outcome, Nick seems to remember Michael seconds before he shoots himself in the head. As various critics have noted, the impact of these scenes is to display the Vietnamese as an evil race taking advantage of innocent Americans and the fall of Saigon as a consequence of the depra-vity of its people.[33]

The three men in *The Best Years of Our Lives* find it hard to pick up their civilian lives but in *The Deer Hunter* the difficulties of readjustment are overwhelming. After escaping from the Viet Cong, Nick is unable to telephone his girl friend Linda or answer a doctor's questions without sobbing. Drug addiction and a compulsion to suicide await him. Back in America, Steven hides away in a hospital and even his wife is apparently struck dumb by his ordeal. Michael, the least 'damaged' of the three friends, avoids a welcome home party and tells Linda (Meryl Streep): 'I feel a lot of distance.'[34] Only the catharsis of the deer hunt, in which he deliberately misses the deer he has in his sights, allows Michael to assert his commitment to life. Even so, when he visits Steven in hospital, the two men are almost inarticulate as Steven admits to feeling: 'I don't fit.'[35] That these difficulties occur despite the absence of anti-war sentiment in the community is an encouraging note of realism – not every city turned against the war. Michael, who continues to wear his uniform after his return home, is welcomed with respect and affection and offered drinks on the house at the local bowling alley even though the war is apparently very close to its end. When Nick's body is rather magically returned to Pennsylvania (getting out of Saigon in April 1975 was difficult enough if you were alive), Michael and Steven meet with their friends to mourn his death. They find consolation and the film finds its moral in the singing of 'God Bless America', an authentic response to events which from the perspective of the friends demanded a closing of ranks. Despite the realism with which the community of Clairton and aspects of the veterans' experience is rendered, however, Cimino's determination to use Nick's experience as the raw material for political symbolism is unhelpful in its simplicity.

During the 1980s the image of the veteran was manipulated even more vigorously in order to persuade Americans to look at the war in a more positive way. Ronald Reagan had recognised the importance of the veteran's reputation during his campaign for the presidency in 1980. As well as challenging the view that the war had been meaningless and justifying those who had supported what he called 'a noble cause', he argued that America's defeat had been a consequence of the timidity of its leaders rather than the fault of its veterans. Americans, he warned, must not repeat the mistake of sending 'young men to fight and possibly die in a war our government is afraid to win.'[36]

Reagan's emergence as 'the chief spokesman for a revisionist history of the Vietnam War', as Richard Slotkin described him, had more to do with his determination to revive enthusiasm for American interventions abroad than with concern about the men who had fought in Vietnam.[37] His hostility towards the anti-war movement, sharpened by his experiences as Governor of California between 1967 and 1975, was a further encouragement. In fact, his economic policies led to the cutting of veterans' benefits and he did not visit the National Memorial to Americans killed in Vietnam until six months after its dedication in November 1982; a memorial, incidentally, initiated by Vietnam veterans rather than by the government. Nevertheless, Reagan's comments endorsed a new view of the war and its veterans and prepared the ground for the development of one of the most powerful myths of 1980s America: the myth of the missing POWs.

The possibility that American servicemen remained imprisoned in South-east Asia after the end of the war had been used to various ends by Presidents Nixon, Ford and Carter but the Reagan administration, according to a joint report by the Departments of Defense and State: 'raised domestic consciousness of this issue to the highest level since the end of the war.'[38] Despite the lack of any firm evidence that Americans were still in captivity, the president stated in January 1983 that the fate of these men was 'the highest national priority'.[39] Reagan continued to use the emotional pull of the notional prisoners' plight throughout his presidency to emphasise the inhumanity of the Vietnamese and to persuade Americans that they and the POWs were the war's true victims. The persistence of the POW myth testifies to the effectiveness of Reagan's work. In 1993, five years after he left office and twenty years after the last official POW had left North Vietnam, a poll showed that two-thirds of Americans continued to believe that there were still prisoners in South-east Asia.[40] A further element of the myth, as H. Bruce Franklin observed in *M.I.A. or Mythmaking in America*, held 'scheming bureaucrats and liberals' responsible for keeping the truth about the prisoners from the president.[41] In this scenario, like the POWs and the veterans, Reagan was fettered by an American enemy committed out of selfishness or pusillanimity to the frustration of national purposes. Thus, during Reagan's presidency, the image of the Vietnam veteran was assimilated into a version of history which accorded a dual status, as a warrior who had been deprived of a victory he could have won and as a victim who symbolised the various betrayals the nation had suffered in Vietnam. Such an image helped to justify more aggressive foreign policies and enabled Reagan to demonise those 'scheming bureaucrats and liberals' who might oppose them.

Reagan's message was reinforced by the appearance during the mid-1980s of several feature films which involved the rescue of American soldiers incarcerated in Vietnam after the end of the war. Sylvester Stallone's return as John Rambo in George P. Cosmatos' *Rambo: First Blood Part II* was the most successful of these, earning fifty-seven million dollars in the first fortnight of its release in 1985 and prompting the president to remark: 'Boy, I saw *Rambo* last night. Now I know what to do the next time'.[42] Franklin's comment that the film 'changed the public climate' indicates its significance but earlier films like Ted Kotcheff's

Uncommon Valor (1983) and the Chuck Norris vehicle *Missing in Action* (1984), directed by Joseph Zito, had anticipated the seductiveness of the ideas in *Rambo: First Blood Part II*.[43] Rubbished by the critics, these films did well at the box office because they insisted that there were American prisoners in Vietnam whose predicament, like America's defeat in Vietnam, was the fault of weak but conspiratorial American politicians. In each of the films the American veteran, freed of constraints, won the victory he had been denied during the war.

Stallone's first appearance as Rambo had been in Ted Kotcheff's 1982 film *First Blood*. Based upon a novel with the same title published by David Morrell in 1972, the film depicts the violent retaliation of a returned Vietnam veteran who is mistreated by the police force of another town bearing the name Hope. Stallone's Rambo, who believes 'There are no friendly civilians', is a stereotype of the alienated veteran. The only survivor of his team in Vietnam, he harbours a resentment that: 'I did what I had to do to win. But somebody wouldn't let us win.' In a rambling final speech which precedes a collapse into tears he makes exactly the same point that John Wayne had made in *The Green Berets*, that only the professionals who had been to Vietnam had a right to an opinion about it:

> I come back to the world and I see all those maggots at the airport, protesting me, spitting, calling me babykiller and all kinds of vile crap. Who are they to protest me, huh? Who are they? Unless they been me or been there and know what the hell they're yelling about.[44]

His military excellence confirmed by his outwitting of the hundreds of men sent to track him down, Stallone's veteran in *First Blood* is presented as the victim of an ignorant and unappreciative nation dominated by those who naïvely believed the war to be wrong and making scapegoats out of the men who had fought and died in Vietnam. The song which plays over the closing credits reminds the audience: 'It hurts when they tear your dreams apart', but in *Rambo: First Blood Part II* the opportunity is provided to put all this right.[45]

At the beginning of the sequel Rambo asks: 'Sir, do we get to win this time?' and Trautman replies: 'This time it's up to you.'[46] An ex-Green Beret of German–Indian parentage, Rambo's eventual triumph is assured by his mythic roots. As Franklin observed in his article 'The Myth of the Missing':

The foundation of American culture is the mythic frontier, with its central images of white captives tortured by cruel non-white savages until they can be rescued by the ... great American hero, the lone frontiersman who abandons civilized society to merge with the wilderness.[47]

Stallone's incarnation of the 'lone frontiersman' bore useful resemblances to another 'great American hero'. Garry Wills' description of a figure who 'combines all these mythic ideas about American exceptionalism – contact with nature, distrust of government, dignity achieved by performance [and] skepticism towards the claims of experts' explains the appeal of Rambo's character even though it was the attractions of John Wayne's screen persona that Wills was summing up.[48] Rambo, like Wayne, is a frontier fighter who has learnt the skills of his indigenous foe and an enemy of the bureaucrats and technology which seek to marginalise the individual soldier. His destruction of the banks of computers at the end of the film and the threat he issues to the bureaucrat Murdock confirm that Rambo is firmly identified with the individualism that Wayne stood for in his westerns. By bringing American POWs out of Vietnam and killing anyone who gets in his way Rambo demonstrates that America, in the right hands, can be omnipotent once more.

However, in Rambo's final conversation with Trautman he returns even more explicitly to the plea for appreciation which had been implied in *First Blood*: 'I want what they want and what every other guy who came over here and spilt his guts and gave everything he had wants: for our country to love us as much as we love it.'[49]

Even those returning from the 'butt end of a bad war' in 1971 were not condemned to the sort of traumas suggested by Hollywood, however, and it is important to distinguish between the immediate feelings of veterans upon their arrival home and the way their experience in Vietnam affected them later. A surprising number would claim to have enjoyed their war. A 'comprehensive' survey of Vietnam veterans found that '74 per cent enjoyed their time in the military'.[50] In 1984 William Broyles, Jr wrote an essay entitled 'Why Men Love War' which expressed the deep attraction which fighting in Vietnam held for him and for other Marines with whom he served in 1969 and 1970. He revelled in the intensity of the experience which provided 'enough "I couldn't fucking believe it" 's to last a lifetime' and in the opportunities it offered to play 'a game, the best there is', one which enabled an exploration of 'regions of your soul that in most men will always remain uncharted.'[51] His essay also admits to 'more troubling reasons why men love war': the 'thrill of killing'; the joy 'in being alive when so many around you are dead'; the beauty of the weaponry and its effects and the way that most men 'who have been to war ... remember that never in their lives did they have so heightened a sexuality.'[52] A chance meeting at the Vietnam Veterans Memorial with Hiers, a Marine with whom he had served, apparently provided the stimulus for Broyles' essay. His description of Hiers at a later meeting underlines Broyles' point: '"What people can't understand," Hiers said, gently picking up each tiny rabbit and placing it in the nest, "is how much fun Vietnam was. I loved it. I loved it, and I can't tell anybody."'[53] The contrast between Hiers' sensitivity with the 'tiny rabbit' and his feelings about the war enables Broyles to suggest that soldiers did not have to be psychopaths to enjoy their experience in Vietnam. The fact that, on his return home, Broyles demonstrated against the war indicates that they did not have to be convinced of the rightness of America's cause either.[54] In his memoir *Brothers in Arms* Broyles, a successful journalist, argues that service in Vietnam often proved beneficial to veterans, many of whom 'came home, put the war behind them, and proceeded with their lives'. His idea that 'instead of blaming the war for our problems, many Vietnam veterans give it credit for their success' is not, however, one which has appealed to Hollywood.[55]

Manipulation of the screen image of the Vietnam veteran has been directed to different ends. Originally demonised, the veteran has also been used to reinforce diametrically opposed attitudes towards the war. By turning to the veteran as a stereotype for enlistment in support of a political perspective or to provide convenient dramatic effect, film makers have neglected the sort of detailed accounting of the variety of Vietnam veterans' experiences which William Wyler began for World War II veterans in *The Best Years of Our Lives*.

Notes

1. Franklin Fearing, 'Warriors Return: Normal or Neurotic?', *Hollywood Quarterly*, vol. 1, 1945–6 (New York: AMS Reprint Company, 1966), pp. 106–7.
2. The survey taken by the War Department in August 1945 is cited in Joseph C. Goulden, *The Best Years 1945–1950* (New York: Atheneum, 1976), p. 46.
3. Fearing, 'Warriors Return', p. 109.
4. Goulden, *The Best Years*, p. 39; the Revd. Kennedy's comments, which appeared in *Christian Century*, are cited in Eric F. Goldman, *The Crucial Decade – And After: 1945–1960* (New York: Vintage, 1960), p. 34.
5. Goulden, *The Best Years*, p. 38.

6. Mark Baker, *Nam: The Vietnam War in the Words of the Men and Women Who Fought There* (London: Abacus, 1982), p. 205. Stallone's Rambo makes a similar complaint in Ted Kotcheff's *First Blood* (Carolco, 1982): 'Back there ... I was in charge of million dollar equipment. Back here I can't even hold a job parking cars.'

7. Goulden, *The Best Years*, p. 41.

8. The study by the War Department's Research Branch is cited in ibid. p. 47.

9. Tim O'Brien cited in Myra MacPherson, *Long Time Passing: Vietnam and the Haunted Generation* (London: Sceptre Books, [1984] 1988), p. 66. Ron Kovic's *Born on the Fourth of July* also contains the idea that the Vietnam veteran's experience could not be understood by the veterans of other wars. Listening to the Memorial Day speeches made on his behalf by veterans of World War II, the disabled protagonist thinks: 'These people had never been to his war, and they had been talking like they knew everything, like they were experts on the whole goddamn thing'. Kovic, *Born on the Fourth of July* (London: Corgi Books, 1976), p. 82.

10. Baker, *Nam*, p. 193.

11. MacPherson, *Long Time Passing*, p. 55.

12. Lawrence A. Tritle, *From Melos to My Lai: War and Survival* (London: Routledge, 2000), p. 154.

13. MacPherson, *Long Time Passing*, p. 67.

14. The figures are cited in Guenter Lewy, *America in Vietnam* (New York: Oxford University Press, 1978), p. 156. Milton J. Bates has claimed that figures were even higher: 'From 1969 to 1972 alone, 1,016 fraggings were reported in Vietnam ... The figure, which does not include shootings, is thought to represent less than a tenth of the actual number of assaults.' Bates, *The Wars We Took to Vietnam: Cultural Conflict and Storytelling* (Berkeley and Los Angeles: University of California Press, 1996), p. 99.

15. Heinl's article is cited in Marilyn Young, *The Vietnam Wars 1945–1990* (New York: Harper Perennial, 1991), p. 256.

16. The figures are cited in Peter Macdonald, *Giap: The Victor in Vietnam* (London: Fourth Estate, 1993), p. 304.

17. Donald Kirk, 'Who Wants To Be The Last American Killed in Vietnam?', *New York Times Magazine*, 19 September 1971.

18. Robert Jay Lifton, *Home From The War: Learning From Vietnam Veterans* (Boston: Beacon Press, [1973] 1992), p. 35.

19. Ibid. p. 36 and pp. 39–4 0.

20. Ibid. p. xvii.

21. Ibid. p. ix. The study cited by Lifton is Richard Kulka et al., *Trauma and the Vietnam War Generation*.

22. Charles R. Figley and Seymour Leventman (eds), *Strangers at Home: Vietnam Veterans Since the War* (New York: Praeger, 1980), p. 178.

23. Michael Lind, *Vietnam: The Necessary War – A Re-interpretation of America's Most Disastrous Military Conflict* (New York: The Free Press, 1999), pp. 175–6. Lind based his argument upon evidence found in *Shook Over Hell: Post-Traumatic Stress, Vietnam and the Civil War* by Eric T. Dean, Jr and an interview with B. G. Burkett in *Vietnam* magazine, February 1997.

24. MacPherson, *Long Time Passing*, p. 68.

25. Julian Smith, *Looking Away: Hollywood and Vietnam* (New York: Charles Scribner, 1975), pp. 155–6.

26. Smith, *Looking Away*, p. 164 and p. 167 (note).

27. Albert Auster and Leonard Quart, *How the War was Remembered: Hollywood and Vietnam* (New York: Praeger, 1988), p. 42.

28. The hero speaking in *Billy Jack*, directed by Tom Laughlin (Warner/National Student Film Corporation, 1971).

29. Auster and Quart, *How the War was Remembered*, p. 42 and p. 44.

30. Bernard and Billy Jack in *Billy Jack*.

31. Auster and Quart, *How the War was Remembered*, p. 46.

32. The conversation takes place between Homer and a customer at the drug store counter at which Fred works in *The Best Years of Our Lives*, directed by William Wyler (RKO, 1946).

33. For example, Auster and Quart observed that: 'The Vietnamese are viewed almost uniformly as a repellent, savage people' in *The Deer Hunter*. *How the War was Remembered*, p. 63.

34. Michael speaking in *The Deer Hunter*, directed by Michael Cimino (EMI, 1978).

35. Steven speaking in ibid.

36. Reagan cited in Robert Dallek, *Ronald Reagan: The Politics of Symbolism* (Cambridge, MA: Harvard University Press, 1999), p. 58.

37. Richard Slotkin, *Gunfighter Nation: The Myth of the Frontier in Twentieth-Century America* (Norman: University of Oklahoma Press, [1992] 1998), p. 649.

38. The report is cited in H. Bruce Franklin, *M.I.A. or Mythmaking in America* (New Brunswick: Rutgers University Press, 1993), p. 139.

39. Reagan cited in ibid. p. 4.

40. The poll, jointly conducted by *The Wall Street Journal* and NBC News in April 1993, is cited in ibid. p. 197.

41. Ibid. p. 137.

42. The figure of fifty-seven million dollars is cited in Auster and Quart, *How the War was Remembered*, p. 107; Reagan is cited in Franklin, *M.I.A.*, p.151.

43. Franklin, *M.I.A.*, p. 232 (note).

44. Rambo speaking in *First Blood*.

45. 'It's a Long Road', sung by Dan Hill, was written by Jerry Goldsmith and Hal Shafer.

46. Rambo in conversation with Trautman in *Rambo: First Blood Part II*, directed by George P. Cosmatos (Anabasis Investments, 1985).

47. Franklin's article 'The Myth of the Missing', which appeared in *The Progressive* in January 1993, is cited in Donald Ringnalda, *Fighting and Writing the Vietnam War* (Jackson: University Press of Mississippi, 1994), p. 219.

48. Garry Wills, *John Wayne: The Politics of Celebrity* (London: Faber and Faber, 1997), p. 311.

49. Rambo in conversation with Trautman in *Rambo: First Blood Part II*.

50. The poll by Harris is cited in Timothy J. Lomperis, *'Reading the Wind': The Literature of the Vietnam War* (Durham: Duke University Press, 1987), p. 16.

51. William Broyles, Jr, 'Why Men Love War', in Walter Capps (ed.), *The Vietnam Reader* (New York: Routledge, 1991), pp. 71–2.

52. Ibid. pp. 74–8.

53. Ibid. p. 68. It may be coincidental that *hiers* is French for yesterdays.

54. William Broyles, Jr, *Brothers in Arms: A Journey From War to Peace* (New York: Alfred A. Knopf, 1986), p. 269.

55. Ibid. p. 270.

Telling Differences

In September 1963 Marine General Victor Krulak and Joseph Mendenhall, a representative of the State Department, returned from a thirty-six-hour visit to South Vietnam to report their observations to President Kennedy. What they each told Kennedy was so different that he asked them if they had visited the same country.[1] Those who share Steven Kaplan's argument that in Vietnam 'nothing was certain' may find it unsurprising that Kennedy received such dissimilar accounts of a situation which, by 1963, was already confusing. The analyses presented here, however, suggest that the inter-disciplinary study of history, literature and film will aid an understanding of America's 'complicated' war in Vietnam.

It was not just defeat which distinguished the war in Vietnam from America's earlier wars. Having travelled to the other side of the world to fight alongside a people with whom they had little in common, American soldiers found that the methods which had been used with such success during World War II were often irrelevant. At home, after years of social upheaval, a majority of Americans moved from support for the war to the view that the war had been a mistake. Thus, it became tempting to dismiss the Vietnam War as a madness that defied rational analysis. It is true that the details of certain events are unrecoverable and that bitter and frequently inconclusive debate was provoked by a war which, for many Americans, made little sense. Nevertheless, careful investigation does lead to a sharper picture, as Peers' work on the massacres at Son My demonstrates, and those who argue the futility of historical inquiry into the war, deciding like Tim O'Brien's John Wade that there are 'no certainties ... no facts', are in danger of ignoring the reality of the war in all its horror.[2]

President Kennedy's encounter with Krulak and Mendenhall points to another of the tendencies which has obscured the nature of the war. Required to brief the president, the two men selected the evidence necessary to support the views of the departments they represented. Not for the last time a difference of opinion about the war was a consequence of predisposition rather than of the slipperiness of the facts. Scrutiny of the propaganda messages in John Wayne's *The Green Berets*, the fabrications in *Rambo: First Blood Part II* and the misuse of evidence in Oliver Stone's *JFK* reveals that film makers have often shown a similar determination to manipulate their audience in accord with a set of established ideas. As well as indicating their historical weaknesses, however, the study of such films and of books like Robin Moore's *The Green Berets* divulges their usefulness as a record of the prejudices which prompted them, prejudices which sometimes reflected the beliefs of millions of Americans.

The study of film and literature which focuses upon the individual's experience of war offers a more direct benefit. Ward Just's comment that 'Each man had his own Vietnam' should be read as a reminder that each person perceives the world uniquely rather than as a demonstration of the impossibility of establishing truths about the war.[3] Thus, the various perspectives of the men in the valley and the men on the hilltop can be used to broaden one's grasp of the war's complexities instead of compounding its confusion. Irvin's *Hamburger Hill* is devoted to the portrayal of combat from the viewpoint of a single squad and Stone's *Platoon* is persuasive in its depiction of what might have motivated soldiers to commit war crimes in Vietnam. Similarly, oral histories like Hammel's *Khe Sanh*, Michael Herr's reactions to combat in *Dispatches* and the work of journalists who shared, to some extent, the experiences of the soldiers offer a graphic and immediate account of the fighting in which Americans took part in Vietnam.

As John Keene observes in the opening paragraph of his novel *Pettibone's Law*, the telling of stories about America's war in Vietnam presents problems, but opportunities for understanding too:

> It was a time of returning ... he had to wonder if everything had happened as he remembered. Had he dreamed part of it? Embellished or diminished the truth? Fabricated history? And what about the gaps – periods of crucial decisions of which he had no recall. Yes, a time of returning, of trying to re-examine the life that had slipped away. To somehow make sense of it. To look closely at the things he had done and the thing he had become, and try to draw some kind of conclusion. To understand some of it.[4]

There are many obstacles to an understanding of the most complicated of America's wars, a war which has stimulated the telling of many different stories. The study of history, literature and film, each of which tells the stories of the war in its own ways, helps us 'to understand some of it.'

Notes

1. Richard Reeves, *President Kennedy: Profile of Power* (London: Papermac, 1994), p. 595.
2. Tim O'Brien, *In the Lake of the Woods* (London: Flamingo, [1994] 1995), p. 277.
3. Ward Just, *To What End* (New York: Public Affairs, [1968] 2000), p. 166.
4. John Keene, *Pettibone's Law* (London: Bloomsbury, 1992), p. 11.

A Guide to Further Reading

The quantity of material confronting the student of America's war in Vietnam is daunting, especially so because second-hand copies of just about anything published or released on video can be tracked down via the internet. The list of suggestions which follows is a series of starting points.

There are several, lengthy, general histories. Gabriel Kolko's *Anatomy of a War*, and Stanley Karnow's *Vietnam: A History* are both useful and readable and Guenter Lewy's *America in Vietnam* and Marilyn Young's *The Vietnam Wars 1945–1990* offer, respectively, a more sympathetic and a more critical treatment of America's involvement in Vietnam. George C. Herring's *America's Longest War* is expensive but it remains the most helpful of the shorter histories.

The origins of the war have been most recently explored in David Kaiser's *American Tragedy*. Richard Reeves' carefully documented *President Kennedy* details the Kennedy administration's anxieties about events in Vietnam whilst Newman's *JFK and Vietnam* argues that Kennedy was determined to pull out of Vietnam in his second term. Published in 1972, David Halberstam's *The Best and the Brightest* remains a fascinating examination of the men responsible for American policies in Vietnam and Neil Sheehan's *A Bright Shining Lie* uses the experiences of Lieutenant Colonel John Paul Vann, who went to Vietnam in 1962, to explain the mistakes America made in the following decade. Loren Baritz's focus upon the cultural assumptions which led America into the war in *Backfire* and Frances FitzGerald's emphasis on the perceptions of the Vietnamese in *Fire in the Lake* are also valuable.

For those interested in the escalation of the war under Johnson, Herring's *LBJ and Vietnam*, Larry Berman's *Lyndon Johnson's War* and H. R. McMaster's *Dereliction of Duty* are all worthwhile. Lyndon Johnson's presidential memoir *The Vantage Point* is heavy-going but revealing of the thinking behind some of Johnson's decisions. More compelling are the transcriptions of telephone calls made by Johnson from the White House which are to be found in Michael Beschloss' *Taking Charge* and *Reaching for Glory*. A further volume is being prepared by Beschloss to cover the years 1966–8. Another relevant political memoir is Robert S. McNamara's *In Retrospect* which, like the statements he made when he was Secretary of Defense, should be treated with some caution.

It is possible to find studies of almost every aspect of the war. Especially provocative are: *On Strategy* by Harry G. Summers, Jr, an analysis of America's military failures in Vietnam; Robert Jay Lifton's *Home From The War* which assesses the nature and extent of the post-traumatic stress suffered by America's veterans; H. Bruce Franklin's *M.I.A. or Mythmaking in America*, an account of how the unsubstantiated claim that Americans remained captive in South-east Asia after the war was manipulated by America's leaders; and Michael Lind's *Vietnam: The Necessary War*, which concludes that America's attempts to defend the South Vietnamese government were justified. *The Vietnam Reader* edited by Walter Capps includes a number of important essays, notably Broyles' 'Why Men Love War'.

There is a considerable literature devoted to particular events. *We Were Soldiers Once ... and Young* by Lt. Gen. Harold G. Moore and Joseph L. Galloway describes the battles in the Ia Drang Valley in 1965, the first occasion on which the forces of America and North Vietnam met. Don Oberdorfer covers the Tet Offensive and the reactions of the American media to it in *Tet! The Turning Point* and Michael Bilton and Kevin Sim's *Four Hours in My Lai* and the television documentary with the same title directed by Sim are the most illuminating of the shorter works about the massacre. Contemporary journalism is enlightening on a host of incidents and topics and the anthology *Reporting Vietnam: American Journalism 1959–1975*, especially the single-volume paperback, provides convenient access to some of the best writing by reporters. Jonathan Schell's *The Military Half: An Account of Destruction in Quang Ngai and Quang Tin* and Robert Pisor's *The End of the Line: The Siege of Khe Sanh* are also useful and William Prochnau's *Once Upon a Distant War* tells the story of those American reporters in South Vietnam who first became critical of America's conduct of the war.

The thoughts of those Americans who served in Vietnam are available in different forms. Of the oral histories, Mark Baker's *Nam*, Al Santoli's *Everything We Had* and Wallace Terry's *Bloods: An Oral History of the Vietnam War by Black Veterans* are the most instructive. Hammel's *Khe Sanh: Siege in the Clouds* offers a range of perspectives on the battle and *Dear America: Letters Home From Vietnam*, a collection of letters edited by Bernard Edelman, is, like the documentary film of the same title, especially moving. Myra MacPherson's *Long Time Passing* uses oral testimony to portray the experience of the 'Vietnam generation'.

There are hundreds of memoirs and novels based upon the war. Although it may lack literary merit, Moore's *The Green Berets* discloses the way many

Americans thought about their nation's role in South-east Asia. Philip Caputo's *A Rumor of War* and Ron Kovic's *Born on the Fourth of July* are powerful, autobiographical accounts of their service in the Marines and James Webb's *Fields of Fire* and John M. Del Vecchio's *The 13th Valley* provide a wealth of realistic detail. Other writers have been less conventional in their approach. Michael Herr's *Dispatches* and Tim O'Brien's novels *Going After Cacciato*, *The Things They Carried* and *In the Lake of the Woods* are all essential reading. *The Short Timers* by Gustav Hasford, upon which Kubrick based *Full Metal Jacket*, is out of print but available on the internet. Larry Heinemann's *Paco's Story* is amongst the best of the novels which consider the veteran's return to America. On stage David Rabe explored the effect of the war upon the American psyche in *The Basic Training of Pavlo Hummel* and *Sticks and Bones* and John Balaban, W. D. Ehrhart and Bruce Weigl have produced the most memorable of the poems about the war.

Criticism of the war's literature includes Philip Beidler's *American Literature and the Experience of Vietnam* and, interesting because they are in such disagreement, Donald Ringnalda's *Fighting and Writing the Vietnam War* and Jim Neilson's *Warring Fictions*. In *Vietnam, We've All Been There* Eric James Schroeder interviews, amongst others who have written about the war, Herr, O'Brien and Heinemann. Milton J. Bates in *The Wars We Took to Vietnam* and John Hellmann in *American Myth and the Legacy of Vietnam* adopt the perspective of the cultural historian to discuss the ways in which the war has been reflected and debated in literature and film.

Of the films made for general release during the war only Wayne's *The Green Berets* depicted combat in Vietnam. Like *Rambo: First Blood Part II*, it makes interesting viewing because of the political messages it conveys so forcefully. The most important of the films appearing in the late 1970s are Ted Post's *Go Tell the Spartans*, Cimino's *The Deer Hunter* and Coppola's *Apocalypse Now*. Oliver Stone's trilogy of *Platoon*, *Born on the Fourth of July* and *Heaven and Earth*, along with *JFK*, constitutes the most substantial body of work about Vietnam by a single director. Like *Platoon*, and also released in the late 1980s, Kubrick's *Full Metal Jacket* and Irvin's *Hamburger Hill* concentrate upon the traumas of combat for the American soldier. Albert Auster and Leonard Quart's *How the War was Remembered* is the most insightful of several books devoted to critical analysis of the Vietnam War film.

Glossary

America's war in Vietnam generated a vocabulary of its own. An exhaustive glossary would fill several pages but a knowledge of the following will facilitate a reading of this and other books about the war:

ARVN	Army of the Republic of Vietnam – the South Vietnamese Army
CIA	Central Intelligence Agency
CID	Criminal Investigation Division (of the US Army)
CIDG	Civilian Irregular Defense Group
DEROS	Date eligible for return from overseas
DMZ	Demilitarized Zone (which separated North and South Vietnam)
FNG	Fucking New Guy
Fragging	The deliberate killing of another American, usually a superior, with a grenade
Friendly fire	The accidental killing of an ally
Gook	A derogatory name for a Vietnamese, enemy or ally, or anyone else from East Asia
Grunt	An American infantryman
LLDB	Luc-Luong Dac Biet (South Vietnamese Special Forces)
LZ	Landing Zone
MACV	Military Assistance Command, Vietnam
NLF	National Liberation Front
NSAM	National Security Action Memorandum
NVA	North Vietnamese Army
PTSD	Post-traumatic Stress Disorder
R&R	Rest and Relaxation
REMF	Rear Echelon Mother Fucker
VC	Viet Cong

Index

Acton, Lord, 12
Adamson, Al
    Satan's Sadists, 137
Adler, Renata, 49
American soldiers
    described in combat, 22, 84–5, 87–8,
        92–3, 95–100
    perspectives on the war, 28–9, 88,
        93–4, 97–9, 118, 123, 144–5, 149
    and sense of futility, 1, 25, 27, 97–
        100, 135–6
    varied experience, 84, 95, 134–5,
        145
Americans
    and disagreements about the war,
        1, 8, 23–4, 87, 111, 148
    and military invincibility, 6–7,
        42–3, 46, 48, 50, 53
    and relationship with Vietnamese,
        6–7, 43–4, 46–8, 109, 116, 134,
        148
Anderson, David, 115
anti-war movement, 99, 133–5, 140–1
Apocalypse Now (Coppola), 24
Appy, Christian G., 35, 91, 95, 99
Armies of the Night, The (Mailer), 18
Ashby, Hal
    Coming Home, 139–40
Auster, Albert and Quart, Leonard,
    98, 138

Baker, Mark, 133

Baritz, Loren, 91
Barker, Frank, 116
Barnes, Julian, 29–30
Bates, Milton J., 28, 93, 118
Baxter, Charles, 123
Best Years of Our Lives, The (Wyler),
    139–40, 145
Billy Jack (Laughlin), 138
Bilton, Michael and Sim, Kevin, 113
Black Sunday (Frankenheimer), 138
body count, 115–16
Born Losers (Laughlin), 137
Born on the Fourth of July (book:
    Kovic), 140
Born on the Fourth of July (film:
    Stone), 140
Bourke, Joanna, 99, 107, 113, 118
Brothers in Arms (Broyles), 145
Browning, Christopher R., 118
Broyles, William Jr
    Brothers in Arms, 145
    'Why Men Love War', 144–5
Bryan, C. D. B., 90
Bundy, McGeorge, 76–8
Bury, J. B., 12
Bush, George, 23, 79–80

Calley, William L. Jr, 105–7, 110,
    112–13
Capote, Truman, 18
    In Cold Blood, 18
Capouya, Emile, 40, 48

Carabatsos, James, 98
casualties during the war, 8
Cawley, Leo, 121
Central Intelligence Agency (CIA), 46
Charley Varrick (Siegel), 138
Chrome and Hot Leather (Frost), 137
Cimino, Michael
    Deer Hunter, The, 139–41
cold war, 8
Coming Home (Ashby), 139–40
Compton, Richard
    Welcome Home, Soldier Boys, 138
Coppola, Francis Ford
    Apocalypse Now, 24
containment, policy of, 78
conventional journalism, 21, 89, 94, 96
Costner, Kevin, 60–1
counter-insurgency *see* Kennedy,
    John F.
'credibility gap', 19
Cosmatos, George P.
    Rambo: First Blood Part II, 42,
      138, 142–4, 149

Dean, Eric T., 137
Deer Hunter, The (Cimino), 139–41
Defense Department *see* United
    States Department of Defense
Didion, Joan, 50
Diem, Ngo Dinh *see* Ngo Dinh Diem
Dien Bien Phu, battle of (1954), 7, 86,
    94
Dispatches (Herr), 15, 25–7, 88, 90–6,
    149
domino theory, 6
Donaldson, Roger
    Thirteen Days, 80
Dwan, Allan
    Sands of Iwo Jima, 10, 98–100

Eisenhower, Dwight D., 5–7, 74
Ellsberg, Daniel, 107

Elton, G. R., 13
Emerson, Gloria, 47
End of the Line, The (Pisor), 87, 95–6

Fearing, Franklin, 131
First Blood (Kotcheff), 143
Ford, John, 49
Four Hours in My Lai (book: Bilton
    and Sim), 113
Four Hours in My Lai (film: Sim), 113
fragging, 134
France, 74, 86
    history of colonialism in Indo-
      china, 6–7
Frankenheimer, John
    Black Sunday, 138
Franklin, H. Bruce, 123–4, 142–4
free fire zone, 114–16
Frost, Lee
    Chrome and Hot Leather, 137
Full Metal Jacket (Kubrick), 7, 98
Fuller, Jack, 24
Fussell, Paul
    criticism by historians, 16–17
    Great War and Modern Memory,
      The, 15–17

Galloway, Joseph L., 89
Geneva Conference (1954), 7
Going After Cacciato (O'Brien), 25
'Good Form' (O'Brien), 11
Goulden, Joseph C., 132
Gray, J. Glenn, 120
Great War and Modern Memory, The
    (Fussell), 15–17
Green Berets *see* Special Forces
Green Berets, The (Moore), 33, 40–8,
    54, 149
Green Berets, The (Wayne), 34, 48–
    54, 143, 149
Greenshaw, Wayne, 105
Gulf of Tonkin Incident (1964), 77–8

Gulf of Tonkin Resolution, 77

Haeberle, Ronald, 106–7
Halberstam, David, 10, 38, 45, 74
    One Very Hot Day, 25
Hamburger Hill, battle of (1969), 85,
    97–8
Hamburger Hill (Irvin), 98–100, 149
Hamilton, Nigel, 73
Hammel, Eric
    Khe Sanh, 87, 96–7, 149
Harkins, Paul D., 45
Heinl, Robert, 134–5
Hellmann, John, 27, 39–40, 49, 90
Henderson, Oran, 110
Herr, Michael, 15, 26, 88–9
    Dispatches, 15, 25–7, 88–96, 149
    'Khe Sanh', 87–8, 90–5
Herring, George C., 46, 69, 74, 78, 113
Hersh, Seymour, 105, 114
history, 11, 14, 22, 65, 77
    changing ideas about, 11–13
    and combat, 12–17
    and film, 10–11, 15, 24, 28–9, 64–
       7, 119
    and literature, 10–11, 13, 15–16,
       18–19, 20–3, 28–9, 91, 119
    and Vietnam War, 19, 21, 24–9,
       89–91, 95, 113, 118
Ho Chi Minh, 6
Ho Chi Minh trail, 86
'How to Tell a True War Story'
    (O'Brien), 11, 123

In Cold Blood (Capote), 18
In the Lake of the Woods (O'Brien),
    119, 121–6, 148
Irvin, John
    Hamburger Hill, 98–100, 149

Jaglom, Henry
    Tracks, 138

James, Henry, 2, 29
JFK (Stone), 58–67, 71, 75–6, 78–80,
    149
Johnson, Lyndon B., 51
    and concern about Khe Sanh, 86
    and escalation of war, 6, 58, 74,
       76–8
    and Gulf of Tonkin Resolution,
       77–8
    and justifications for the war, 52–
       3, 74–5
    and Vietnam policy, 6, 68, 75–8,
       134
Joint Chiefs of Staff *see* United States
    Joint Chiefs of Staff
Just, Ward, 149

Kaplan, Steven, 123, 148
Karnow, Stanley, 69, 78, 113
Katz, Bob, 65
Keene, John, 149
Kelly, Francis J., 35, 40, 48
Kennedy, Edward, 98, 100
Kennedy, John F., 148
    and cold war, 36, 73
    and Diem coup, 69–71
    and escalation of the war, 58, 74
    and interest in counter-
       insurgency, 35–7
    and relationship with military
       leaders, 37–8
    and Special Forces, 37
    and *Ugly American*, 35–6
    and Vietnam policy, 68–74, 77–8,
       134
Kennedy, Robert F., 71
Kerrey, Robert, 126
Khe Sanh, battle of (1967–8), 85–7,
    91–7
Khe Sanh (Hammel), 87, 96–7, 149
'Khe Sanh' (Herr), 87–8, 90–5
King, Richard, 29

Kinney, Judy Lee, 98, 100
Kirk, Donald, 135
Klann, Gerald, 126
Kotcheff, Ted
    First Blood, 143
    Uncommon Valor, 142
Kovic, Ron
    Born on the Fourth of July, 140
Kubrick, Stanley
    Full Metal Jacket, 7, 98
Kurosawa, Akira
    Rashomon, 67

Laughlin, Tom
    Billy Jack, 138
    Born Losers, 137
Lederer, William J. and Burdick,
    Eugene
    Ugly American, The, 35–7
Lemnitzer, Lyman, 37–8
Lewis, R. W. B., 2
Lewy, Guenter, 38, 97
Life, 48, 51, 87, 106
'Life in the V Ring' (Wheeler), 87–8
Lifton, Robert Jay, 116–17, 135–6
Lind, Michael, 23, 73, 137
Lodge, Henry Cabot Jr, 69–70
Lomperis, Timothy J., 23

M (Sack), 19–22
McGovern, George, 112
McMaster, H. R., 78
McNamara, Robert S., 6, 70, 75
McNamara–Taylor report (1963), 70–1
MacPherson, Myra, 112, 134, 137
Mailer, Norman, 18, 59
    Armies of the Night, The, 18–19
Marwick, Arthur, 10
Meadlo, Paul, 106, 119–20
Mecklin, John, 89
media reaction to the war, 33, 49, 89,
    134–5

Medina, Ernest, 112–13
Meos see Montagnards
Meyers, Kate Beaird, 24
Minh, Ho Chi see Ho Chi Minh
Missing in Action (Zito), 143
missing POWs, 142–4
Montagnards, 35, 46–7
Moore, Harold G., 89
Moore, Robin, 45–6
    Green Berets, The, 33, 40–8, 54, 149
Murphy, Audie, 10, 107
My Hoi see My Khe 4
My Khe 4, 105, 112, 114
My Lai massacre, 104–126, 135
    and cover-up, 104–5, 109–10, 115
    and congressional investigation,
        111–12
    and Peers Report, 105, 107, 109–
        10, 112–16, 126, 148

National Liberation Front (NLF), 86,
    115, 117
National Review, 107
National Security Action
    Memorandum #263, 60, 68,
    71, 78
National Security Action
    Memorandum #273, 63, 68,
    75–8
Neilson, Jim, 23, 27, 43, 123
New Journalism, 13, 18–22
Newman, John M., 67–78
New York Times, 116
Ngo Dinh Diem, 69–71
Nixon, Richard M., 107, 110, 134, 142
No Gun Ri, 126
North Vietnamese Army (NVA), 86
Novick, Peter, 12

O'Brien, Tim, 24, 117–18, 122–3,
    125–6, 132
    Going After Cacciato, 25

'Good Form', 11
'How to Tell a True War Story',
    11, 123
In the Lake of the Woods, 119, 121–
    6, 148
The Things They Carried, 123
O'Donnell, Kenneth, 68
official sources, 21, 89, 94, 96, 116
Oman, Sir Charles, 13
One Very Hot Day (Halberstam), 25
origins of the war, 5–8, 27

Peers, William, 110, 112, 114, 117
Peers Report *see* My Lai massacre
'Pinkville' *see* My Lai massacre
Pisor, Robert, 95
    End of the Line, The, 87, 95–6
Platoon (Stone), 10, 78, 98, 119–21,
    126, 149
Polan, Dana, 67
postmodern perspectives on the war,
    24, 26–8
post-traumatic stress disorder, 136, 138
Prior, Robin, 17
Prochnau, William, 33, 45
Prouty, L. Fletcher, 59
public opinion, US, 33–5, 40–1, 48,
    86, 106–7, 142, 148

Quang Ngai, 109, 115, 117

racism, 43–4, 46–8, 99, 114, 116,
    134–5, 140
Rambo: First Blood Part II
    (Cosmatos), 42, 138, 142–4, 149
Ransom, Robert C., 117
Rashomon (Kurosawa), 67
Reagan, Ronald W., 141–2
Reeves, Richard, 36, 38, 71, 75
Remarque, Erich Maria, 15
Ridenhour, Ronald, 104, 106, 112
Ringnalda, Donald, 24, 26–8, 40

Roberts, Jay, 116

Sack, John, 20, 22
    M, 19–22
Sadler, Barry, 34, 53
Sale, Roger, 90
Sands of Iwo Jima (Dwan), 10, 98–100
Santoli, Al, 28, 46–7
Satan's Sadists (Adamson), 137
Schell, Jonathan, 117
Schlesinger, Arthur M., 76–7
Schroeder, Eric James, 33
Schulzinger, Robert D., 69
Scorsese, Martin
    Taxi Driver, 138
search and destroy, 115, 117
Sheehan, Neil, 45
Siegel, Don
    Charley Varrick, 138
Sim, Kevin
    Four Hours in My Lai (film), 113
Simpson, Varnado, 113, 126
Sledge, Eugene B., 15
Slotkin, Richard, 46, 50–1, 106, 141
Smith, Elizabeth A., 13
Smith, Julian, 137
Somekawa, Ellen, 13
Son My *see* My Lai massacre
Sorlin, Pierre, 65
Special Forces, 33–54
    Kennedy's interest in, 35, 37–8, 51
    origin of, 34
    popular perception of, 35, 38–4
    role in Vietnam, 35, 37–8
    self-image of, 39–40, 50
    US Army's relationship with, 35,
        37–40, 44–5, 48
    in US media, 35, 38–9
Spiller, Roger J., 2, 4
Stanton, Shelby L., 34–5, 37, 39–40,
    45, 47–8
Steiner, George, 118

Stone, Oliver, 10, 23, 58, 66, 73–4, 78, 126
  Born on the Fourth of July, 140
  JFK, 58–67, 71, 75–6, 78–80, 149
  Platoon, 10, 78, 98, 119–21, 126, 149

Taxi Driver (Scorsese), 138
Taylor, A. J. P., 10
Taylor, Maxwell D., 45
Tet Offensive (1968), 34, 49, 86, 134
The Things They Carried (O'Brien), 123
Thirteen Days (Donaldson), 80
Thompson, Sir Robert, 86
Thomson, David, 58
Thoreau, Henry David, 11
Time, 10, 33, 38–9, 45, 86, 107, 126
Tonkin Gulf Incident see Gulf of
  Tonkin Incident (1964)
Tonkin Gulf Resolution see Gulf of
  Tonkin Resolution
Toplin, Robert Brent, 71
Tracks (Jaglom), 138
Tritle, Lawrence A., 134
Truman, Harry S, 5, 7, 74–5

Ugly American, The (Lederer and
  Burdick), 35–7
Uncommon Valor (Kotcheff), 142
United States Department of
  Defense, 46, 51, 142
United States Joint Chiefs of Staff,
  37–8, 45

Valenti, Jack, 51
Vann, John Paul, 45
Viet Cong see National Liberation
  Front
Viet Minh, 6–7, 117
Vietnam veterans, 132–45
  attitudes of Americans towards,
    133–7, 141–2, 144
  in media, 134–5, 137–45

problems of, 133–7, 144–5
Vietnam Veterans' Memorial, 141
Vietnamese
  history, 6
  relationship with Americans, 7–8,
    134

Wall Street Journal, 49
Walzer, Michael, 13–14
Wayne, John, 10, 48–51, 96, 99–100,
  144
  Green Berets, The, 34, 48–54, 143, 149
Wayne, Michael, 50
Webb, James, 24
Welcome Home, Soldier Boys
  (Compton), 138
westerns, 49–51
Westmoreland, William C., 86, 104, 116
Wheeler, Earle G., 38
Wheeler, John T.
  'Life in the V Ring', 87–8
White, Hayden, 13, 66, 121
Whitman, Walt, 14
'Why Men Love War' (Broyles), 144–5
Widmer, Fred, 113, 126
Wills, Garry, 50
Wilson, Trevor, 17
Wilson, William V., 104
Wolfe, Tom, 19, 21
World War II, 25, 26, 49, 131
World War II veterans, 84
  attitudes of Americans towards,
    132, 139
  in media, 131–2, 137, 139
  problems of, 131–2, 137, 139
Wyler, William
  Best Years of Our Lives, The, 139–
    40, 145

Zais, Melvin, 98
Zito, Joseph
  Missing in Action, 143

The British Association for American Studies (BAAS)

The British Association for American Studies was founded in 1955 to promote the study of the United States of America. It welcomes applications for membership from anyone interested in the history, society, government and politics, economics, geography, literature, creative arts, culture and thought of the USA.

The Association publishes a newsletter twice yearly, holds an annual national conference, supports regional branches and provides other membership services, including preferential subscription rates to the *Journal of American Studies*.

Membership enquiries may be addressed to the BAAS Secretary, Jenel Virden, Department of American Studies, University of Hull, Hull HU6 7RX.